John

A PRE-RAPHAELITE IN CORNWALL

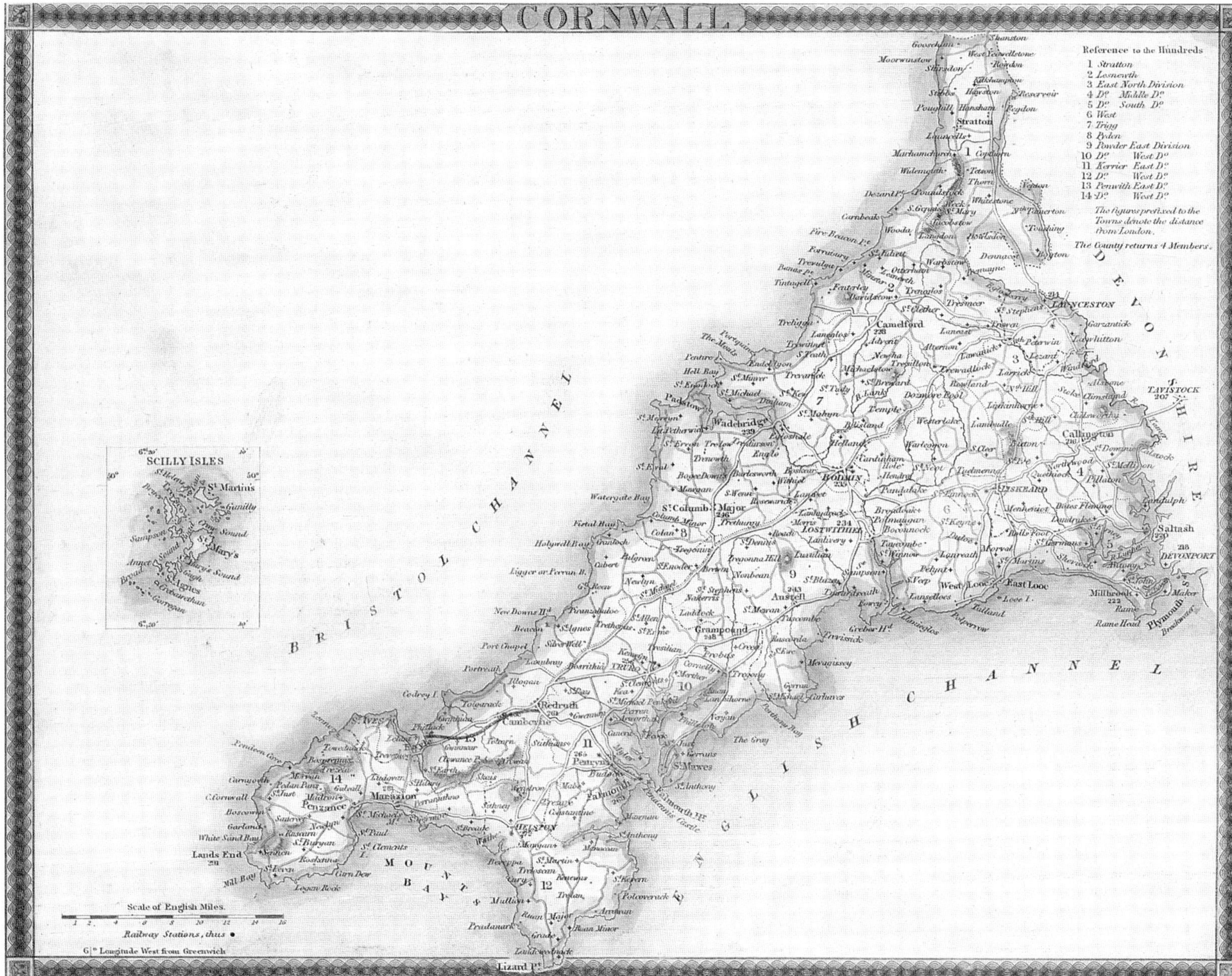

CORNWALL
Reference to the Hundreds
1 Stratton
2 Lesnewth
3 East North Division
4 Dº Middle Dº
5 Dº South Dº
6 West
7 Trigg
8 Pyder
9 Powder East Division
10 Dº West Dº
11 Kerrier East Dº
12 Dº West Dº
13 Penwith East Dº
14 Dº West Dº
The figures prefixed to the Towns denote the distance from London.
The County returns 4 Members.
SCILLY ISLES
BRISTOL CHANNEL
ENGLISH CHANNEL
DEVONSHIRE
MOUNTS BAY
Scale of English Miles.
Railway Stations, thus •
6|° Longitude West from Greenwich
LAUNCESTON
BODMIN
TRURO
Penzance
Lands End
Lizard Pt.

John Brett

A PRE-RAPHAELITE IN CORNWALL

Sansom & Company

Penlee House
Gallery & Museum

Charles Brett | Michael Hickox | Christiana Payne

FIG. 1
John Brett by himself.
Dated Oct 29/1857. Pen & ink
Inscribed *'Mein Selbst (ganz wahr)'*
Private Collection

NEXT PAGE
Rocks, Scilly
1873, Oil on board
35.8 x 61.2cm (14½ x 24ins)
Inscribed *'Scilly July 7 73'*
National Museums Liverpool
(The Walker)
Provenance: Rev E.C. Dewick
Presented by him to the
Gallery 1919

First published in 2006 by Sansom & Company Ltd
81g Pembroke Road, Bristol BS8 3EA

www.sansomandcompany.co.uk
www.artdictionaries.com

ISBN 1 904537 51 0

British Library Cataloguing in Publication Data:
A catalogue record for this book is available from the British Library.

Designed and typeset by Gendall Design, Falmouth, Cornwall and printed by Gutenberg Press, Malta.

Text set in Dante MT and Abadi MT.

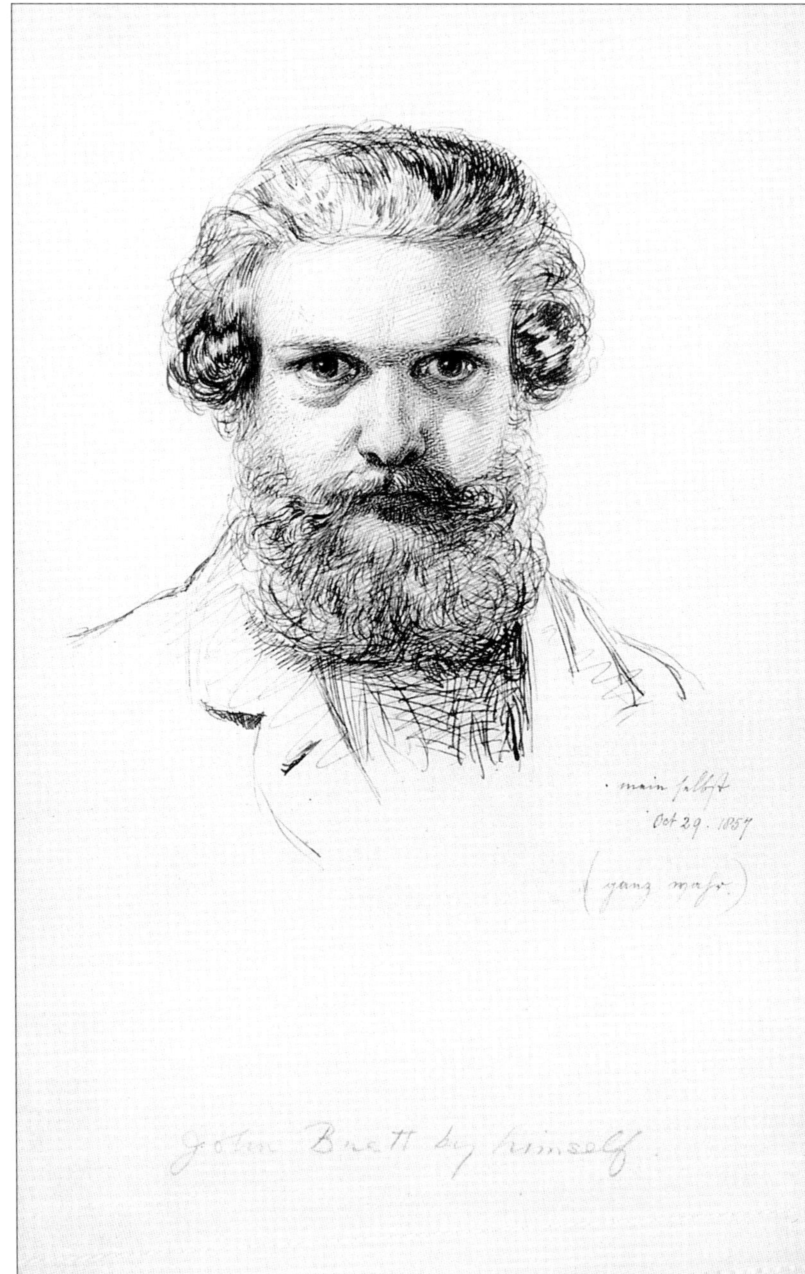

CONTENTS

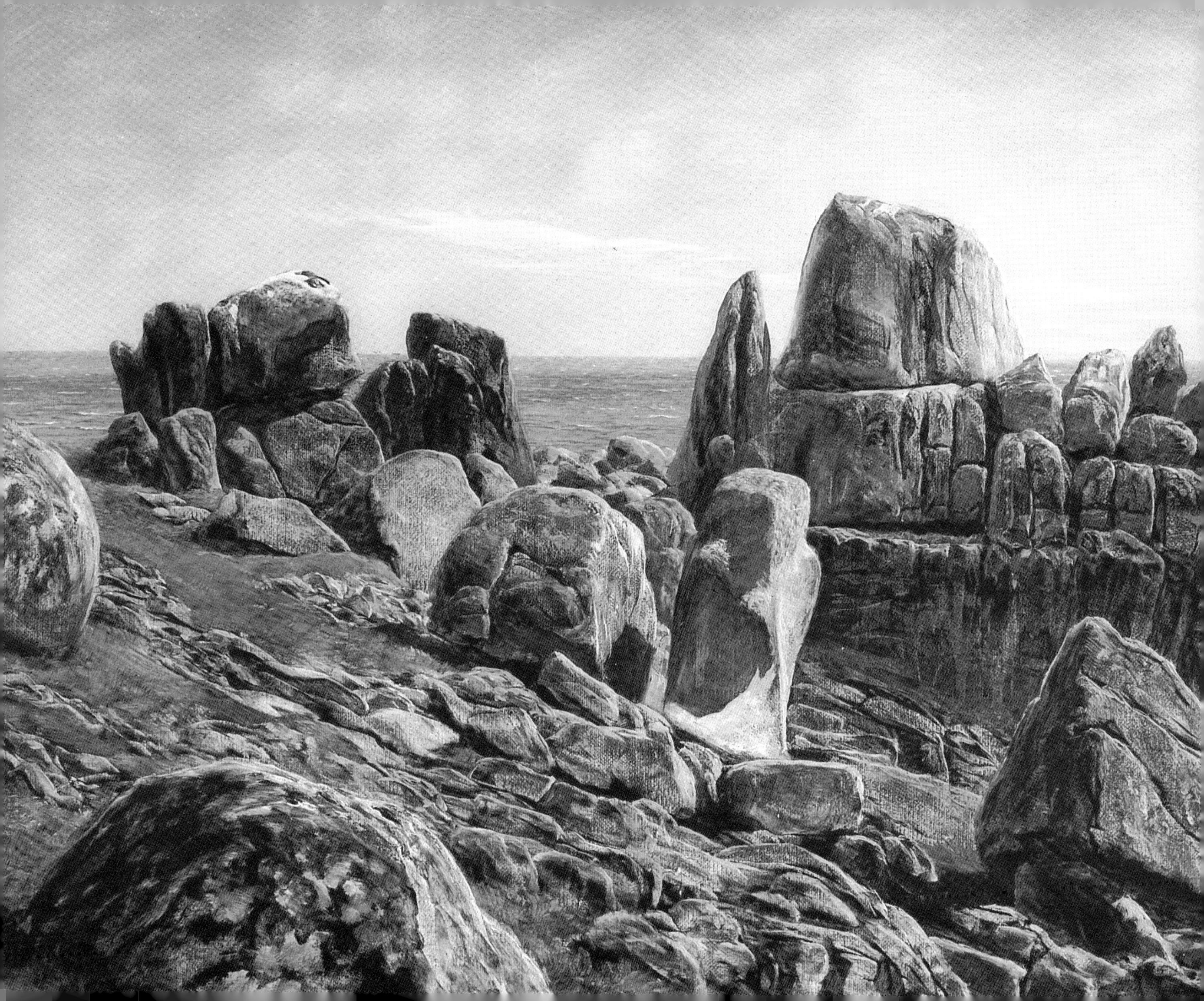

PREFACE

The great champion of the Pre-Raphaelite Brotherhood, John Ruskin, wrote of the particular beauty arising from a coast made up of granite rock. The lustrous sands and sparklingly clear seas he alluded to as resulting from this geological feature are key attributes of the Cornish coast, so it is unsurprising that several of the Pre-Raphaelites painted the county.

For John Brett, Cornwall provided a lasting source of inspiration, drawing him back again and again over the course of three decades. The legacy of these visits is an astonishing body of work, detailing both well-known and obscure coastal views, capturing the spectacular splendour of the Cornish scenery. A selection of these paintings have been brought together in this book, and for the exhibition which accompanies its launch.

We are greatly indebted to Charles Brett, the artist's great-grandson, both for being the instigator of this project and for travelling, with his wife Cécile, to most of the places depicted to record their exact locations. Whilst much of Cornwall has changed greatly since Brett's time here, many of the coastal locations he depicted have barely been touched, either by mankind or by elemental forces, as Cécile's 21st-century photographs prove.

We would also like to thank Christiana Payne and Michael Hickox for their insightful essays, giving this sumptuous publication further depth of interest and enjoyment.

Penlee House Gallery & Museum are grateful to all the private and public collections who have lent works to the exhibition and to those who provided images for this publication. We also acknowledge the inspiration of the exhibition and book *John Brett – A Pre-Raphaelite on the Shores of Wales,* National Museum of Wales, 2001.

Finally, we are delighted once again to be working in partnership with the publishers, Sansom & Co., to highlight yet another aspect of Cornwall's rich artistic heritage.

Alison Bevan

Director, Penlee House Gallery & Museum, Penzance

FURTHER ACKNOWLEDGEMENTS

Jane Ashe, Richard Barlow, Chris Beetles, Dr Martin Brett, Brian Brooke-Smith, Jenifer Brooke-Smith, Mary Chibnall (Royal Astronomical Society), Dr David Cordingly, Sue Daley (Sotheby's), Caroline Dakers, Sir James Devitt Bt, Peter Finch (National Maritime Museum), Peter Greenslade, Christopher Gridley, Monica Grose-Hodge (Art Workers Guild), Richard Guise, Diana Harding (Royal Yacht Squadron), Alison Keating, Rupert Maas (Maas Gallery), Lynda McLeod (Christie's Archives), Amanda Martin (Isles of Scilly Museum), Steven Miller (Archivist, Art Gallery of New South Wales), Christopher Newall, Susan Oliver, Elizabeth Padmore, The Paul Mellon Centre for Studies in British Art, Alan Powers (Art Workers Guild), Michael Scott, Professor Allen Staley, Oliver Swann (Tryon Gallery), Barbara Thompson (Witt Library), Simon Toll (Sotheby's), Robert Wallers, Gillian Watson, Jack Watson, Peter Watson, Stewart Young.

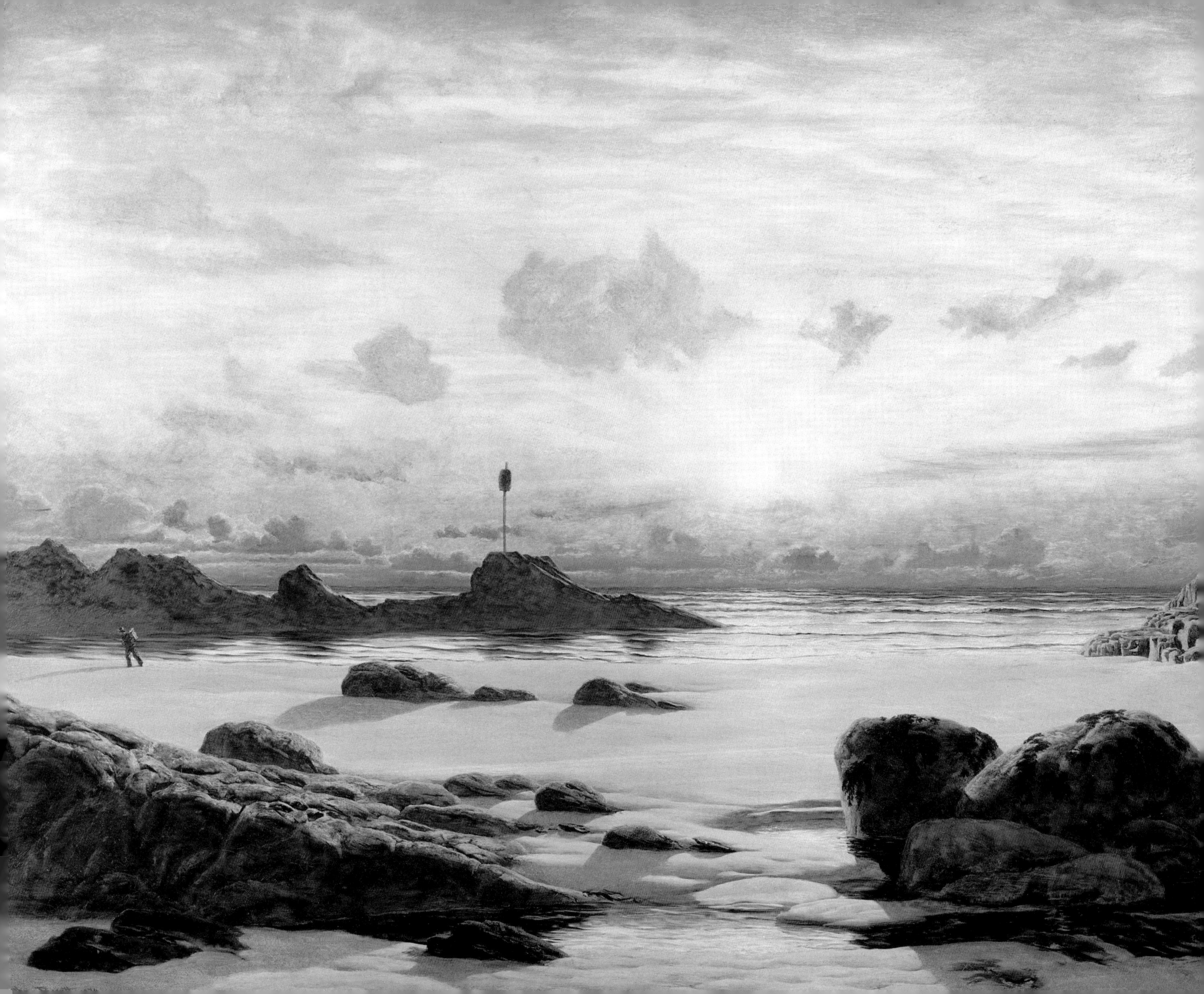

1 FROM PASSIONATE PRE-RAPHAELITE TO SUCCESSFUL MARINE PAINTER: **THE LIFE OF JOHN BRETT**

Christiana Payne

In retrospect, John Brett seems like an artist who had two careers – the first as a struggling Pre-Raphaelite landscape painter and aspiring figure painter in the 1850s and early 1860s, the second as a successful marine painter from the late 1860s until the 'lean years' of the 1890s. A survey of his life reveals strong contrasts between these two periods, not only in his paintings but also in his personality and values.[1] This contrast is borne out by portraits and photographs. The self-portraits of the late 1850s (see fig. 1 p.4) show a young man who is sensitive, vulnerable, intense, visionary; in later life he looks like a fierce, uncompromising person, hardened by experience.

There are two major documentary sources of evidence of Brett's character and beliefs: his early diary, which is very detailed from 1851 to 1854, and then increasingly sketchy until 1861; and the 'Memoranda of the Early Travels of our Children', written alternately by Brett and his 'wife' Mary in their summer holidays from 1879 until 1897.[2] There is a large gap for the 1860s and 1870s, made more acute by the disappearance of most of Brett's correspondence. The early diary and the 'Memoranda' are documents written for very different purposes: the 'Memoranda', as the title implies, was intended as a record for Brett's children, and thus presents a more public and

OPPOSITE
Bude Sands at Sunset [detail]
1874, Oil on canvas, 74 x 124cm
Detroit Art Institute

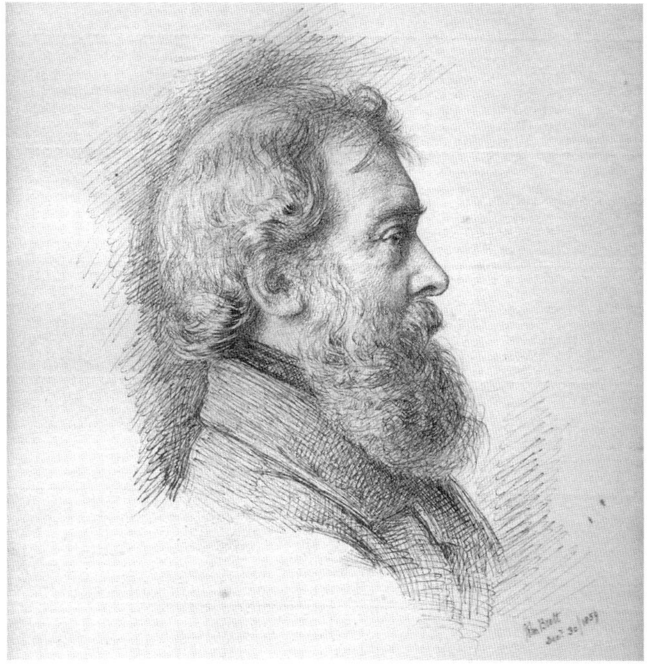

FIG. 2
Portrait of Charles Curtis Brett
Dated Dec 30/1859, Pen and ink
Private Collection

factual account than the early diary, in which he records his private thoughts and aspirations. However, even taking these differences into account, the contrast between the two texts is striking. The young Brett is passionate, effusive, deeply religious, a voracious reader, caught up in the excitement of a new movement in art. The older Brett is practical, hostile to the church, devoted to his growing family and hence to the need for regular sales of his work to support them. In artistic terms, he became, by the 1890s, an isolated reactionary, railing against the new art of Impressionism, which he regarded as a side-effect of decadent eyesight brought on by 'the pernicious habit of wearing spectacles to alleviate a temporary disability which a little perseverance would overcome.'[3] Brett's published writings date from this later period in his life, when he ventured to express his opinions (not very successfully) as an art historian and art critic. In losing (or altering) his religious beliefs Brett was like many intellectuals of his time, troubled by Darwinism, sectarianism, and the restrictive morality of Evangelicalism. He was unusual, however, in adhering to the artistic principles which had first fired his enthusiasm, long after fashions had moved on. In both periods of his life, he was passionately committed to art and fiercely independent in his views.

John Brett was born on December 8th 1831, into a closely-knit and supportive family. He was the second child of Charles Curtis Brett, an army veterinary surgeon and an amateur painter of marines: it is likely that he taught both John and his elder sister Rosa to paint. A diary kept by Charles Curtis between 1863 and 1865, when all his children were grown up, provides a vivid glimpse of a close family circle. Apart from observations on the weather, the diary is mainly devoted to recording the receipt and sending of letters, which were then circulated amongst other family members.[4] A pen-and-ink drawing, dated December 30 1859 (fig. 2), is evidence both of John's assured technique and of his deep affection for his father: he wrote in his diary for January 1 1860 that he had 'made a drawing of his head a few days ago, never more beautiful and fresh, and with elastic curls in his lovely grey locks'.[5] John was protective towards his younger brothers, Theodore, Arthur and Edwin and extremely fond of Rosa, his 'diamond sister', who was a gifted artist in her own right (fig. 4).[6] Rosa's talent lay in extremely finely detailed studies, such as her recently rediscovered *Hayloft* of 1858 (fig. 3). The family circle was something he sought to replicate in his own life after 1870, when, as he wrote, 'whereas I was formerly an individual and lived only one life now I am become multiform and live several lives at once'.[7]

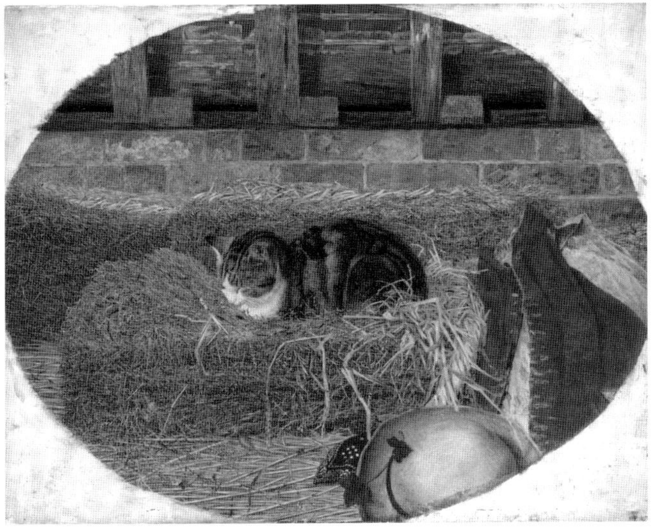

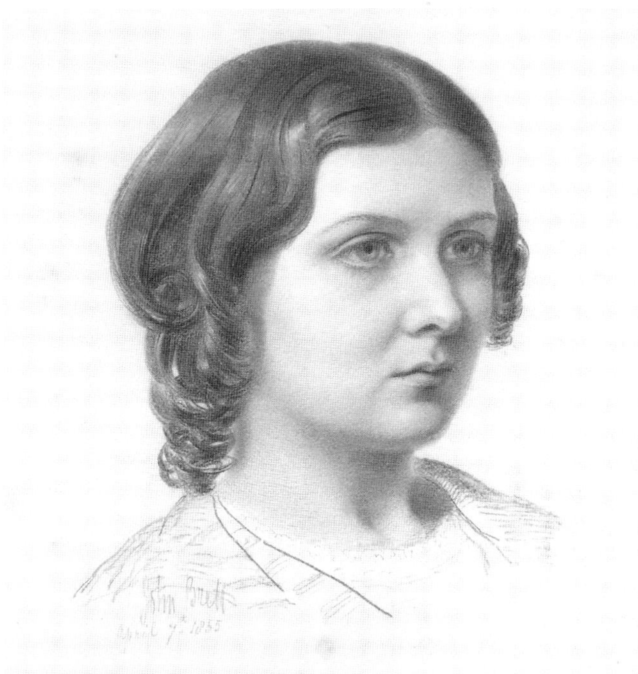

As a young man, Brett was keen to become self-supporting: it grieved him that he was still financially dependent on his father in his 20s, when his siblings also required expenditure on medical and educational needs. The early diaries show him pursuing scientific as well as artistic interests, and experimenting with a number of schemes to bring in income, including the invention of a sketching-seat. He established a good practice as a drawing-master, with many female pupils, with the unfortunate side-effect of emotional turmoil as he was constantly falling in love with them. However, he wanted to be more than a drawing-master: as he wrote in his diary, 'I indulge a strong hope to be one day a great artist'.[8] Following a spell in Dublin, he grew up in and around Maidstone, and his early diaries repeatedly express his love for the lush Kent countryside. In January 1853, at the age of 21, he moved to London to prepare for entry to the Royal Academy Schools, a change of scene which caused him much homesickness.

Quite early on, he read Ruskin's writings and met members of the Pre-Raphaelite Brotherhood (initially, it seems, through the Ormes, to whom he was related by marriage), but he had a somewhat uneasy relationship with them. Brett was aware that he was awkward in society, sufficiently well-connected to meet 'men of genius' but wanting to prove his ability first. He records the books that he read, often lives of potential role models, including Goethe, Jean Paul Richter, John Constable and Benjamin Robert Haydon. A major theme of the early diary is his religious life: he was a regular attender at Congregationalist services, and once he moved to London he visited different chapels, trying to decide which one to join. In September 1853, when he recorded the making of two new acquaintances, William Holman Hunt the artist and Thomas Toke Lynch the Congregationalist minister, it was, rather surprisingly, the

FIG. 3
Rosa Brett
The Hayloft
1858, Oil on canvas
Bridgeman Art Library

FIG. 4
Portrait of Rosa Brett
Dated April 7th 1855, Pencil
Private Collection

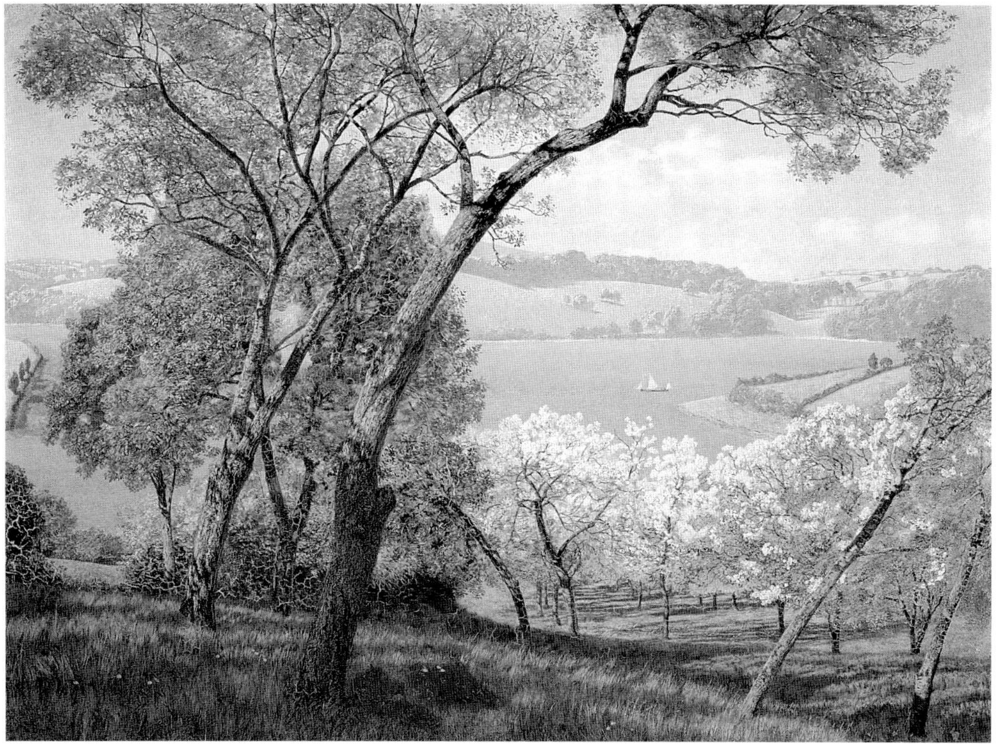

FIG. 5
The River Dart
1866, Oil on canvas, 46 x 61cm
© Sotheby's Images Ltd

latter he was most excited by.[9] Lynch became famous in 1856, when his publication, *The Rivulet* (1855), a collection of poems which could also be sung as hymns, led to a bitter controversy within the Congregationalist church. Lynch's writings express a rapturous appreciation of the beauties of nature, seen in symbolic terms. Flowers are emblems of God's goodness, mountains represent hope and valleys are visions of Paradise. The poems also use the waves of the sea and rock pools to illustrate devotional themes.[10] Lynch's opponents accused him of pantheism or Deism. Brett, however, evidently found his approach highly congenial: he bought books by Lynch and illustrated themes from his writings in his sketchbooks, particularly in 1857 and 1858. In 1858, for example, he made a drawing of himself, or one of his brothers 'under our garden wall at Detling' and wrote on it lines from Lynch beginning: 'I sat at evening in the shade, a Bible on my knee:/Still heaven beautiful above, cool air around me free.'[11] At this stage in his life Brett was a teetotaller and a strict sabbatarian – he was troubled by an invitation from J. D. Harding, who gave him drawing lessons, to call on a Sunday as 'the greatest temptation I have had'.[12] Like John Constable and Samuel Palmer before him, he considered the painting of landscape as an act of worship, one that would bring his viewers to a sense of peace and delight, similar to the feelings he himself experienced from his enjoyment of the natural world. 'A work of Art', he wrote, 'is the reflection of the soul, in nature.'[13]

Brett's religious beliefs in the 1850s help to explain the visionary quality of his best paintings: at this period of his life he might have agreed with Caspar David Friedrich, William Blake and Samuel Palmer in their shared belief that we see more clearly with the spiritual than with the physical eye. In April 1852, he was asking himself whether the Ideal was 'the exaltation of nature above its own intrinsic naturalness by the inspiration of the spirit of man? – That spirit expanding itself into pure nature – becoming its living vivifying principle adopting it as its second tabernacle entering into and inspiring every leaf of the tree & herb of the field – and speaking through them as the organs or faculties of his soul? – Is not this the Ideal man assimilating [sic] himself with his companion nature and feeling himself part of God's creation? Is not this the true vocation of the Painter and Poet, to embody & render permanent in a language to be known & read of all men – these glorious feelings?'[14] There is strong evidence that the landscape paintings of the 1850s were imbued, like Lynch's poems, with religious symbolism. We know from his drawings that Brett regarded the boy in *The Stonebreaker* (1857) as being 'outside Eden', separated by thistles and brambles, and by the oppressive nature of his work, from the idyllic landscape beyond.[15] The productive mountain valley of the *Val d'Aosta* (1858) looks like another Eden, to which the sleeping girl has access only through her belief in the cross on her breast. Many of Brett's landscapes of the 1860s, such as the recently rediscovered *Norbury on the Mole* (1862, fig. 32 p.41) and *The River Dart* (1866, fig. 5) show a fertile, productive countryside, with trees in blossom and corn in the ear – a sense of 'God's creation' in its most benign aspect, capable of embodying those 'glorious feelings' that Brett himself had experienced in the countryside.

His later seascapes replace this kind of detail with a careful study of the movements of the waves, the variety of rock types and vegetation, and the clouds in the sky. They seem less obviously 'visionary', but Lynch, like other religious writers of the time, had also used such subjects to illustrate the love of God. Brett's 'Memoranda' show that his attitude to religion changed completely between the 1850s and the 1870s. Instead of going to church or chapel, in 1879 the Bretts were devoting their Sundays to photography; their children were not baptized; church services are described as being like the superstition of monkeys.[16] Previous writers on Brett have claimed that he was an atheist in later life. This does not seem quite the right term for a man who writes repeatedly of his children's souls and says they are 'as beautiful as heaven'.[17] The sea was commonly seen in the nineteenth century as a symbol of eternity, and Brett's seascapes have a sense of stillness, of wonder, that has led some observers to compare them with the work of Caspar David Friedrich. *Bude Sands at Sunset* (1874, fig. 6), with its solitary figure walking across a deserted beach at twilight, is particularly evocative. It may be, then, that although he was hostile in later life to organized religion, he retained, nonetheless, his basic faith in nature as a source of the spiritual.

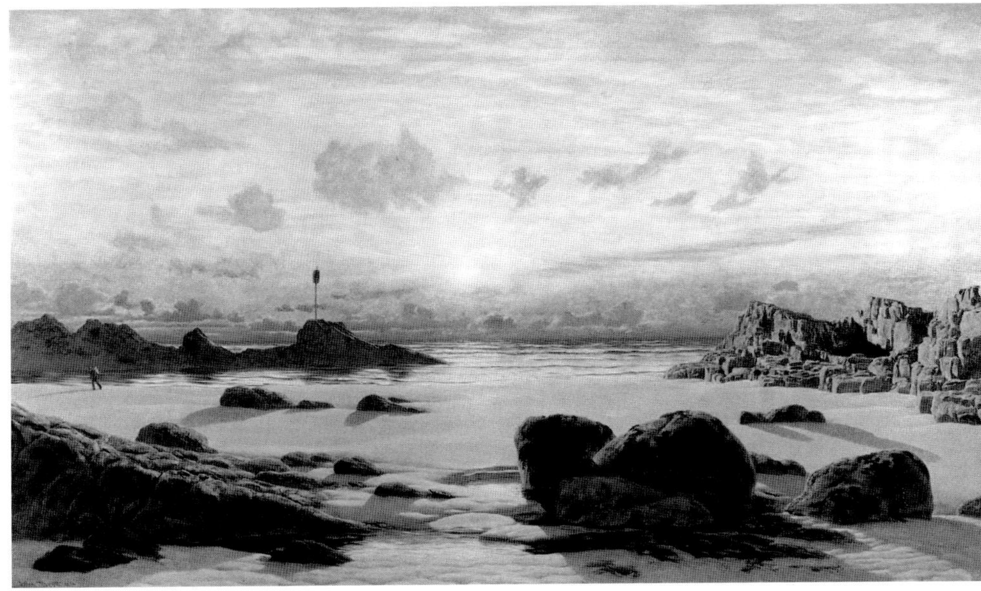

FIG. 6
Bude Sands at Sunset
1874, Oil on canvas, 74 x 124cm
Detroit Art Institute

Brett wrote in his diary in March 1853: 'where there is uphill work there only can I thrive'.[18] It is a feature of his artistic career that he was repeatedly going back to first principles, beginning his apprenticeship all over again. He did this when he went to the Academy as a student in 1853, and drew from the cast and then from the life model, going back to basics although he was already proficient as a painter of landscape watercolours. On meeting John William Inchbold in the Alps in 1856 and watching him paint, he recorded in his diary that he 'there & then saw that I had never painted in my life, but only fooled and slopped; & thenceforth attempted in a reasonable way to paint all I could see'.[19] His response to reading Ruskin's *Elements of Drawing* in 1857 was to try the exercises recommended for beginners; and yet again, on his voyage to Naples in 1863, he set himself to learn how to draw and paint the sea.[20] He eagerly embraced the artistic credo of Ruskin with its emphasis on laborious work in difficult conditions, hauling his canvases up steep hillsides and spending so much time painting in sunlight that his hands became 'gypsyish' in colour.[21] The great Pre-Raphaelite pictures, however, represented so much labour that a failure to sell one painting would be disastrous. In the years 1858, 1859, 1860 and 1861 he showed only one painting in the annual exhibition of the Royal Academy, each the product of several months' intensive outdoor work and priced accordingly. It is not surprising that his later practice was to produce plenty of finished sketches alongside the large paintings, so that more modest buyers could provide a steady source of income.

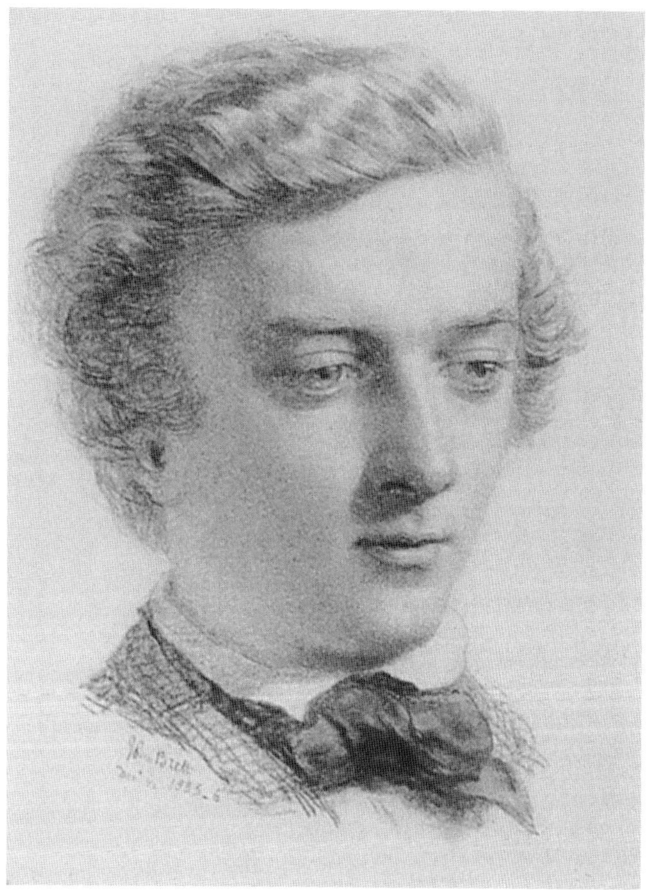

FIG. 7
Portrait of Arthur Brett
1855–6, Pencil, 19 x 16.5cm
Private Collection

Brett first exhibited at the Academy in 1856, and all three of his exhibits were portraits, including a recently rediscovered portrait of his brother Arthur (fig. 7), in a meticulously detailed style which rivalled the new precision of the daguerreotype. With his scientific interests, Brett was drawn to photography from early on in his life, and he may have begun taking photographs himself as early as 1857. This was the year in which he exhibited his first landscape, *The Glacier of Rosenlaui* (fig. 18 p.33), painted in Switzerland in the summer of 1856; Brett records that Dante Gabriel Rossetti told him Ruskin had praised it, but neither Ruskin, nor any other critic, mentioned it in their reviews of the exhibition, and it remained unsold until June 1860, when Hunt persuaded his patron Sir Thomas Fairbairn to buy it.[22] It is now recognized as a weirdly beautiful painting, which typifies the intense interest taken by Brett and many of his contemporaries in geology in the 1850s. Geology, like astronomy, another science in which Brett was passionately interested, occupied a central place in the religious debates of this decade. Ruskin included rapturous accounts of the beauty of rocks, which he saw as proof of God's Providence, in his fourth volume of *Modern Painters* (1856), which was probably the immediate stimulus to Brett's visit to Switzerland. Ruskin argued that the hardest rocks were the most beautiful, because God had so ordered the world that they would be visible in the mountains. He also remarked on the beauty of the sand and the sea on a granite coast: he wrote that granite decomposes into the purest sand or clay 'the sand often of the purest white, always lustrous and bright in its particles';

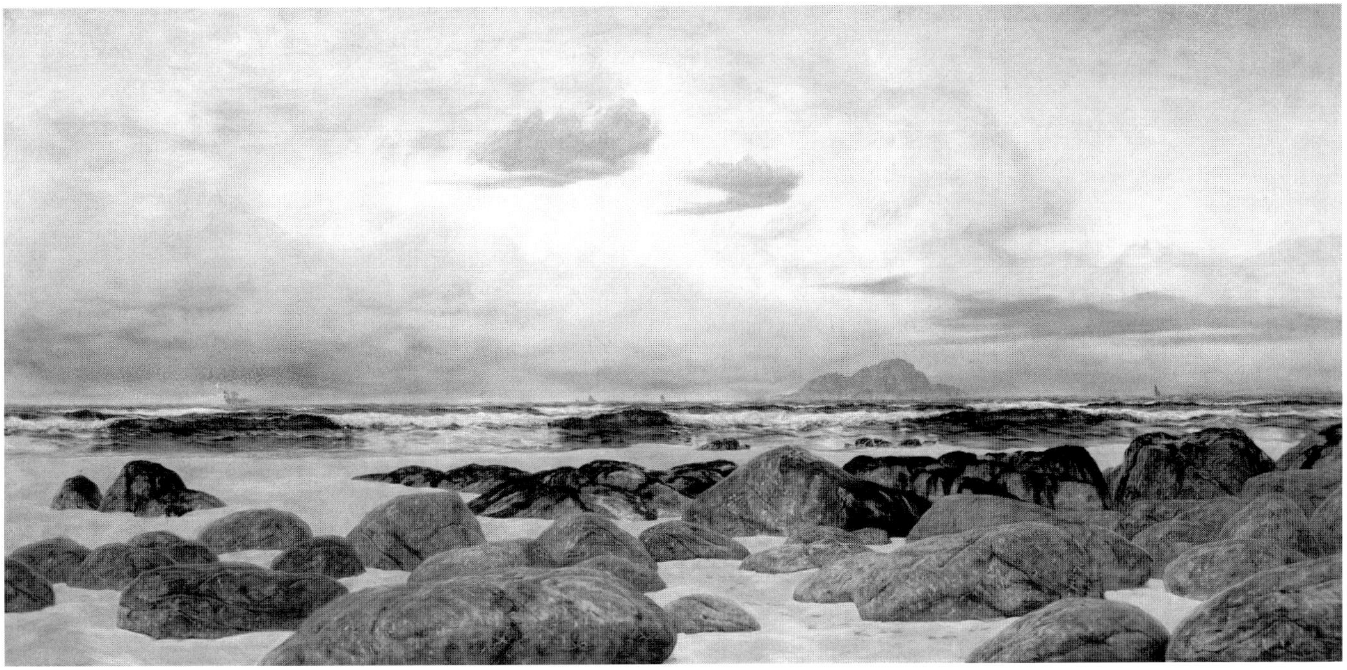

FIG. 8
A Morning amongst the Granite Boulders
1873, Oil on canvas, 104 x 211cm
© Sotheby's Images Ltd

while 'the sea which washes a granite coast is as unsullied as a flawless emerald'.[23] Brett was to continue his interest in geology in his coastal landscapes, showing a preference for the hard rocks which Ruskin had admired, the granite, serpentine and porphyry of the Penwith and Lizard peninsulas. The title of one of his earliest exhibited Cornish landscapes, *A Morning amongst the Granite Boulders* (1873, fig. 8) draws attention to the material of the rocks, in a painting which, like Ruskin's writings, brings out the beauty of their contrasting colours. Ultimately, however, a knowledge of geology could conflict with religious belief, as the Biblical accounts of creation became increasingly difficult to reconcile with the great age of the earth. This may have been one of the reasons for the change in Brett's attitude to religion in the late 1850s and 1860s.

1857 was the year in which Brett was most closely associated with the Pre-Raphaelites, exhibiting with them in two special exhibitions, at Russell Place in London and in a travelling exhibition which went to Philadelphia and Boston. There is strong circumstantial evidence that he was courting Christina Rossetti, the poet and sister of Dante Gabriel Rossetti, at this time. As Jan Marsh has pointed out, Christina's poem, 'No, Thank You, John' (1860) implies that he was more smitten than she was, yet an earlier poem, 'A Birthday' (1857), which begins 'My heart is like a singing bird', suggests that she, too, was deeply in love. An unfinished, jewel-like portrait of her by Brett (fig. 9) is still in the family. Her face and hair are delineated in meticulous detail against a background of ultramarine and delicately painted feathers – an echo of the references to birds in

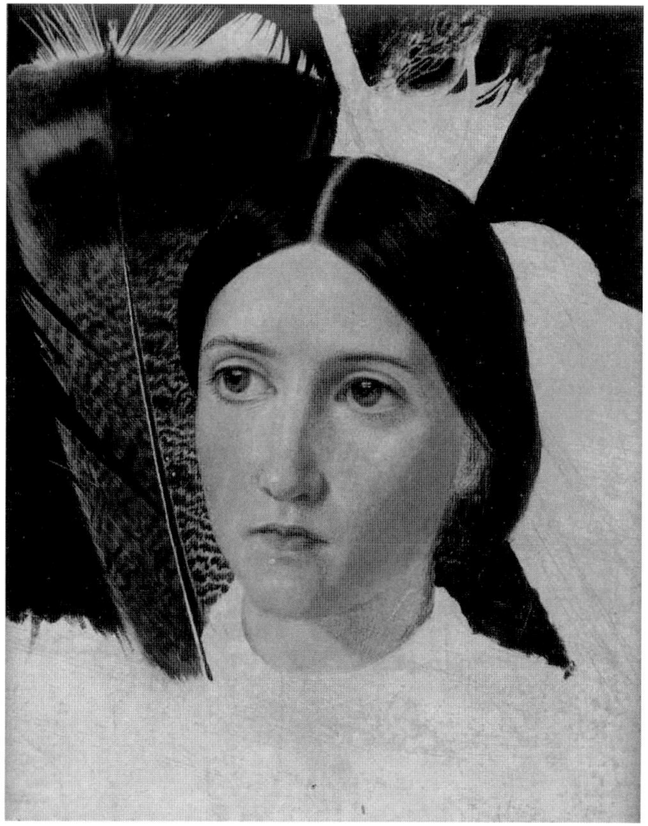

FIG. 9
Portrait of Christina Rossetti
1857, Oil on panel, 13.3 x 10.1cm
Private Collection

her poem. Jan Marsh has also observed that the social theme of Brett's *Stonebreaker* (fig. 20 p.36), painted this summer, matches the themes that occur in her poetry.[24] There would have been religious obstacles to their marriage, however, as Christina's High Church Anglicanism was far removed from Brett's allegiance, at this point in his life, to the Congregationalists. In early 1858 the two families were on visiting terms, but the abortive relationship may have caused a later coolness between Brett and Dante Gabriel Rossetti, which contributed to Brett's move out of the Pre-Raphaelite orbit in the 1860s.[25]

The first critical notice of Brett's work as a landscape painter was in a review of the 1857 Russell Place exhibition, anonymous but known to be by Coventry Patmore. This sounds a note of caution, which was to become a major theme in reviews of Brett's work. Like Thomas Seddon, Brett's eyes were compared to 'simple photographic lenses'; his two watercolours were 'wonders of laborious and effective finish', but Inchbold's paintings were 'that and a good deal more' and 'the most valuable landscapes' were those of William Davis 'who paints less the scene than the feeling of the scene before him'.[26] Patmore sets up a hierarchical mode of judging landscape painting which ultimately goes back to academic theory and the idea that merely copying nature was an inferior quality. The advent of photographs sharpened this debate, because it became important to promote the claims of art to be superior to photography. Brett's landscapes were notable for their fine detail, and it became an easy criticism to say that they lacked 'feeling' or 'sentiment'. However, another critic in the same year described Brett as 'a painter of thought and feeling'.[27] Ultimately, the analysis of feeling in a landscape painting depends on the subjective judgment of the viewer, but Brett's early diary certainly proves that, for him, the natural world was a source of deep joy. The idea that his meticulously naturalistic technique was emotionless seems to have originated in an attempt to put Brett down, to remind him of his lowly status in relation to other artists. F. G. Stephens reiterated this implication in 1859 when he wrote (also in an unsigned review) that Brett, in his *Val d'Aosta,* had taken 'a grand subject' and treated it with 'the finicking spirit of a drawing-master'.[28] Both Patmore and Stephens were friends of Brett, who knew his personal history. It was, indeed, as a drawing master that he had first come to London, and he was interested in photography from a very early stage. The art world was tremendously competitive, and Brett probably did not help his position in relation to other artists and critics by being self-evidently proud of his achievements. As he wrote in his diary in 1856 'I am conceited & proud in my inmost nature and affected in my external deportment… but I can't help it – I do hate it eternally'.[29]

The most famous statement of the charge that Brett's work lacked feeling came, ironically, in the review which established his reputation – Ruskin's commentary on the *Val d'Aosta* (fig. 17 p.30). This review damaged Brett's prospects in two diametrically opposed ways: those who had reason to dislike Ruskin (such as Millais) were repelled by Ruskin's extravagant praise of Brett as the artist who had made it possible 'for the first time in history' to provide as much knowledge about a place as if the viewer of the picture were actually there; others, more sympathetic to Ruskin, accepted the latter's argument that too literal a transcription of landscape could not communicate emotion. As Michael Hickox points out in his essay in this volume, Ruskin's relationship with Brett was fraught with tensions, and it seems that Brett quite often ignored Ruskin's forcefully given advice. The negative part of the review, therefore, may reflect Ruskin's personal disappointment in Brett as much as an objective analysis of the painting. *The Stonebreaker,* the *Val d'Aosta* and the *Hedger* (1858–60, fig. 22 p.36) all show human figures oppressed by the need to labour in surroundings which are full of beauty and fertility. They invite us to admire the productiveness of the earth – proof of God's benevolence – at the same time as evoking sympathy for fallen human beings. In *The Stonebreaker,* the bird sings, the puppy plays, the foreground foliage is intricate and the distance exhilarating to the viewer – but the boy is a pauper, doomed to labour. The sleeping girl in the *Val d'Aosta*, similarly, is a child labourer whose slumber could be interpreted as the result of exhaustion. In the *Hedger,* an adult labourer patiently exercises a well-known rural skill, while his daughter, saddled with responsibilities beyond her years, stands a little way off holding baby and lunch. Brett was very fond of children: his early diary is full of expressions of affectionate concern for his younger brothers, Arthur and Edwin (and it was Edwin who posed for the boy in *The Stonebreaker*). Later on, when he had his own children, he and Mary not only devoted a great deal of attention to the development of their children but also adopted unusually progressive notions of child-rearing. They chose not to punish the children for naughtiness, believing that they would learn good behaviour through kindness and good example rather than through chastisement.[30] Ironically, Ruskin exerted his influence to turn Brett away from figure painting, yet in these early landscapes it is the tension between the figure and the landscape which provides both the symbolism, and much of the emotional impact of the picture.

Ruskin's relationships with artists, as Robert Hewison has pointed out, followed a particular pattern, originating, perhaps, in his relationship with his own father, John James Ruskin, who, incidentally, seems to have been a much more steady friend to Brett than was his son. Lavish praise was followed by criticism, often of a deliberately hurtful and rather personal kind.[31] This was certainly the pattern followed by Ruskin in his review of the *Val d'Aosta*. Brett asked a high price for the work, 450 guineas (perhaps on Ruskin's advice); when it did not sell, Ruskin bought it for £200. Characteristically, Brett sold it for this knock-down price because he needed to raise money for his younger brother Arthur, who had gone into the army. Some months later John James called on Brett and 'brought me £50

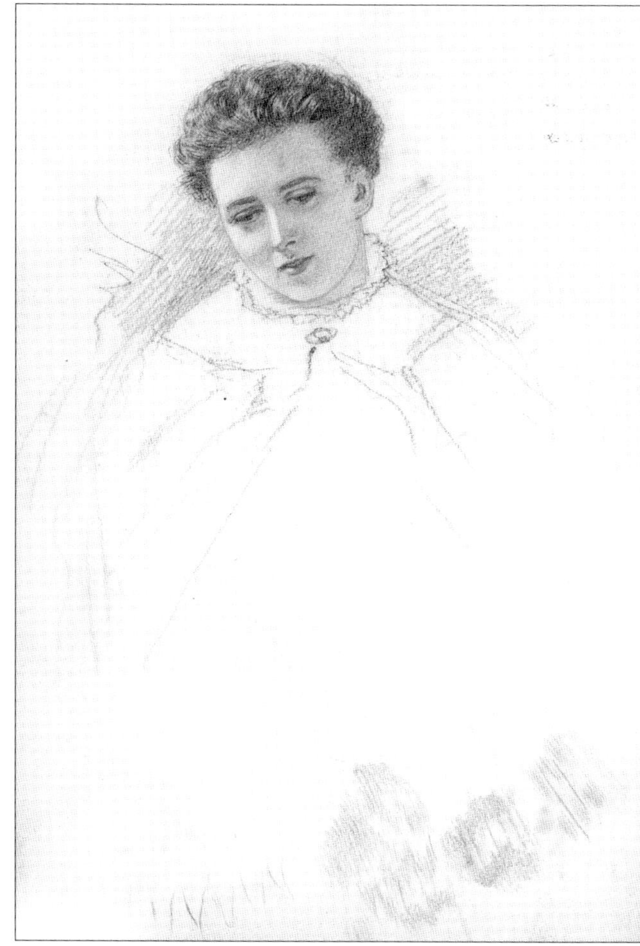

FIG. 11
Georgina Weldon
December 1866, Graphite pencil
Sketchbook No. 21, *'Towyn 1866–7'*

protesting he couldn't keep the Val d'Aosta at the price I had received'.[32] It may be significant that the final break between Brett and Ruskin occurred in 1864, around the time of Ruskin's father's death. John James Ruskin had taken a paternal interest in Brett, inviting him to dinner on several occasions when his son was away, and even lending him money in 1862.[33] As Michael Hickox points out in his essay, Ruskin was dismissive of the subject of Brett's next major painting after the *Val d'Aosta,* the *Hedger.* Rather pathetically, however, Brett wanted to wait for Ruskin's opinion before deciding what price to ask for the *Hedger.*[34] It remained unsold until 1863, when B. G. Windus bought it for £150; Brett had originally asked £300.[35]

Despite these setbacks, Brett continued to drive himself 'uphill', embarking on an ambitious painting of a medieval knight and his lady crossing a river in front of Warwick Castle, which has been lost since 1865, although Brett caught a brief glimpse of it in a shop window in 1887.[36] This time he was successful in achieving a price commensurate with the labour involved: Thomas Plint agreed to buy *Warwick Castle* for £420 in January 1861. This was a turning point for Brett: as soon as the Academy exhibition was over he was off to Paris with £60 in his pocket, and for the first half of the 1860s he spent long periods of time abroad. This also seems to have been a period when his strict religious and moral beliefs were giving way to a more secular and permissive way of life. There is no mention of church or chapel in the diary entries after the end of 1854. A gap of over two years is followed by summaries at the end of each year up to 1859, and the diary then peters out into brief one-line entries for selected dates. There are a few tantalizing hints of his state of belief. At Christmas 1858 he rejoices that he is 'secluded from the chief snare of the Devil', but by July 1859 he comments 'How deeply dyed life is with death, how much better never to have known either!'[37] 1859 was the year of the publication of Darwin's *On the Origin of Species,* a time when many found their Christian faith sorely shaken.

In the 1860s Brett appears to have had affairs with at least two married women, Mathilde Loeser and Georgina Weldon. Most of the evidence for these relationships comes from the diary kept by Georgina Weldon, who writes in February 1865

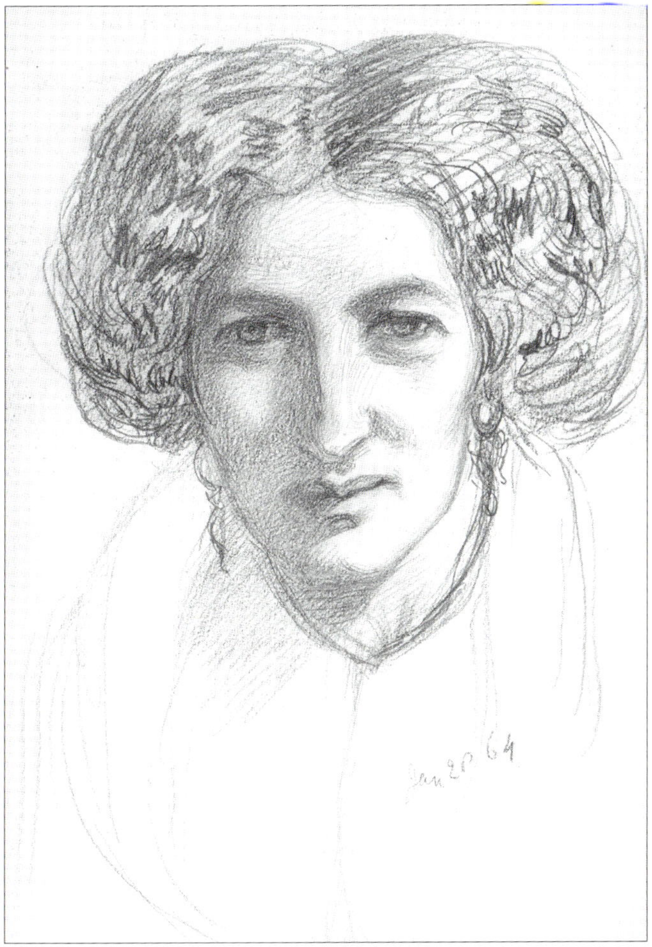

FIG. 10
Mathilde Loeser
Dated Jan 28 1864,
Graphite pencil , 25.7 x 17.5cm
Sketchbook No. 14, *'Capri 1863'*
© National Maritime Museum, London

that Madame Loeser has warned her that Brett is 'a most dangerous seducteur': this is corroborated, however, by a series of intimate, seductive portrait drawings he made of both women (figs. 10 and 11).[38] In the drawings of Georgina he brings out her childlike, petulant beauty, often with delicate effects of lighting; Mathilde, by contrast, appealed to him for her abundant hair and exotic features, at times looking like his own version of Rossetti's Janey Morris. Ruskin's father, John James, may have been thinking of Brett's drawings of Mathilde when he asked if he could buy one of his sketches of 'the lovely Lady of Florence', adding perceptively 'for in Human Countenance your great Strength lies'.[39] Mathilde Loeser was the subject of his only full-length portrait, *Lady with a Dove* (1864, fig. 12), in which he juxtaposes his loved one's features with the delicate feathers of a bird, just as he had done in the earlier portrait of Christina Rossetti.

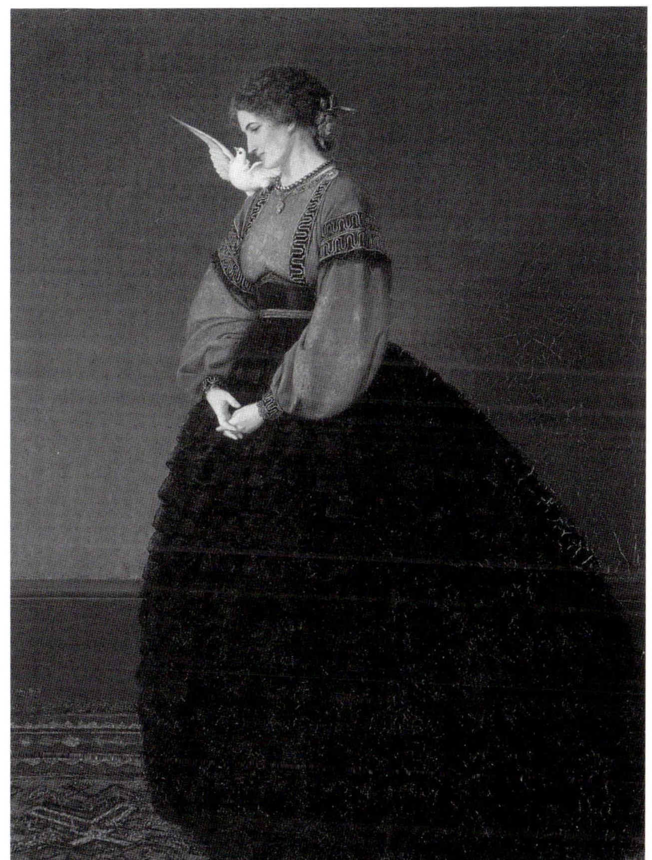

FIG. 12
Lady with a Dove
1864, Oil on canvas, 61 x 46cm
© Tate, London, 2005

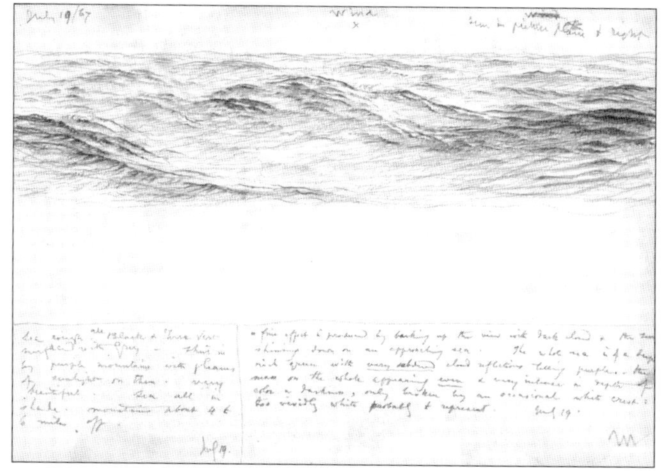

FIG. 13
Drawing of the sea, with annotations
Dated July 19 1867
Graphite pencil, 17.8 x 26cm
Sketchbook No. 23, *'Victoria 1867'*
© National Maritime Museum, London

In 1861 Brett was in the Alps again, in Champéry, where he painted another picture (now lost) of a fertile valley – described in his Diary as 'the truest paradise I have yet seen' – and evidently had a sociable time with other travellers, from the United States, France and Germany (Brett was a good linguist, who taught himself French and German). A sudden death of one of the party ended the 'dream', however, and Brett never painted in the Alps again.[40] He went on to Florence: when he returned to England in March 1862, he had been away for nine and a half months. He was back in Florence the following winter, from late November until the end of March 1863. Here he seems to have moved in literary circles, becoming acquainted with Isabella Blagden, the close friend of Robert Browning. Brett had always taken a keen interest in poetry, even writing some himself in his early diaries, and he asked Browning's permission to include lines from one of his poems in the Royal Academy catalogue to go with his picture of *Florence from Bellosguardo* (fig. 31 p.40).[41] However, this was destined not to be shown at the Academy: it was rejected, an event which caused a scandal in the art world and stimulated other rejected artists to hold an exhibition in the Cosmopolitan Club in London, an English 'salon des refusés' in the same year as the famous French one. Brett's work had often been badly hung at the Academy, but this was a worse insult and suggests some resentment, of his artistic ambition, perhaps, or his ability to winter abroad, or his involvement in elevated social circles. Holman Hunt and Coventry Patmore were both active on his behalf, although John Ruskin did less than Brett might have expected. In the event Brett showed that he did not need the approval of the Royal Academicians, as his painting sold immediately to Lord Overstone.[42] This was the start of a period in which he gradually acquired a wide circle of loyal patrons, mainly from the worlds of finance, industry and the professions, freeing him both from the need to depend on the kindness of his acquaintances in the Pre-Raphaelite movement, and also from relying, as so many of his contemporaries did, on dealers.[43] Many of his contacts would seem to have been made through gentlemen's clubs: he was an active member, first of the Hogarth Club, then, later on, of the Savile Club and the Athenaeum.

The sale to Lord Overstone enabled Brett to go back on his travels, and in August 1863 he took a passage on a ship, sailing round Gibraltar to Sorrento, possibly to rendezvous with Mathilde Loeser, whom he seems to have met for the first time in Florence earlier that year. Two successive winters were spent with Mathilde in Capri, a place for physical rather than spiritual pleasures, between 1863 and 1865. Brett's love life was further complicated by the presence of Georgina Weldon and her husband (who seem to have had a flexible approach to marriage), with Georgina goading Mathilde into displays of jealousy. It was in this period that Brett began his intensive study of the sea. Yachting was becoming popular at the time, and instantaneous photography had made it easier for artists to achieve accuracy in their depictions of moving waves. A market was developing, not just for the traditional type of marine painting of ships (often warships) against conventionally painted waves, but for studies of the sea for its own sake, in compositions which would remind viewers of their holidays, of travels in their yacht or walks along the beach. Henry Moore, a contemporary of Brett's, was also moving into this area of art in the 1860s. Moore's seascapes, however, show land, if at all, only in the distance; Brett's skill in painting rocks enabled him to incorporate detailed studies of headlands and boulders, thus capitalizing on the popular interest in geology, which was often pursued at the seaside.

His sketchbooks from the 1860s reveal his determined attempts to master his new subject matter, both visually and scientifically: careful drawings of the surface of the sea (fig. 13) are accompanied by verbal observations on its appearance and colours, and mathematical diagrams to convey his understanding of the profiles of the waves. In a sketchbook used on a trip to Achill Island on the west coast of Ireland, in 1869, he made intensive studies of rough seas, with waves breaking on the rocks (fig. 14), which he drew in closely observed detail. In his later sketchbooks, such features are indicated in a much more summary fashion, but this was because he had spent years perfecting his knowledge.

In the 1860s Brett produced some hauntingly beautiful watercolours, such as *February in the Isle of Wight* (1866 Birmingham Museums & Art Gallery), in which the early blossoming of the trees, delineated in extremely fine

FIG. 14
A Cove in the promontory of Dooagh
Dated Sep 10 1869.
Graphite pencil
Sketchbook No. 32, *'Ireland 1869'*
© National Maritime Museum, London

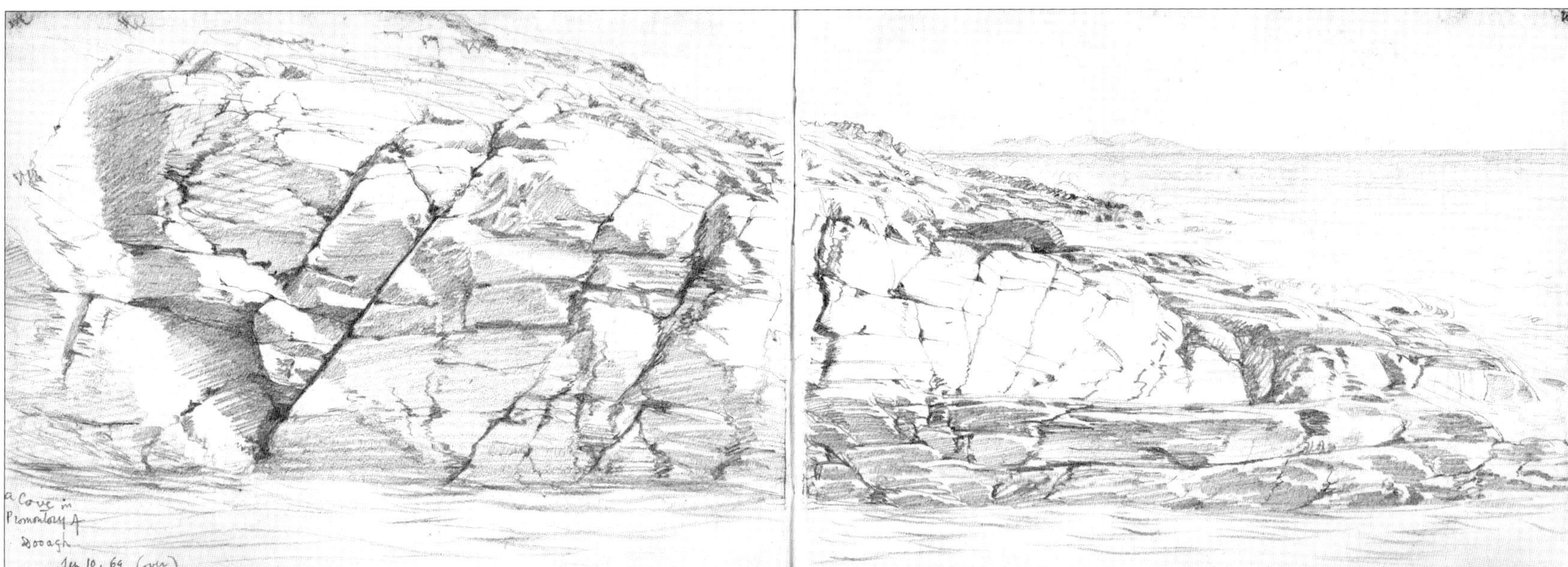

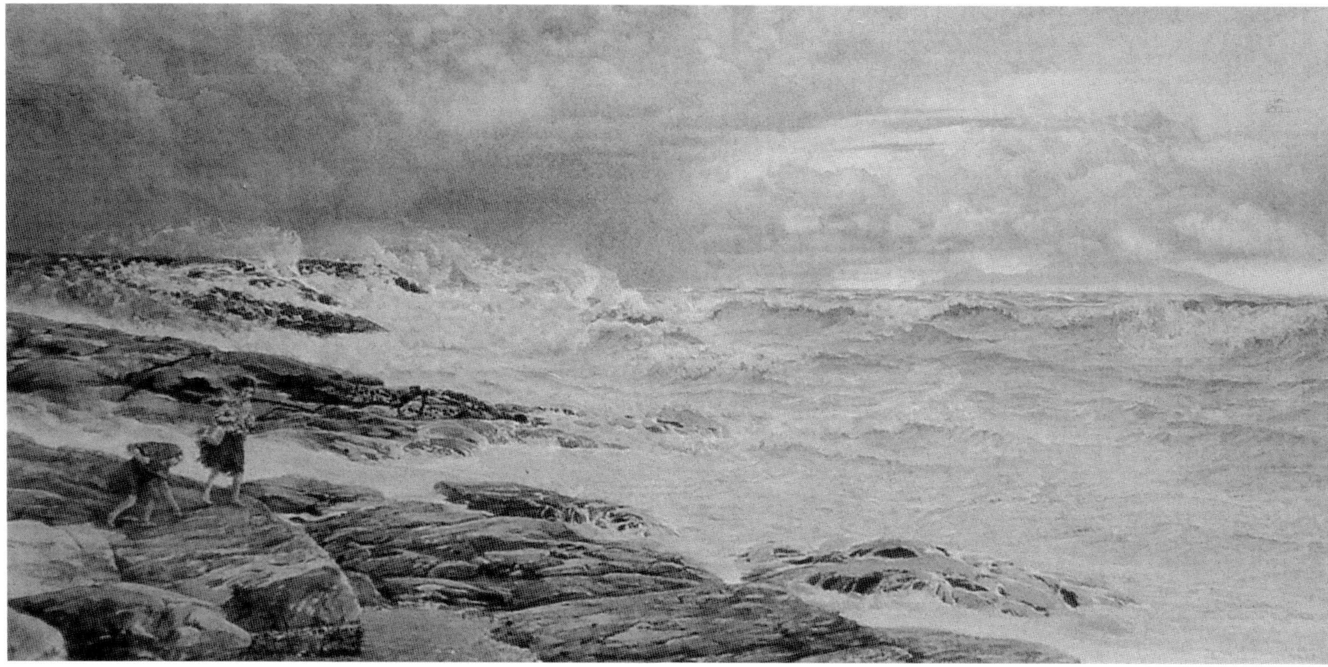

FIG. 15
The Wreckers' Paradise, Achill Island
1869. Watercolour. 24.1 x 49.5cm
Private Collection

brushstrokes, has all the appearance of a natural miracle, and a ghostlike sailing ship is just glimpsed in the bay below. This was a companion to *November in the Isle of Wight*, now lost. The studies on Achill Island also bore fruit in a watercolour (fig. 15) in which two girls, inmates of a colony set up to convert Irish Catholics to Protestantism, watch the waves breaking on the rocks. However, such watercolours are rare after 1870: Brett may have felt that they required too much work in relation to their saleable value. In these works the theme is still man in the landscape, as in the Pre-Raphaelite paintings of the 1850s, but the figures are becoming progressively less important, and in most of his landscapes after 1870 Brett dispensed with them altogether.

Brett appears to have been constantly on the move in these years. In March 1865, just after he received the news of the sudden death of his father, Brett's relationship with Mathilde Loeser ended, and by July he had commissioned a yacht, the *Baby*, which he sailed to Devon in the summer of 1866. He travelled to Holyhead in the winter of 1866–7, spending Christmas with the Weldons, and the following summer he went in the cutter *Victoria* to the west coast of Scotland for two months, a trip he was to repeat in the *Viking* in 1883. In September 1867 he sailed in another vessel, the *Royal Charlotte*, from Liverpool as far south as Lundy Island, returning to the Weldons in Beaumaris for Christmas. The resulting sea paintings were critically acclaimed and found willing buyers, but it must have been a strangely unsatisfying life for someone of Brett's close family background and early religious convictions. We know from her diaries that Georgina Weldon was petulant and capricious, and it must have been with some relief that Brett, in his late thirties, met and settled down with Mary Ann Howcroft.

Mary Brett (as she became) was of lower social standing than John: her father was a coachman, and in the 1881 census her parents are recorded as living in London, with another daughter, Eliza, a dressmaker, and a lodger (by this time the Bretts had six children and two servants, a cook and a housemaid). However, there is no evidence of any contact with her family after Mary began living with John, and oral tradition within the family relates that Mary's relatives refused to have anything more to do with her after this time. We do not know how the couple met, but it seems that Mary was quite well educated: she contributed regularly to the 'Memoranda', and in 1879 she records that she has been teaching the children French.[44] In family photographs she often looks anxious and worn, but occasionally we see a more relaxed side to her character (fig. 16). This photograph was taken in the gallery of the house that Brett designed himself in Keswick Road, Putney, with progressive features such as labour-saving built-in furniture, a burglar alarm and central heating. In the gallery, oil sketches from nature were arranged just above the dado, with portraits of the children on the next level. Both this house and the later Daisyfield embodied many of the idiosyncracies of the increasingly eccentric Brett. Flat roofs were designed to accommodate telescopes so that he could make astronomical observations (which were sufficiently distinguished to earn him a place on an expedition to Sicily to record the solar eclipse of December 1870, and fellowship of the Royal Astronomical Society in 1871). Domestic servants were kept to a minimum, and the children were provided with workbenches so that they could learn a trade, but at the same time the family crest over the door (fig. 31 p.53) proclaimed Brett's pride in his Anglo-Irish ancestry. The burglar alarm enabled the family to go away for long periods each summer, but was also the result of Brett's distrust of servants. Brett's ideas were remarkably original. As Mark Girouard has pointed out, Daisyfield was an astonishingly early example of an open-plan design, without precedent in England.[45]

After 1870 Brett's life settled into a regular pattern: painting campaigns on the coast in the summer, which soon began to double as family holidays, followed by winters in London preparing his works for exhibition. Although there is no record of a marriage, he was a devoted partner and father, and there is no hint of any further dalliances like those he enjoyed with Georgina Weldon and Mathilde Loeser in the 1860s.[46] While he was obviously captivated by the beauties and the challenges of painting rocks and sea, it also became more important to him to achieve a steady income through his art, and he developed what some have seen as an almost mechanical way of working.

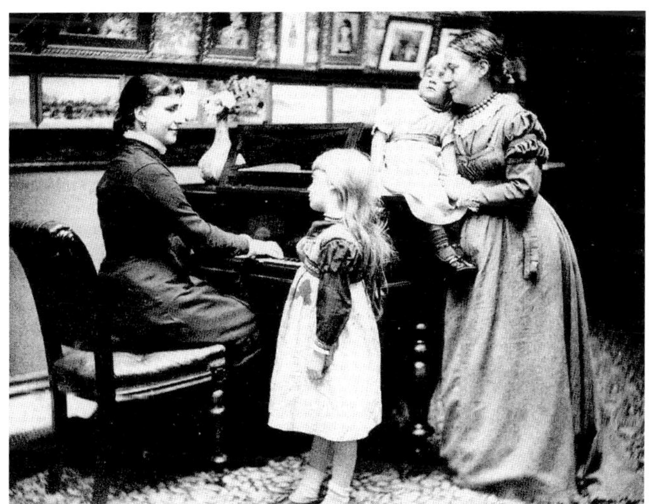

FIG. 16
Photograph of Mary Brett with Miss Christie, Daisy and Alfred, c.1878
Private Collection

In this later period of his life, only the sketches were painted out of doors. He often chose viewpoints that were difficult to get to or even dangerous, but the sketches were painted quite rapidly. The best ones have a freshness that is reminiscent of Constable, whose oil sketches were beginning to be exhibited and appreciated at about this time. The large paintings for exhibition, however, were worked up in the studio. They attracted favourable comments from reviewers: Tom Taylor, for example, wrote in *The Times* that *A Morning amongst the Granite Boulders* (fig. 8) was a 'wonderful painting' which he commended to 'all lovers and students of seaside nature' who would 'admire the wonderful skill with which the colour and surface of granite sands, the colour and movement of sea, and the conformation of cloud are here represented.'[47]

In contrast to the difficulties Brett had in selling his work in the late 1850s, his patrons paid high prices in the late 1870s and early 1880s. His best year was 1881, when his total sales came to £ 2,800; a single painting, *Golden Prospects*, sold for £1,200. His family grew rapidly, and in July 1882 Brett was able to write: 'We now have seven children and they are all in superb health and not a cloud shows on their horizon… They radiate pleasure on all they meet and fill the lives of their parents with delightful days and their outlook with delightful dreams'. At this stage he was investing about £1,000 a year towards his children's inheritance, and 'all anxiety about keeping the wolf from the door has disappeared'.[48] It was also in 1881 that he achieved his ambition of being elected an Associate of the Royal Academy, although he never made the status of full Academician. These were the years of his idyllic painting campaigns in Cornwall, which are described in detail in Charles Brett's essay in this catalogue. The resulting paintings are less intense, perhaps, than the laborious works of the late 1850s, but they continue the theme of his early work: a delight in the natural world and a desire to communicate that feeling to his audience.

NOTES

1 This essay represents work in progress, my intention being to write a full-length study of Brett's life and work. I am extremely grateful to all those scholars and Brett family members who have allowed me access to their collections and have generously shared the results of their own research. Special thanks are due to Charles Brett, Martin Brett, David Cordingly, Michael Hickox, Christopher Gridley and Christopher Newall. I am also very grateful to the Paul Mellon Centre for Studies in British Art, for a research grant which enabled me to travel to public and Private Collections.

2 'John Brett. Diary 1851–61', typescript, edited by Charles Brett; and 'Memoranda of the Early Travels of our Children, written for them by John Brett and Mary Brett, on alternate Sundays commencing in the Autumn of 1879 at Penally', typescript, edited by Charles Brett. The original documents are in a Private Collection.

3 John Brett, 'Realism in Painting', *The Contemporary Review*, no. 402, June 1899, p.830.

4 'Charles Curtis Brett. Diary, 1863–5', typescript, edited by Charles Brett. The original is in a Private Collection.

5 Diary, p.66 (New Year's Day. 1860).

6 He describes her thus in his Diary, p.43 (August 16 1853). On her work as an artist, see Pamela Gerrish Nunn, 'Rosa Brett, Pre-Raphaelite', *Burlington Magazine* 126, October 1984, pp.630–2.

7 Memoranda, p.2 (September 7 1879).

8 Diary, p.4 (August 28 1851).

9 'The chief mile stone that marks this period is...the formation of 2 new acquaintances those of Thomas T Lynch & Holman Hunt... the former at least I regard with a peculiar hopefulness... to have any degree of intimacy with so powerful & exquisite a mind is a great privilege & cannot be fruitless'. Diary, p.46 (September 14 1853).

10 See T. T. Lynch, *Memorials of Theophilus Trinal, Student* (London: Longman, Brown, Green and Longmans, 1850). Brett records that he fell in love with this book and bought it in September 1853, 'perhaps imprudently for I certainly had not 5/6 to spare'. Brett also knew Lynch's book of poems, *The Rivulet: a Contribution to Sacred Song* (London: Robert Theobald, 1855).

11 The drawing is in an album of sketches in a Private Collection. Its state of finish (including indications of a frame) suggest that Brett was thinking of it either as an idea for an exhibition picture, or as part of a series for an illustrated edition of the book.

12 Diary, p.31 (March 17 1853).

13 Ibid, p.45 (September 8 1853).

14 Ibid, p.11 (April 4 1852).

15 M. Hickox and C. Payne, 'Sermons in Stones: John Brett's *The Stonebreaker* reconsidered', in Ellen Harding, ed., *Re-framing the Pre-Raphaelites: Historical and Theoretical Essays* (London: Scolar Press, 1995), pp.99–114.

16 Memoranda, p.2: Brett writes that photography is 'at present the particular divine service set apart in this establishment for Sundays' (September 7 1879). When 14-year-old Daisy had to go to church for the first time in her life, she found it 'beastly' and Brett sympathised, 'thinking the superstition only worthy of monkeys' (p.44–5, July 10 1887).

17 For example, he writes of Daisy: 'She has always been encouraged to succeed, and has plenty of bright and healthy spirits, but her gentle little soul likes to draw a veil over itself' (Memoranda, p.5, October 5 1879). In 1887 he writes: 'The small children who are with us... are enjoying their little lives thoroughly and are as beautiful as heaven.'

(Memoranda, p.45, July 10 1887). Christopher Newall writes of Brett that 'eventually he adopted a determined atheism': 'John Brett – the Pre-Raphaelite Years', in John Brett: a *Pre-Raphaelite on the Shores of Wales* (National Museum and Gallery, Cardiff, 2001), p.23.

18 Diary, p.30 (March 14 1853). He was referring to Mr Allon's 'flourishing' chapel, but the remark applies equally well to his artistic practices.

19 Diary, p.64 (December 9 1856).

20 See Charles Brett, 'John Brett and Ruskin's *The Elements of Drawing*', *Burlington Magazine*, September 2005, pp.613–6. The studies of the sea off the coast of Naples are in Sketchbook no. 13, 'Scotia, Bay of Naples +c', National Maritime Museum, Greenwich.

21 Letter from John Brett to his sister Rosa, from Mickleham, dated Oct 7/57. This has been published in full in Michael Hickox, 'John Brett's *The Stonebreaker*', *Review of the Pre-Raphaelite Society*, Vol IV, No. 1, 1996, pp.3–7. The original is in a Private Collection.

22 On this occasion Brett's friendship with Hunt was very productive: on June 7 he records 'wrote to Hunt to try to raise the wind for me'; Hunt came to visit two days later, and by the 23rd of the month Brett had received a letter from Hunt containing a cheque from his patron, Sir Thomas Fairbairn, for 50 guineas. (Early Diary, p.66).

23 E. T. Cook and A. Wedderburn, eds., *The Works of John Ruskin*, Library Edition, Vol. 6, pp.143–4.

24 On Brett's relationship with Christina, see Jan Marsh, *Christina Rossetti: a Literary Biography* (London: Jonathan Cape, 1994), pp.200–217. The second verse of 'A Birthday' reads 'Raise me a dais of silk and down;/Hang it with vair and purple dyes; Carve it in doves and pomegranates,/And peacocks with a hundred eyes;/Work it in gold and silver grapes,/In leaves and silver fleurs-de-lys;/Because the birthday of my life/Is come, my love is come to me.'

25 M. Hickox, 'John Brett and the Rossettis', *The Journal of Pre-Raphaelite Studies*, Vol V, No. 2, May 1985, pp.105–110.

26 Anon., 'A Pre-Raphaelite Exhibition', *Saturday Review*, July 4 1857, pp.11–12. Judging from this review, Brett's exhibits were two watercolours, *The Engel's Horner and Glacier from Rosenlaui*, and *Moss and Gentians from the Engel's Horner.*

27 Anon., 'Fine Art Gossip', *The Athenaeum*, July 11 1857, p.886.

28 *Dublin University Magazine*, August 1859, p.248. Quoted in David Lewis, 'Pondered Vision: the Art and Life of John Brett, A. R. A., 1830–1902', unpublished PhD thesis, Indiana University, 1995, p.127.

29 Early Diary, p.63 (December 9 1856).

30 According to family tradition, they were never punished, only told to go away and stay by themselves till they felt like being nicer. In the Memoranda, Brett notes: 'They always express themselves without reserve – a habit we have never checked' (p.24, September 19 1884).

31 Robert Hewison, ed., *Ruskin's Artists: Studies in the Victorian Visual Economy* (London: Ashgate, 2000), pp.10–11.

32 Diary, p.66 (New Year's Day, 1860 and June 11 1860).

33 R. Hewison, op. cit., p.12.

34 Letter to Rosa, dated March 22 1860 (Private Collection).

35 In 1860 the picture was exhibited at the Liverpool Academy, priced at £300. Charles Curtis Brett records in his diary that it has been sold for £150 (p.17; August 7 1863). The buyer was presumably B. G. Windus, since the picture reappeared in his executors' sale at Christie's, February 15 1868.

36 In an address book dating from 1874 to c.1897 (Private Collection), Brett notes 'Warwick Castle picture in the shop window of Messrs Richardson, 448 Kingsland Road 22 June 1887.'

37 Diary, p.64 (December 25 1858) and p.65 (July 31 1859). One can only speculate as to what Brett meant by 'the chief snare of the Devil'. Was it debt? Or women? The abrupt end to the first sequence in the Diary comes after he has fallen in love with the sister of a

clergyman, and at the end of 1858 he was out of debt, and confident that he would sell the Val d'Aosta for £450 in the following summer

38 Georgina Weldon, Diary 1864–71 (extracts): typescript by Charles Brett, taken from the Treherne Family MSS by kind permission of Dr Joanna Martin, p.3 (February 8 1865). There are many drawings by Brett of both women, in Private Collections as well as in the sketchbooks.

39 Letter to John Brett, postmarked London July 31 1863 (Private Collection).

40 Diary, pp.70–71 (September 1861).

41 On Brett and the Brownings, see D. Lewis, op. cit., pp.156–165, and Charles Brett, 'John Brett and *Aurora Leigh*', *The Review of the Pre-Raphaelite Society*, Vol XI, No I, Summer 2003, pp.14–20. It may be significant that both the Brownings were Congregationalists.

42 The circumstances surrounding the rejection of *Florence from Bellosguardo* and the Cosmopolitan Club exhibition have been described in the following articles: M. Hickox, 'The Royal Academy's rejection of Brett's *Florence*', *Review of the Pre-Raphaelite Society*, Vol III, no. 1, 1995, pp.10–16; P. McEvansoneya, 'More light on the Royal Academy's rejection of Brett's *Florence*', *Review of the Pre-Raphaelite Society*, Vol IV, no. 1, 1996, pp.19–23; and P. McEvansoneya, 'The Cosmopolitan Club Exhibition of 1863: the British *salon des refusés*', E. Harding, ed., op. cit., pp.27–42.

43 On Brett's patrons, see the comprehensive article by Charles Brett, 'John Brett and his Patrons', *The Review of the Pre-Raphaelite Society*, Vol XII, Summer 2004, pp.1–22.

44 Memoranda, p.3 (September 14 1879).

45 Anon., 'Artists' Houses', *The Art Journal*, 1882, pp.57–8; Mark Girouard, 'An Open Plan in the 1880s', *Country Life*, March 29 1962, pp.720–722.

46 There is no record in the registers of any marriage between John Brett and Mary Ann Howcroft. This is puzzling, because they certainly behaved as if they were married: in the photographs, Mary wears a wedding ring, and in the census return for 1881 she is described as the wife of John Brett. In 1874 John presented Mary with a cabinet of eight sketches 'made during our Honey-moon' (Private Collection). Previous writers on Brett have linked the apparent absence of a marriage with Brett's opposition to religion, but there is no reason why they should not have had a civil ceremony.

47 Quoted in David Lewis, op. cit., p.237.

48 Memoranda, pp.11–12 (July 27 1882).

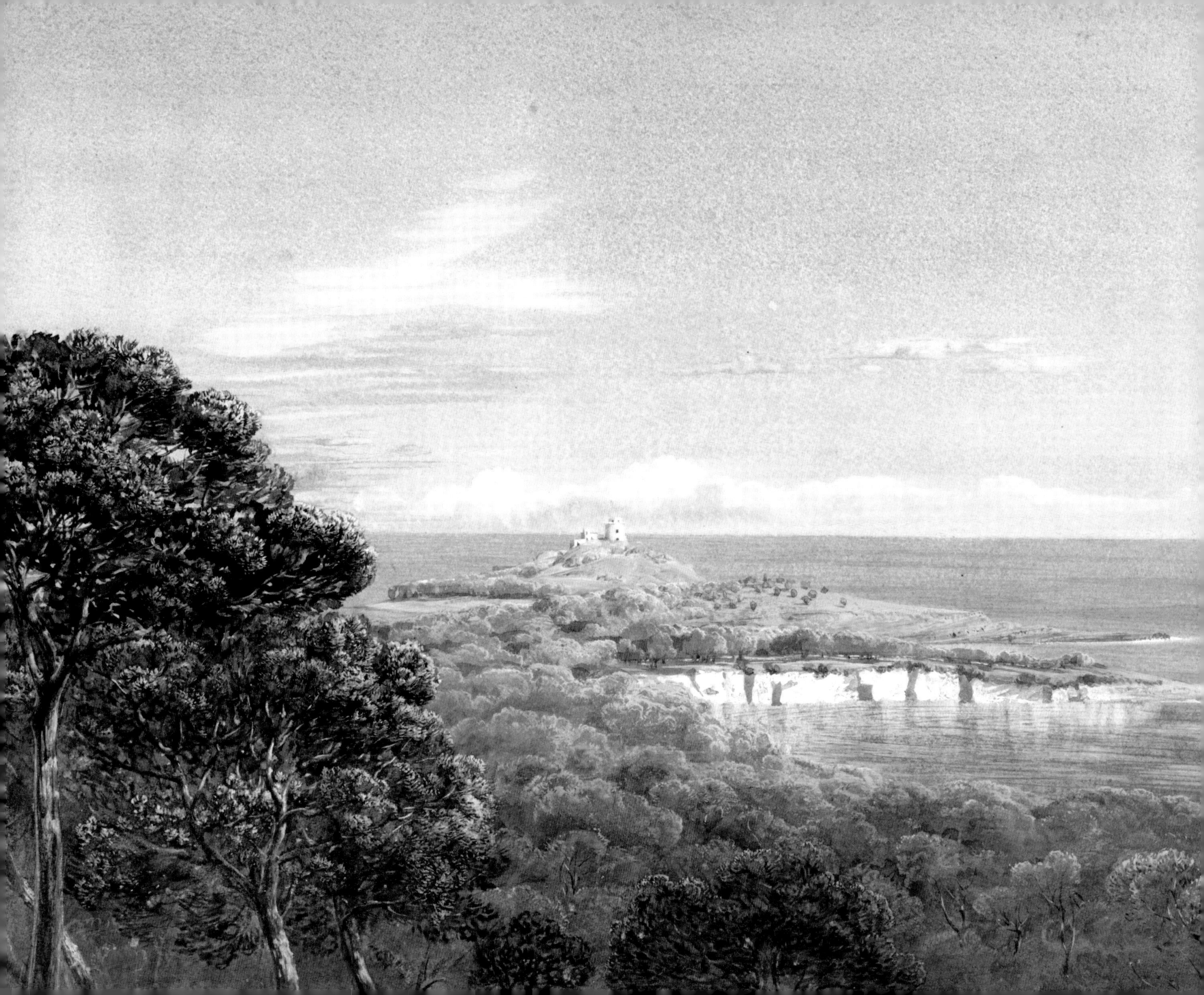

2 JOHN BRETT AND RUSKIN

Michael Hickox

In Ironside and Gere's pioneering post-war *Pre-Raphaelite Painters*, Ruskin is depicted as a kind of Svengali who took up Brett and then destroyed him as a result of the exertions needed to complete *The Val D'Aosta*.[1] (fig. 17) Thus, in an edition of Ruskin's works published in 1964, Kenneth Clark could refer to the 'wretched Brett'.[2] A mark of the change in attitudes since that period is Brett's emergence as one of the major figures in the recent Tate Pre-Raphaelite Landscape Exhibition.[3] This change has had much to do with the rediscovery in recent decades of a number of Brett's works of fine quality from the post-*Aosta* period, showing he did not go into an immediate decline, and also of documentation enabling one to take a more balanced view of the relationship between the two men.

John Brett's detailed early family diaries, which run from 1851 until August 1854, reveal an intelligent, ambitious, deeply religious and, to a large degree, self educated young artist opening himself to a wide range of intellectual and aesthetic influences.[4] Among these Ruskin's writings played an important role. Brett's first reference to these occurs in an entry for May 20 1852: 'The day before, I got Ruskin's pamphlet on Preraphaelitism and read it through, gloriously written and containing much earnest sound healthy thruth [sic], but

OPPOSITE
Pointe St Hospice, Cap Ferrat, from St Jean [detail]
1864. Watercolour and bodycolour, 23 x 32cm
Private Collection

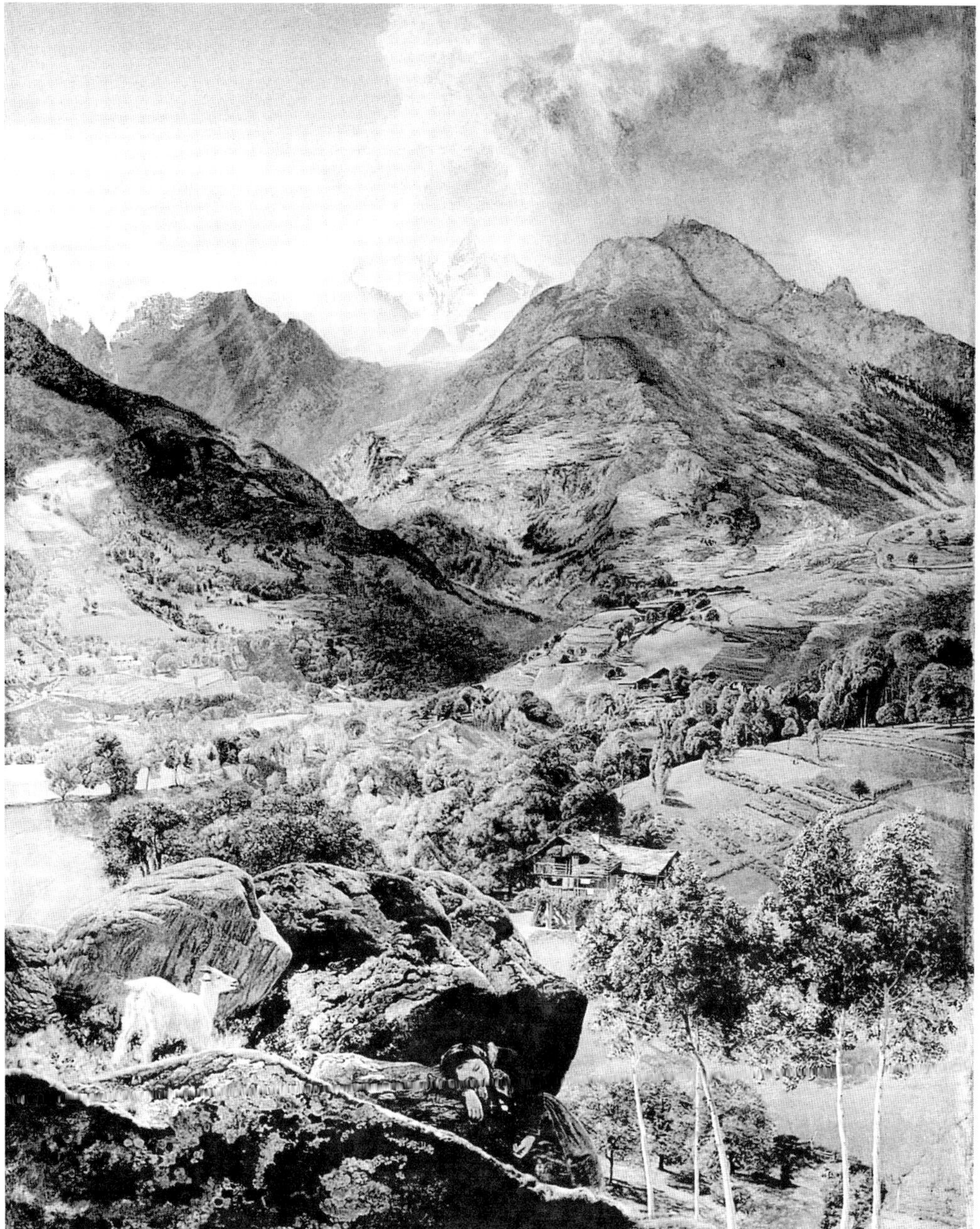

much also that is false and senseless-wrong'. However his next reference to Ruskin, dated May 27, is more unqualified in its praise: 'last Saturday I got Ruskin's 1st Vol Mn Painters and have begun it greedily – think it admirable'. A number of other references to Ruskin's works, including *Modern Painters II*, follow. In an entry dated November 30 1853 he writes: 'During the last week or two I have again come into contact with my great Joy, Ruskin, with renewed delight – this time it is the Stones of Venice in which there are some glorious overflows of genius.' Also, in 1851 Brett received tuition from the painter James Duffield Harding, who had been Ruskin's tutor in the early 1840s. Moreover, the diaries show an increasing interest in the Pre-Raphaelite movement. In an entry for May 18 1853 he notes: 'I am going on fast towards Pre-Raphaelitism. Millais and Hunt are truly fine fellows'.

Unfortunately, documentation is lacking covering the crucial period leading up to his first major Pre-Raphaelite work, *The Glacier of Rosenlaui* (fig. 18), for which one preliminary watercolour study survives. (fig. 19) However, in a short diary entry dated December 9 1856, Brett provides a summary of the events of the year. He had rushed off to the Swiss Alps 'in obedience to a passion that possessed me', probably as a result of reading Ruskin's *Modern Painters IV* published in April 1856. On the Wengern Alp he had encountered Inchbold who had himself previously been tutored by Ruskin. Brett's account is written in terms of a Conversion Experience. Until his meeting with Inchbold he had 'only fooled and slopped'. With respect to *The Glacier* he notes excitedly: 'Ruskin has seen it and praised it unreservedly'.

In *The Pre-Raphaelite Landscape*, Allen Staley views *The Glacier* as the most Ruskinian of all Pre-Raphaelite paintings and links it directly to Ruskin's section on Mountain Beauty in *Modern Painters IV.* This has given rise to a critical debate concerning the meaning of the painting.[5] Bendiner points to the fact that the glacier itself, the subject of the painting, is not mentioned in Ruskin's work and suggests that Brett may have been attempting to illustrate a recent theory of geological evolution advanced by the Swiss geologist Agassiz. Could it have a symbolic significance contrasting the truths of religion and science? Even if this were the case, it would not be to deny Ruskin's influence since his analysis of typological symbolism in *Modern Painters II* had been a major influence on the Pre-Raphaelites. Despite his praise of the painting Ruskin did not review *The Glacier,* which was also included in the Russell Place Pre-Raphaelite exhibition, when it was exhibited at the 1857 Royal Academy.

We know little of the background to what is often regarded as Brett's major Pre-Raphaelite work, *The Stonebreaker* (fig. 20), painted in Mickleham in late summer/autumn 1857. However, a long letter survives from Brett to his sister and fellow Pre-Raphaelite artist Rosa Brett, dated Mickleham Oct 7 57, detailing his progress on the painting.[6] Brett starts the letter:

'Darling R, received yours yesterday, but why didn't you send the PreRaphaelitism pamphlet? I went the other day to Kensington and had a study of the Mulreadys, in the Sheepshanks collection, and want to read what Ruskin says of them'.

Later he adds 'Do send me the pamphlet, you can keep the Ruskin letters for the present – but no longer please than they are really of use'. Charles Brett persuasively suggests that the 'Ruskin letters' refers to Ruskin's *The Elements of Drawing*, published in that year, and that the work had an important influence on Brett's artistic practice. One can link a number of recommendations made by Ruskin to a series of fine, detailed Dürer-like (an artist whom Ruskin especially commends) sketches from nature made by Brett in this period, several of which seem to have formed the basis for exhibited watercolours[7]. For example, Ruskin recommends drawing 'a piece of rock with its variegated lichens'. This may be represented by a beautiful watercolour study of this subject, together with a milestone, in one of Brett's sketchbooks[8] (fig. 21) from about this date. Generally, Brett seems to have been concerned to maintain the dramatic improvement in terms of technique he had made the previous year while painting *The Glacier,* which may explain the impact Ruskin's work had on him. Thus, he notes in his letter to Rosa sending to the village for a model in order to make 'a pen drawing for improvement'.

The reference to Ruskin's *Pre-Raphaelitism* pamphlet is also significant given the evidence suggesting Brett may

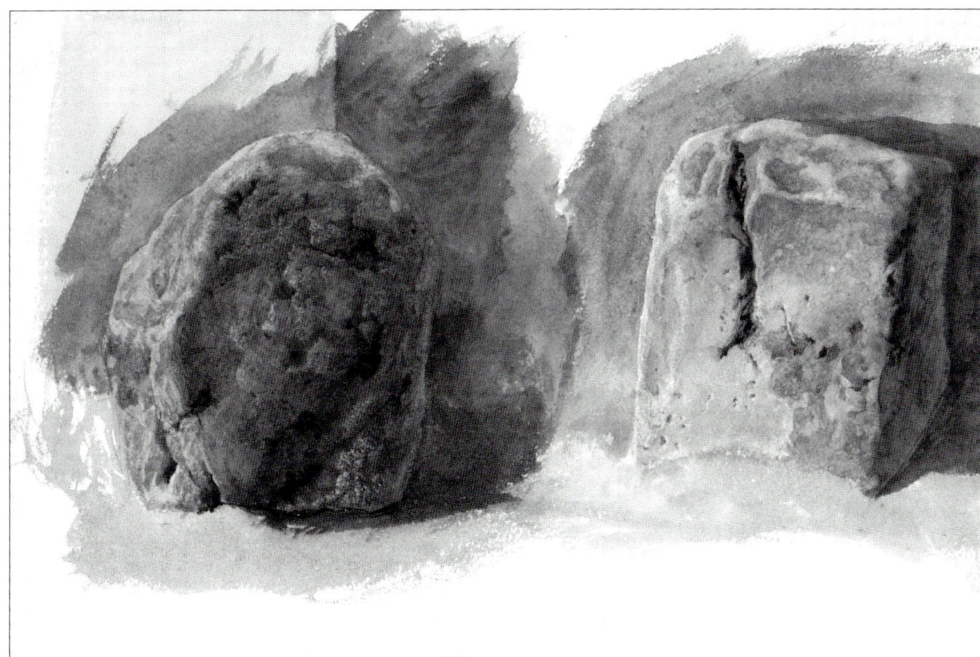

OPPOSITE
FIG. 17
The Val D'Aosta
1858, Oil on canvas, 88 x 68cm
Private Collection
© Sotheby's Images Ltd

FIG. 21
Studies of Stones
1856, Watercolour
Sketchbook No I ,*'Various, 1856–7'*
© National Maritime Museum, London

FIG. 23
Sketch for The Hedger
c. 1859, Monochrome wash and bodycolour, 25 x 18.5cm
Private Collection

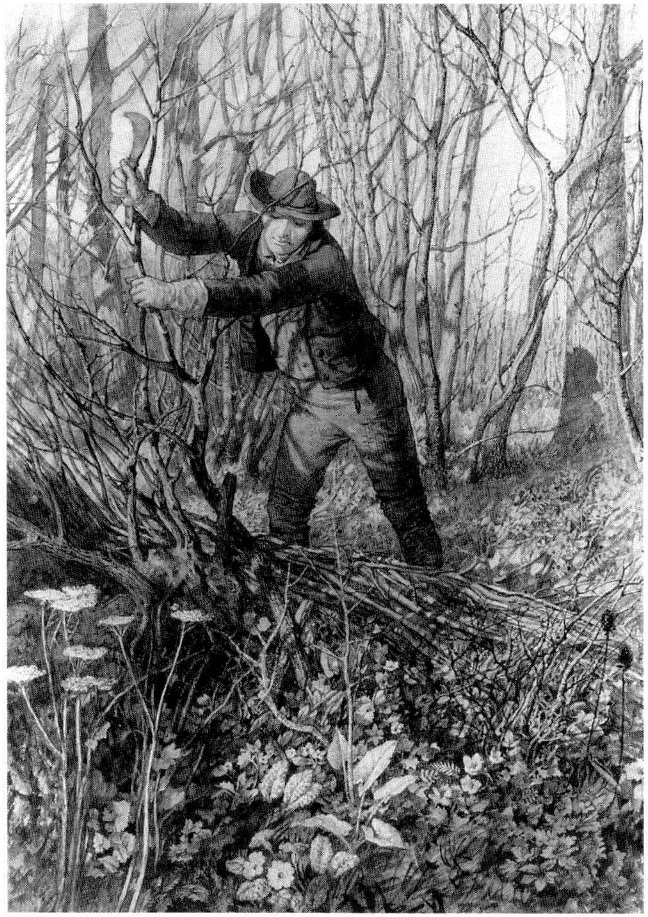

have intended *The Stonebreaker* to be a symbolic landscape, carrying a religious message in the Millais-Hunt tradition[9]. In *PreRaphaelitism*, published in 1851, Ruskin had defended Millais and Hunt against the attacks of contemporary critics comparing these attacks to those made on Turner. At one point he writes of Turner's second period: *'Every subject thenceforward was primarily conceived in colour'*. (Ruskin's italics) This may explain Brett's adoption of a typical Pre-Raphaelite use of heightened colour in *The Stonebreaker* and the concern with colour he displays in his letter to Rosa. Finally, Ruskin's focus on Turner may explain Brett's choice of subject for his next painting *The Hedger* (fig. 22) since Ruskin recommends 20 plates from Turner's *Liber Studiorum* one of which is entitled *Hedging and Ditching*.

Ruskin did review *The Stonebreaker* in his 1858 *Royal Academy Notes*.[10] It may be significant, given his later criticism of Brett for persisting in figure painting, that, while praising Brett's meticulous handling of the landscape, he makes no reference to the figure subject. Nor does he refer to the – possibly symbolic – dead box tree surmounted by fresh growth; an omission that again may be significant given he was later to attack Brett for having ' ideas'. While criticising aspects of Brett's composition, particularly the handling of the sky, he concludes:

'For all that, it is a marvellous picture and may be examined inch by inch with delight… If he can paint so lovely a distance from the Surrey downs and railway-traversed vales, what would he not make of the chestnut groves of the Val d'Aosta! I heartily wish him good speed and long exile'.

The reference to the subject of Brett's next painting, *Val D'Aosta*, indicates they must already have met. Indeed, Ruskin's reference in his first surviving letter to Brett, dated August 14 1858 to the latter's love of argument suggests that they may have met on more than one occasion.

His meeting(s) with Ruskin seems to have persuaded Brett to postpone *The Hedger* until the following year and to change the subject to that of flowers in spring. Thus, in his 1858 *Academy Notes* Ruskin comments: 'How strange that among all this painting of delicate detail there is not a true one of English spring!'[11] A fine detailed monochrome study for the picture, in a wintry setting with the trees barren of leaves, indicates what may well have been

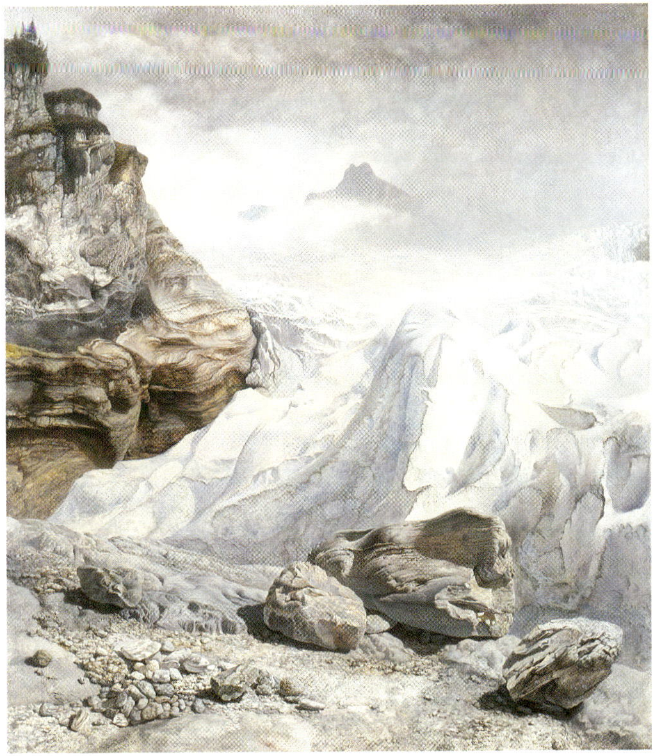

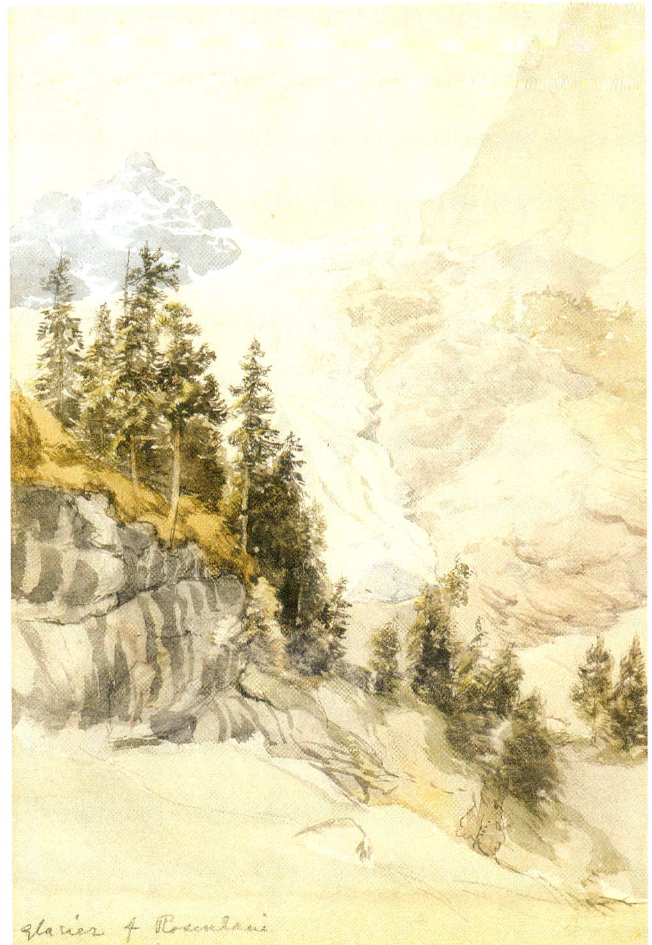

FIG. 18
The Glacier of Rosenlaui
1856. Oil on canvas, 44.5 x 41.9cm
Tate, London, 2005

FIG. 19
Preliminary watercolour sketch
for *The Glacier of Rosenlaui*
Private Collection

Brett's first idea for the picture, dating perhaps from early 1858. (fig. 23) A pen-and-ink outline sketch for the picture, dated May 18 1858, showing flowers in spring may show Brett's change of plan incorporating Ruskin's advice.[12] Since by then it was too late to complete the picture that year, the sketch may have served as an aide memoire for when he resumed work on it the following year.

After arriving in the Val D'Aosta Brett discussed his progress on the painting in a letter to his sister from the Château de St Pierre. His comments regarding his use of colour show the continuing influence of Ruskin's *Elements*.[13] The first of the surviving letters from Ruskin dated August 14 invites Brett to join him at Turin[14] and sheds light on an often quoted letter from Ruskin to his father dated August 26 1858:

'I mentioned that Mr Brett was with me at La Tour. He has been here a week today. I sent for him at Villeneuve, Val d'Aosta, because I didn't like what he said in his letter about his present work, and thought he wanted some lecturing like Inchbold… He is much stronger and tougher than Inchbold, and takes more hammering, but I think he looks more miserable every day'…[15]

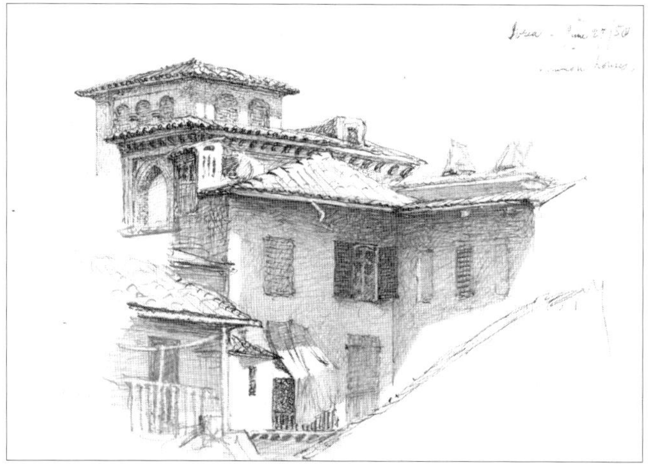

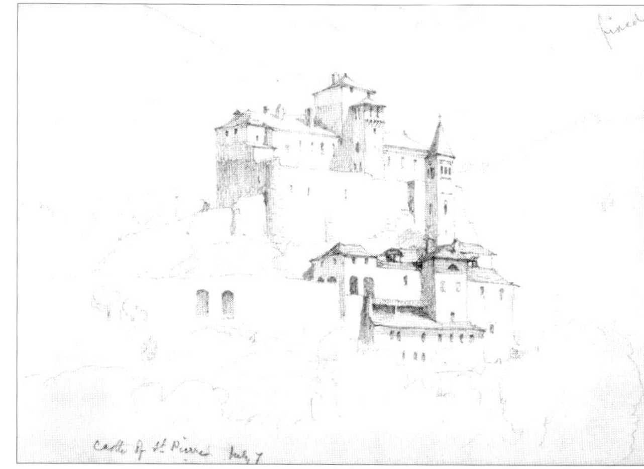

FIG. 24
Ivrea
June 27 1858, Pencil
Sketchbook No. 2,
'Various, Piedmont 1858'
© National Maritime Museum, London

FIG. 25
Castle of St Pierre
July 7, Pencil, Sketchbook No. 3,
'Val d'Aosta 1858'
© National Maritime Museum, London

Ruskin's letter commences:

> You must positively come and help me with some scrapes I've got into with Paul Veronese, and take a little dose of Paul yourself – he's good for all complaints – especially for that ridiculous Pre-Raphaelite love of painting people with purple cheeks and red noses by way of being in the sun.

This appears to be a sarcastic reference to the figure subject in *The Stonebreaker*, suggesting that Brett's determination to achieve success as a Pre-Raphaelite figure painter was already a bone of contention between them. More generally it may reflect Ruskin's aversion to what he perceived to be Ford Madox Brown's choice of ugly, modern subjects. Ruskin adds that persisting in 'the blue cheek style' is unlikely to bring commercial success. This criticism can be related to Brett's membership of the recently formed Hogarth Club, in which Brown played a central role, designed to encourage the painting of subjects from modern life.

Ruskin's playful reference to Brett's 'toughness' and to his love of argument shows his relish in a making a new friend. Thus, he writes to his father on June 28 1858; 'I am exceedingly glad that Brett has sold his painting, for he is a fine fellow as well as a good painter...' Undoubtedly their conversation must have covered a wide range of topics and religion is likely to have been one of them given that Ruskin was losing his early evangelical religious faith precisely at this time, while the inscriptions on the preliminary sketches for *The Stonebreaker* show Brett to have been still intensely religious. Indeed, Brett's range of intellectual interests, covering geology as well as literature and religion, may explain why Ruskin valued his friendship and refers to him as 'one of my keenest minded friends.'[16]

The sketchbooks covering *Val d'Aosta* show Brett's determination to maintain good Ruskinian practice since they contain a number of fine, minutely detailed observations of the geology and natural life of the area. They also include delicate architectural studies of Ivrea dated June 27 (fig. 24) and of the Castle of St Pierre, where Brett stayed while completing the picture, dated July 7 (fig. 25). Staley notes a pen and ink drawing, apparently in Ruskin's hand, dated August 25, which points to

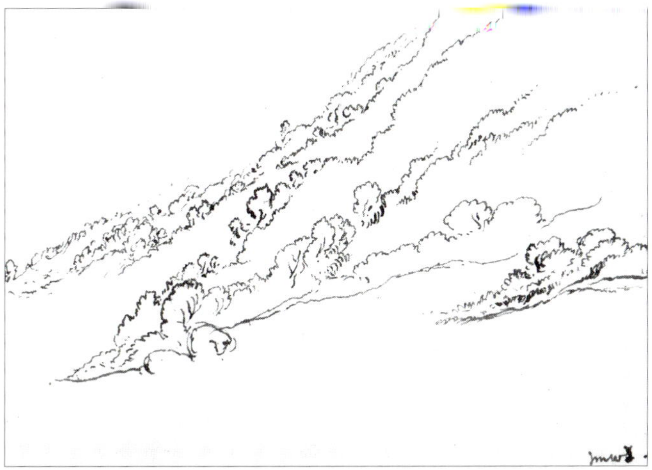

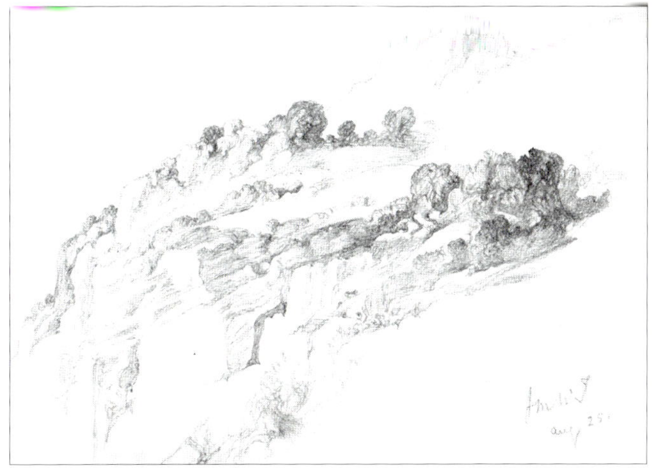

FIG. 26
Drawing of a mountain slope
1858, Pen and ink
Sketchbook No. 4, *'Aosta 1858'*
© National Maritime Museum, London

FIG. 27
Drawing of a mountain slope
1858, Graphite pencil
Sketchbook No. 4, *'Aosta 1858'*
© National Maritime Museum, London

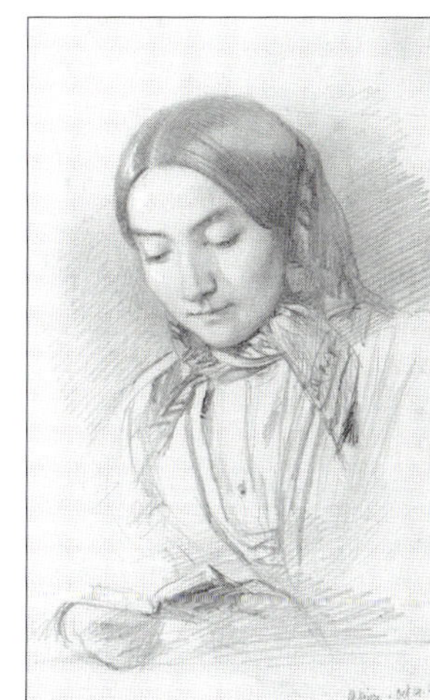

FIG. 28
Pauline Rivaz
1858, Pencil
Private Collection

the kind of artistic advice Ruskin may have been offering Brett. Diagrammatic in character, it bears Turner's initials JMWT (fig. 26) and suggests that Ruskin was criticising Brett for concentrating too much on detail and ignoring the grand lines of nature.[17] A sketch in Brett's hand also inscribed JMWT shows his own, much more carefully modelled, attempt at the same subject (fig. 27).

A beautiful Dürer-like portrait of Pauline Rivaz, the model for the figure in *Val D'Aosta*, inscribed 'St Pierre Oct 14 58', (fig. 28) dates from after his meeting with Ruskin. Upon his return to England, Brett notes Ruskin's approval of the finished picture in his December 25 1858 diary entry and expresses high hopes, no doubt anticipating a favourable review from Ruskin, that it will fetch £450 when exhibited at the Royal Academy. However, he adds: 'it is as I plan at present my last landscape'. This comment is significant in the light of Ruskin's later criticism of Brett for ignoring landscape in favour of figure painting.

A determination to succeed as a Pre-Raphaelite figure painter marks Brett's work in the immediate post-*Aosta* period, for example in *The Hedger* and especially the lost *Warwick Castle*. The latter, which was commercially but not critically successful, was Brett's one venture into medievalist History Painting. This interest in historical subjects is demonstrated by a fine watercolour study of armour dated Oct 16/60 (fig. 29) relating to this picture. Brett's choice of subject may have been reinforced by the failure of the *Val d'Aosta* to sell, despite the qualified approval Ruskin gave it in his 1859 *Royal Academy Notes*.[18] In these he gives high praise for its Dürer-like fidelity to nature: 'And here, accordingly, for the first time in history, we have by help of art, the power of visiting a place, reasoning about it, and knowing it, just as if we were there…' However, he goes on to criticise the painting for its lack of empathy.

> Yet not, in the strong, essential meaning of the word, a noble picture. It has a strange fault, considering the school to which it belongs – it seems to me wholly emotionless… He has cared for nothing, except as it was more or less pretty in colour and form. I never saw the mirror so held up to Nature, but it is Mirror's work, not Man's.

Staley notes that this criticism is curious given that hitherto

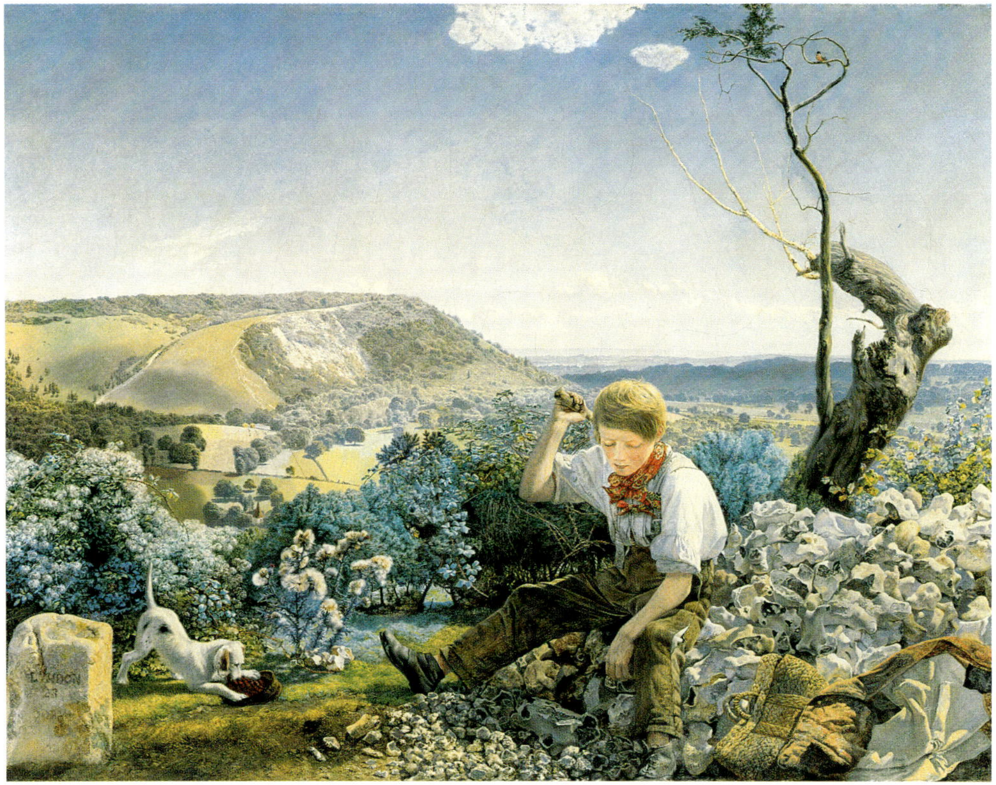

FIG. 20
The Stonebreaker
1857–8, Oil on canvas,
51.3 x 68.5cm
National Museums Liverpool
(The Walker)

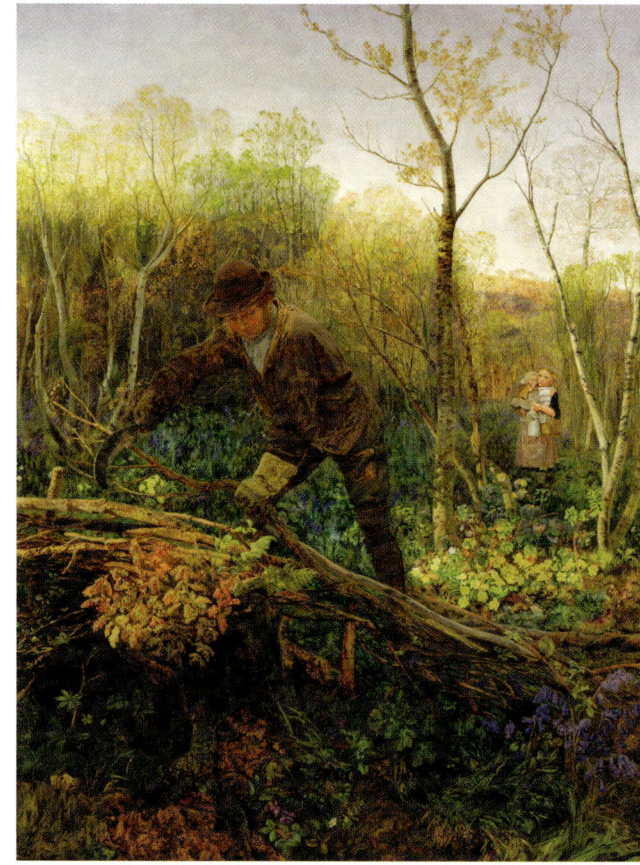

FIG. 22
The Hedger
1858–60, Oil on canvas, 90 x 70cm
Private Collection/Bridgeman
Art Library

Ruskin seems to have wished to encourage the kind of detached, scientific observation of nature which the picture exemplifies. Ruskin concludes his review:

> Think of all that this Italian life might be among these sacred hills, and of what Italian life has been, and yet is, in spite of silver crosses on the breast, and how far it is your fault and mine that this is so; and the picture may be serviceable to you in quite other ways than by pleasing your eyes with purple and gold.

The allusion to the detail of the sleeping girl wearing a cross, which seems to have been added after Brett's meeting with Ruskin, suggests there may be an allegorical religious meaning in the picture. One notes, for example, the cross on the mountaintop at the very highest point in the landscape. Given that Ruskin's comment seems, if in an oblique fashion, to deprecate the role of religion (it is the hills which are 'sacred') could it contain a reference to debates he might have had with Brett? Christopher Newall suggests that the goat and the sleeping girl may contain a reference to the section on 'mountain gloom' in *Modern Painters Volume IV* where Ruskin

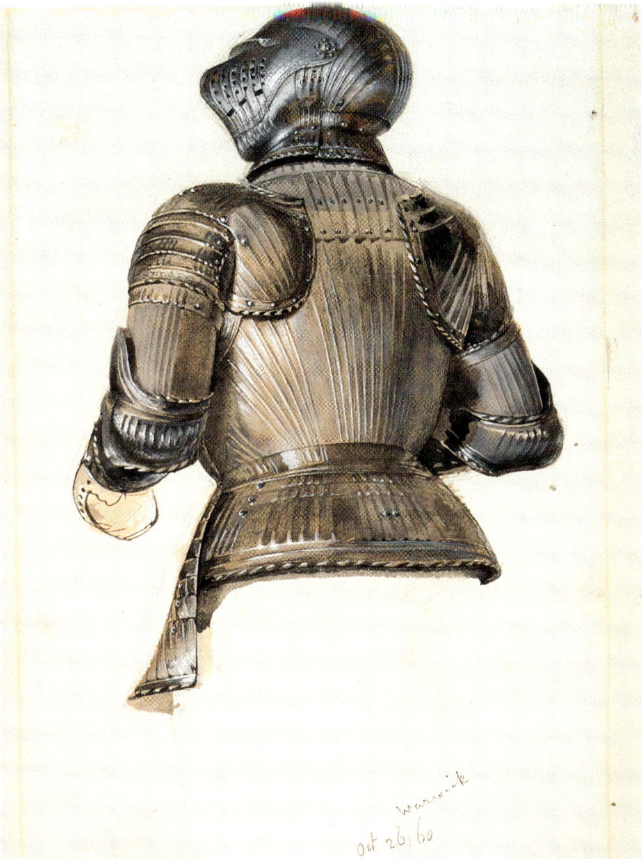

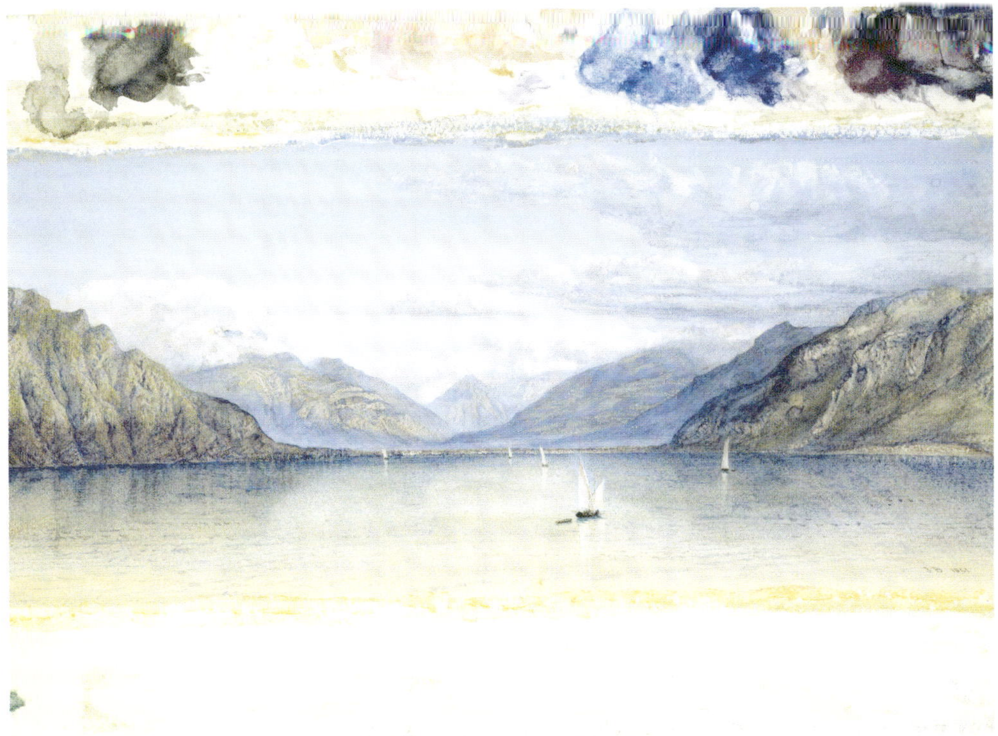

FIG. 29
Sketch of armour
Dated Oct 16 1860, Watercolour
© British Museum, London

FIG. 30
The Mountains of St Gingolph
Watercolour and bodycolour
15.2 x 34.3cm
Fitzwilliam Museum, Cambridge

savagely attacks the role of the Church in the Catholic areas of Switzerland, reflecting his own Evangelical Protestant background. This interpretation would imply that Brett was turning Ruskin against himself since, by the summer of 1858, Ruskin's loss of his early evangelical religious faith meant that he no longer wished to deprecate Catholicism in favour of Protestantism. Against this interpretation one should note that the girl is wearing a plain cross rather than a crucifix, so it may be intended to symbolise Christian belief in general.[19]

The picture's failure to sell, dashing Brett's high hopes for its success, meant that in the end Ruskin had to act as a buyer of last resort. Brett bitterly notes in his Jan 1 1860 diary:

> Ruskin bought my *Val d'Aosta* a little while ago for £200 when he understood I grievously wanted money, an affair this that made me sing very very small.

The evidence points to a marked change in Brett's artistic practice in the post-Aosta period which involved abandoning the numerous extremely detailed sketches he had made for that picture. Thus, the surviving sketches relating to both *The Hedger* and *Warwick Castle* show a decline both in quantity and to some extent in quality, although he continued to produce detailed sketches throughout his career. This shift in Brett's practice continued even when he returned to landscape after the critical failure of *Warwick Castle*. Thus we see a move away from the highly detailed foreground of *The Val d'Aosta* to the empty foreground typified by *The Mountains of St Gingolph* (fig. 30) exhibited at the RA in 1862. This shift may partly be explained by the extreme degree of labour that *Val d'Aosta* had required. Thus in his July 31 59 diary he writes of his progress on *The Hedger*:

> It wants yet a good fortnight's work. I hope it will be more felt than the Aosta[20]; it is much more strongly painted, and is deeper in color; not half so delicate and refined perhaps but I can't think how I ever got the Aosta done.

This change was picked up by Ruskin in a root and branch attack on the direction taken by Brett's art after *Val D'Aosta* in his letter of May 2 1863. He criticises Brett for his failure to 'make quantities of black and white studies'. Interestingly, he also makes this criticism of Holman Hunt: ' Hunt with all his tremendous powers will never paint a picture but by chance for want of it', hinting that Hunt may have been an alternative source of inspiration for Brett in this period. Ruskin gave up his Royal Academy reviews after 1859 so his views of Brett's post-*Aosta* work must be derived from his later May 1863 letter and from two letters replying to enquiries from the collector Thomas Plint who purchased *Warwick Castle*. In one Ruskin advises him not to purchase *The Hedger* since it had an unsuitable subject:

> As for Brett I believe he is going to paint a good picture of Warwick Castle this year: I cannot advise you to buy his Woodcutter – though it has beautiful qualities; the subject being totally uninteresting.[21]

This contempt for the picture's subject reflects his earlier attack on the 'blue cheek style'. However, John James Ruskin echoes the reference to its 'beautiful qualities' in a letter to Brett of July 31 1863. After praising Brett's abilities as a portrait artist he adds (almost certainly referring to *The Hedger*), 'forgive me ye wood hyacinths and all the other Beauties of your marvellous foreground'. In another letter to Plint Ruskin notes 'Rossetti is far greater than Brett' but goes on to justify Brett in terms of the tremendous effort he had put into painting *Val D'Aosta*, and concludes:

> He looks upon himself only as a student yet and hopes to do good things eventually; so that I think that he would quite concur in a modest view of prices at present. He is a thoroughly good and worthy fellow.[22]

Despite Brett's rejection of his artistic advice Ruskin continued on good terms with him in the period after the *Aosta* painting, revealing perhaps how much he valued Brett's friendship. Eight letters survive covering 1859 and 1860.[23] These are friendly and chatty in tone and Ruskin seems to studiously avoid giving direct artistic advice. The nearest he comes to this is in a letter of July 1860: 'One good I have got out of German art is greater respect for the PRB, including you, though you defy the title'. This letter also touches on the religious issue, which is likely to have been a subject of debate during their Turin meeting. Ruskin comments on *The Dwelling Place*, written by Brett's friend James Hinton offering an allegorical interpretation of the Bible. Ruskin dismisses the possibility of such an interpretation:

> ...It seems to me that the Bible must mean pretty well what common people reading it would think it meant, or be useless.

This offers an interesting pointer to the evolution of Brett's own religious beliefs in this period. In the letter Ruskin seems concerned to avoid religious debate and to move quickly on to talk about art. A further hint, perhaps, that Brett did not as yet share his new agnosticism.

After a fragmentary letter of November 16 1860, the correspondence lapses. However, this does not appear to indicate any falling out since Ruskin seems to have left his father to keep a watching eye over Brett. John James Ruskin's diary records a number of visits paid by Brett to his house in this period.[24] Ruskin's letters resume with his May 2 1863 critical attack on Brett's art. The occasion for this was the Royal Academy's rejection of Brett's two submissions for the year, *Florence from Bellosguardo* (fig. 31) and *Norbury on the Mole* (fig. 32) This rejection, together with that of the works of a number of Pre-Raphaelite landscape artists, caused a furore in the artistic community and created a division between the supporters and opponents of the Royal Academy decision. Holman Hunt, always an opponent of the Royal Academy, organised a Salon des Refusés of the rejected works at the Cosmopolitan Club. Brett himself remained aloof from this group preferring to exhibit his works at his own studio.[25]

Ruskin might have been expected to come out publicly in favour of the rejected artists as he had previously done with respect to Hunt and Millais. Thus on April 30 Coventry Patmore wrote to Brett concerning the issue: 'The absurdity is so manifest that the 'Times' would at once insert anything by Ruskin and Hunt about it.'[26] However, Ruskin's response to the crisis was decidedly cool and, instead of coming out publicly in Brett's defence, he took the opportunity to launch an attack on Brett's art, implying that the RA may have been correct in its decision.[27] Linking Brett with Inchbold he writes: 'You had to go wrong; and there an end; but I couldn't stand by to see it – so kept out of the way till you should find it out for yourselves'. As well as criticising his failure to make black-and-white sketches, Ruskin attacks Brett for persisting in his attempt to become a figure artist and for 'making big studies and supposing they are pictures'. He adds that, like Ruskin himself, Brett is incapable of having 'ideas', implicitly denying his aspiration to be seen as a major Pre-Raphaelite artist. In a following letter, dated May 21, Ruskin discusses the Academy issue in general terms without offering Brett any sympathy, and adds sarcastically at the end, 'I'm so glad to hear Florence is sold. But how bad it must be to get sold so soon.'

In another letter relating to the Royal Academy issue John James Ruskin supports his son's position. He refuses what appears to have been an approach by Brett to lend a picture (perhaps *Val D'Aosta*) to the Cosmopolitan Club exhibition: 'I cannot let my picture go to any Club House to be destroyed by Gas' and adds in the margin, 'I don't consider your picture as a rejected one until you confirm it by your exhibition of it in that character'. In a subsequent letter, dated July 31, he offers to purchase £20 of sketches and adds, 'If Mr W Vokins will take your picture for £150 I will guarantee him from Loss.'[28]

The letters from Ruskin conclude with five short notes referring to 'an experiment in oils' the last of which is dated July 21 1863. The final breakdown of their friendship is recorded by Ruskin in a letter to Dante Gabriel Rossetti dated July 1865:

> Brett told me a year ago, that a statement of mine respecting a scientific matter (which I knew à fond before he was born) was 'bosh'. I told him in return he was a 'fool'; he left the house, and I will not see him again 'until he is wiser.[29]

On the basis of this letter and the fact that Ruskin is among a list of Brett's correspondents which he took with him to Italy in September 1863, one can probably date this falling out to spring 1864 upon Brett's return to England. In the event Brett

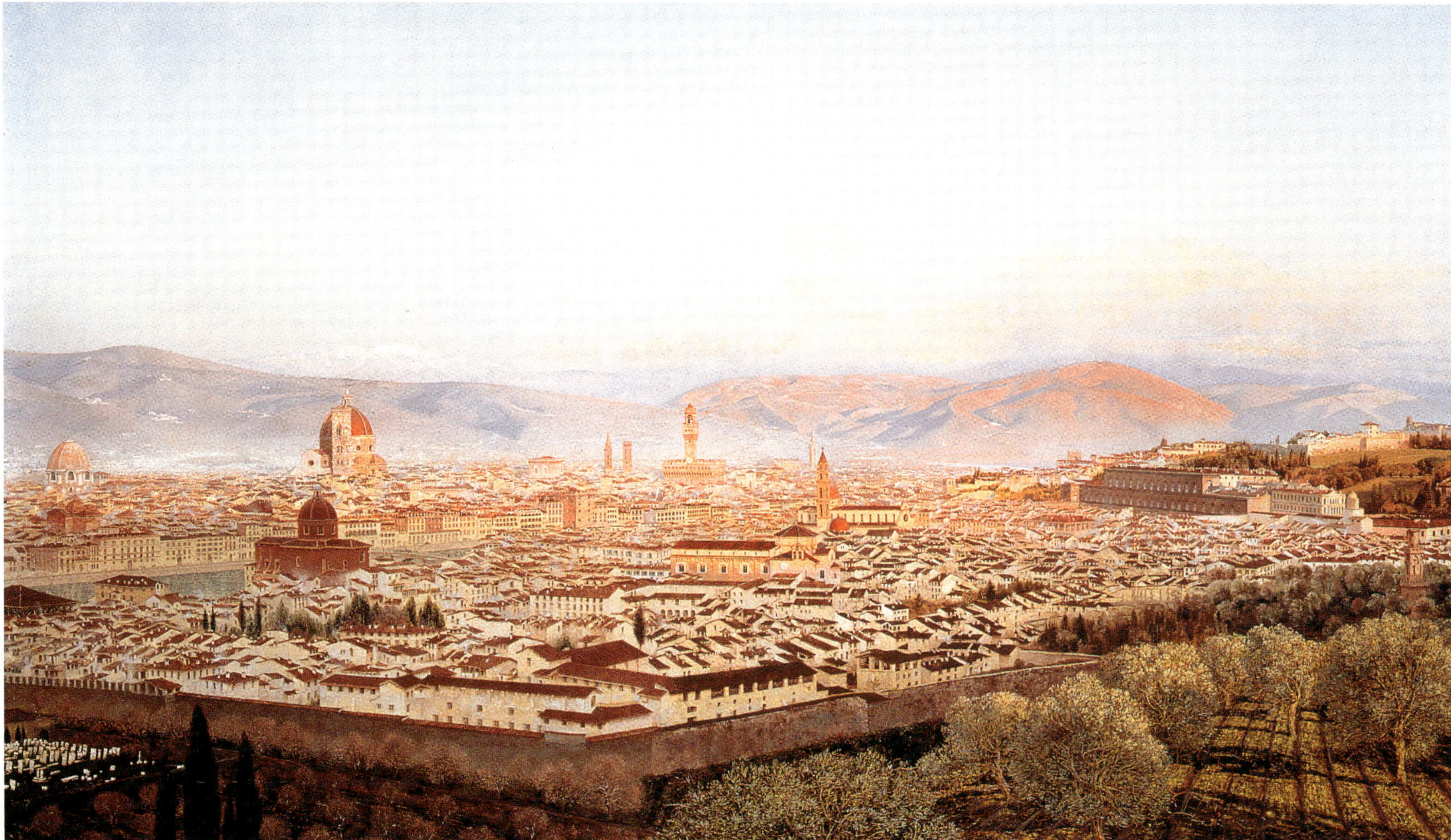

FIG. 31
Florence from Bellosguardo
1863, Oil on canvas, 60 x 101.3cm
© Tate, London, 2005

clearly never did become 'wiser' and there is no record of further contact between them. By this time, ironically partly as a result of the sympathy aroused by the RA's rejection of his works, Brett was selling his pictures and was no longer dependent on Ruskin family patronage.[30] Possibly he may have resented Ruskin's lack of support with respect to the RA's rejection of his works. Finally, the death of John James Ruskin, who seems to have had an especial affection for Brett, on March 3 1864 may have been a barrier to any later reconciliation.

This episode is reminiscent of W. J. Stillman's account of his friendship with Ruskin which lasted until 1870, 'when it was terminated by a trivial personal incident to which his morbid state of mind at that time gave a false colour'.[31] Stillman's account of the friendship sheds an interesting light on the relationship between Ruskin and Brett with which it has a number of close parallels. He recalls that in the 1850s they 'had as many conversations on religion as on art, the two then being to me almost identical and to him closely related'. In 1859 Ruskin forced Stillman to remove the figure subjects from his painting *Bed of Ferns* with the result that it was ruined and rejected by the RA. He then invited him to spend the summer with him in Switzerland where they clashed continually. Ruskin's hammering put such a strain on Stillman's eyes that it was two years before he recovered sufficiently to work again.

Certainly Ruskin's attitude towards Brett hardened over time. In his catalogue notes for the *Val d'Aosta* when it was exhibited at Douglas in 1880 he wrote:

> I at that time hoped much from his zeal and fineness of minute execution in realising, with Dürer-like precision, the details of Swiss landscape. Had he sympathised enough with Swiss and Italian life, his work might have become of extreme value; but, instead, he took to mere photography of physical landscape and gradually lost both precision and sentiment.[32]

There is a final irony here. In terms of his artistic practice Brett, of all Victorian artists, remained throughout his career faithful to Ruskin's precepts, producing large numbers of detailed geological studies.[33] Nevertheless, Ruskin's damning verdict has tended to shape much later critical opinion. It is only in recent years that the emergence of a number of Brett's works from the 1860s, in particular the series of superb watercolour studies exemplified by *Pointe St Hospice Cap Ferrat from St Jean* dated March 1864 (fig. 33), has modified this perception.

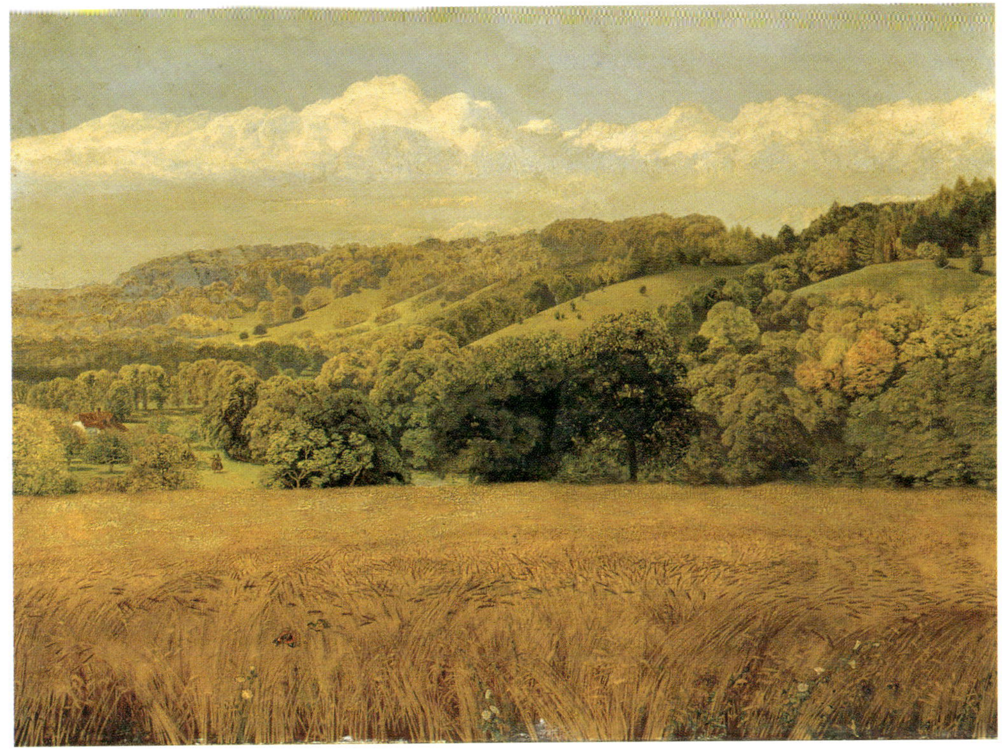

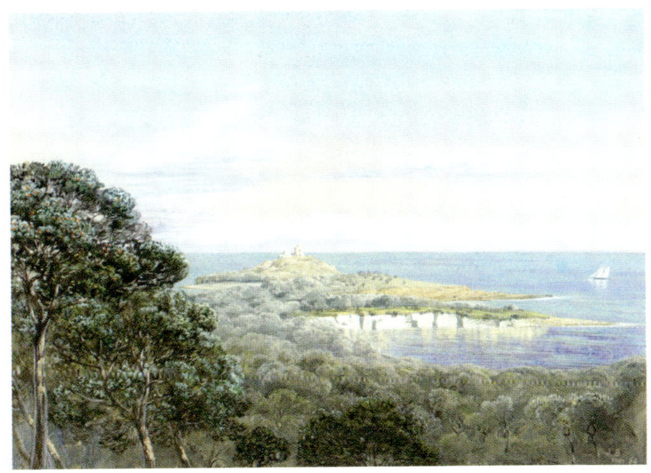

FIG. 32
Norbury on the Mole
1862, Oil on canvas, 51 x 68.5cm
Private Collection
© Sotheby's Images Ltd

FIG. 33
Pointe St Hospice, Cap Ferrat, from St Jean
1864, Watercolour and bodycolour, 23 x 32cm
Private Collection
© Sotheby's Images Ltd

NOTES

1 Robin Ironside and John Gere, *Pre-Raphaelite Painters*, London: Phaidon , 1948, pp.45–6.

2 Kenneth Clark, *Ruskin Today*, London: Penguin, 1967 p.127.

3 Allen Staley and Christopher Newall, *Pre-Raphaelite Vision: Truth to Nature*, London: Tate Publishing, 2004.

4 Private Collection .

5 Allen Staley, *The Pre-Raphaelite Landscape*, New Haven and London: Yale University Press, 2001; Kenneth Bendiner, *An Introduction to Victorian Painting*, New Haven and London: Yale University Press, 1985; Michael Hickox , 'Religion and Science in the Pre-Raphaelite work of John Brett', *The Victorian Web*.

6 Private Collection. Published in Michael Hickox, 'John Brett's *The Stonebreaker*', *The Review of the Pre-Raphaelite Society*, Vol III, No 1, spring 1995, pp 1–8.

7 Charles Brett, 'John Brett and Ruskin's *The Elements of Drawing*', *The Burlington Magazine* Vol CXLVII, No 1230, September 2005, pp 613–616.

8 Possibly a study for the milestone in *The Stonebreaker*.

9 Michael Hickox and Christiana Payne, 'Sermons in Stones: John Brett's *The Stonebreaker* reconsidered', in Ellen Harding (ed), *Re-framing the Pre-Raphaelites: Historical and Theoretical Essays*, Aldershot: Scolar Press, 1996. pp.99–114.

10 E. T. Cook and Alexander Wedderburn (eds), *The Works of John Ruskin*, London: George Allen, 1903–12, Vol. XIV, pp.171–2.

11 Ibid p.154.

12 Christopher Newall '*The Hedger*' in *Pre-Raphaelite Vision*, op cit p.186.

13 Charles Brett, op cit.

14 Michael Hickox , ' John Brett and Ruskin', *The Burlington Magazine*, Vol 138, 1996 pp.521–5.

15 E. T. Cook and Alexander Wedderburn, op cit, Vol XIV, pp.XXXIII–XXXIV.

16 Ibid, pp 360–1.He refers to Brett's definition of 'vulgarity' as ' only one of the forms of death'.

17 Allen Staley, *The Pre-Raphaelite Landscape*, op cit, p.174.

18 E. T. Cook and Alexander Wedderburn, op cit, Vol. XIV, pp.234, 236–7.

19 Christopher Newall, ' John Brett's Alpine Landscapes', talk given as part of the Tate Symposium 'Pre-Raphaelitism and Science' 19 March 2004. For another interpretation see Michael Hickox, 'Religion and Science in the Pre-Raphaelite work of John Brett', *The Victorian Web*.

20 Perhaps a reaction to Ruskin's criticism of *Val d'Aosta*.

21 Brian Lewis, 'Thomas E. Plint – a Patron of Pre-Raphaelite Painters', *The Pre-Raphaelite Review*, May 1980, vol III no 2, endnote 86, p.98.

22 Virginia Surtees (ed), *Sublime and instructive : letters from John Ruskin to Louisa Marchioness of Waterford, Anna Blunden and Ellen Heaton*, Michael Joseph, 1972.

23 Michael Hickox, 'The unpublished correspondence of Ruskin and Brett', *The Ruskin Gazette*, Vol 1, No. 8, 1995 , pp 1–25.

24 Basil Dearden personal communication.

25 Philip McEvansoneya, 'The Cosmopolitan Club Exhibition of 1863: the British salon des refusés' in Ellen Harding (ed) *Re-framing the Pre-Raphaelites*, op cit, 1996.

26. Private Collection.

27. For a comment on this letter cf Allen Staley, op cit, p 179.

28. Probably a reference to *The Hedger.*

29. E. T. Cook and Alexander Wedderburn, op cit, Vol. XXXVI, pp.493–4.

30. Brett sold both the pictures rejected by the RA in 1863.

31. W.J. Stillman, *The Autobiography of a Journalist*, London: Grant Richards, 1931, Vol 1, p.109.

32 E. T. Cook and Alexander Wedderburn, op cit , XIV, p 238.

33. Even after his break with Ruskin, Brett continued to purchase his books. His surviving library is in a Private Collection.

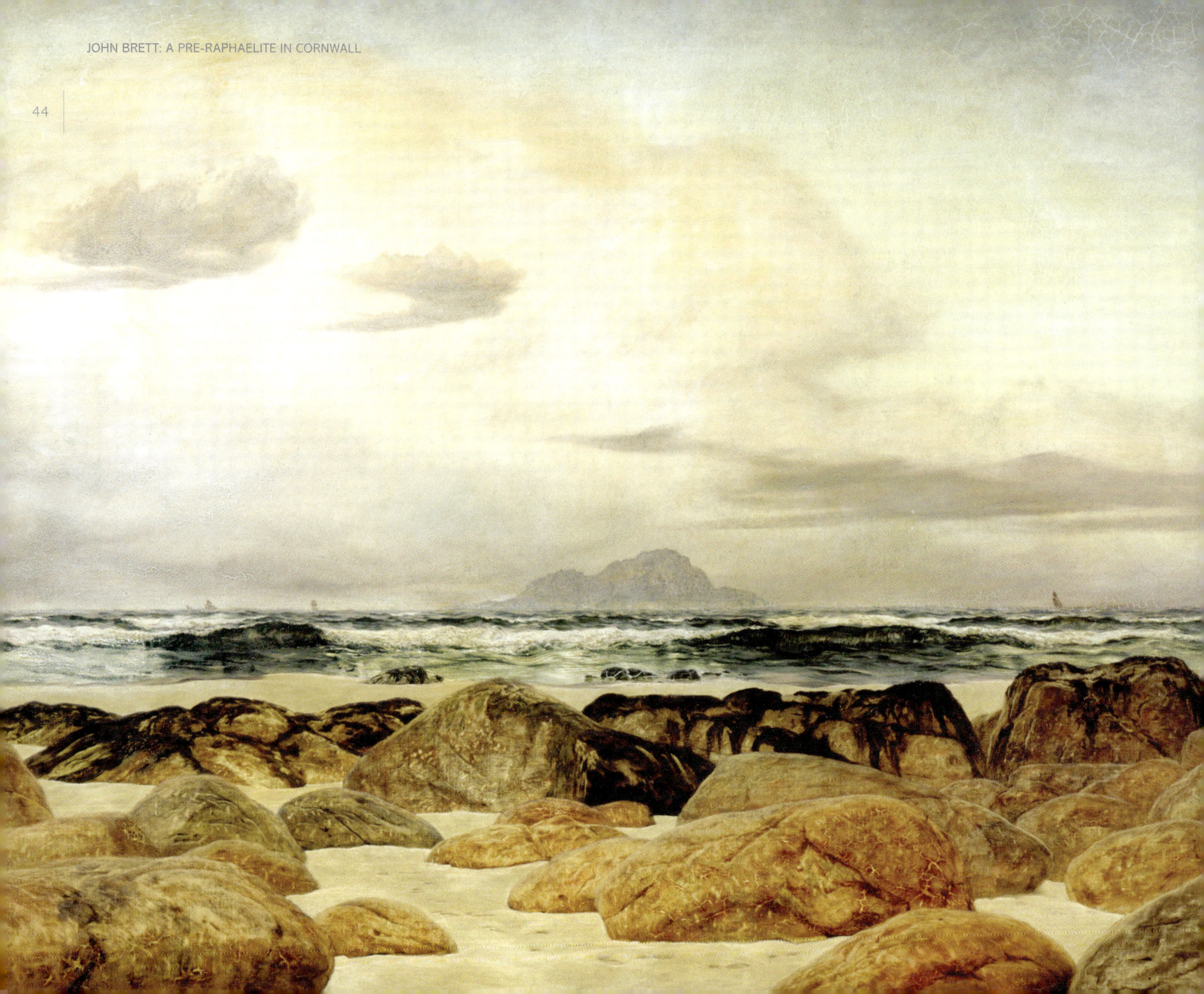

3
JOHN BRETT IN CORNWALL

Charles Brett

OPPOSITE
A Morning amongst the Granite Boulders
1873, Oil on canvas
104 x 211cm.
© Sotheby's Images Ltd

FIG. 35
A north-west gale off the Longships Lighthouse
Signed and dated 1873,
Oil on canvas
104.7 x 212.1cm (41¼ x 83½ins)
Birmingham City Museum and Art Gallery

John Brett discovered Cornwall in 1870, the year he and Mary Ann Howcroft began to live together as man and wife. Their original plan seems to have been to spend their honeymoon in France, and on July 17 they sailed to Le Havre, finding lodgings in nearby Honfleur.[1] But two days later France declared war on Prussia, and they soon concluded, in common with other travellers, that it was wise to return to England.[2] After spending Cowes race week in the Isle of Wight, they headed west, and for the next six weeks explored the Dorset coast from Swanage to Lyme Regis. Brett made a large number of watercolour sketches[3] and detailed studies of sea and sky, particularly from

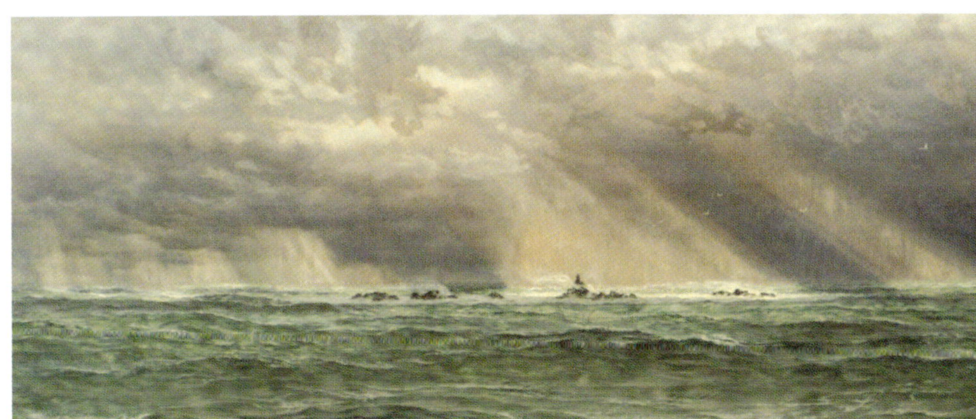

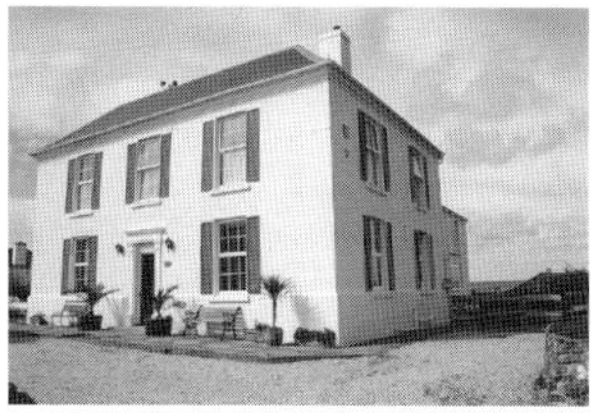

FIG. 34
Park Braws
(formerly Browse), Lizard.
Photograph: Cécile Brett

the cliffs above Lulworth Cove. These later formed the basis for his magnificent 1871 Academy picture *The British Channel from the Dorsetshire Cliffs* (Tate Britain).[4]

By the middle of September they had decided to extend their tour into Cornwall, so they went by train via Plymouth to Falmouth, the terminus of the Great Western Railway. The Lizard was evidently their goal, and from Falmouth they made for the coast at Porthleven. Brett sketched the Lizard from Loe Bar on September 23,[5] and they then established themselves in Lizard Town, staying at Park Browse, (fig. 34), where Thomas and Grace Rowe kept lodgings. There they remained for nearly a month, while Brett made copious pencil sketches of the peninsula.[6] Like Holman Hunt before him, he was especially attracted to Kynance Cove, which made an unforgettable impression. The diarist Kilvert had been there just a few weeks earlier, and marvelled at 'the splendour of the place, the gorgeous blue and beauty of the broad sea, the coloured rocks, the towering cliffs, the coast, the golden swimming mellow light amongst the huge dark rock masses, indescribable.'[7] Strangely, only one watercolour from this visit has been located, though there were certainly others. But the Lizard had worked its magic on Brett, and he would return to the area several times in years to come.

Brett next visited Cornwall two years later. He and Mary had set up home at 3 Mansfield Street, Cavendish Square, his bachelor chambers in Pump Court, Temple, being kept on as a studio. A son, Michael, had arrived in 1871, and he was just over a year old when they left for St Ives at the beginning of September 1872. The railway did not yet reach St Ives itself, but it was possible to get to Hayle or the junction at St Erth, three or four miles away. We do not know where they stayed, but it could have been at the Queen's Hotel in the High Street, a 'Family and Commercial hotel', which advertised 'wines, spirits, and every accommodation at the lowest prices.'[8] St Ives was a substantial town, with a population of about 7,000,[9] and was the most important centre of the pilchard fishing industry.[10] This was no doubt one of its principal attractions for Brett. He always attempted to depict boats as accurately as possible, with precise detail of sails and rigging, and his sketchbooks for this year are full of studies of boats and fishermen at work. He was still working in watercolour in 1872, but oil was beginning to take over, and he made a number of delightful oil studies of the town and its harbour, several in the 7 x 14ins format he had devised the previous year as the most convenient size for oil sketches done rapidly on the spot. Some of these would subsequently be worked up into larger finished pictures in his studio.

Towards the end of September the family moved to Sennen, near the Land's End, lodging with Mary Harvey at Sea View House. Here the rugged granite coast appealed to the geologist in Brett. He concentrated in his sketches on Cape Cornwall, the Land's End, and the rocks offshore – the Armed Knight and Enys Dodman. The former featured in several works later on. He sketched the Longships Lighthouse in a NW gale, later developing this into the seven-foot picture of the Longships now in Birmingham City Art Gallery (fig. 35), and explored the coast to the south as far as Porthcurno and the Logan Rock. He was to paint this area in more detail in 1880. In the middle of October he made a charming study of Michael asleep (Private Collection), and on the 24th a view of Cape Cornwall from Whitesand Bay (p.69), his last recorded sketch of the season. This work is clearly related to his other 1873 Academy exhibit, *A Morning amongst the Granite Boulders* (see fig. 8).

The 1873 summer campaign was one of the most extended and ambitious of Brett's career. There was now a sister for Michael – Daisy, who had been born in January. The family set off on June 17, taking the 11.45 train from Paddington for Plymouth.

Here they broke their journey, probably staying overnight at the Duke of Cornwall Hotel, before proceeding to Penzance the next day. They spent a day or two at Gurnard's Head on the north coast before taking ship for the Scilly Isles on June 24. This took courage, as both the packet boats on the Scilly run had been lost the previous year, and the Isles had no lifeboat until 1874.[11] They stayed on St Mary's until the end of July, at the hotel Benjamin Holgate had recently opened in Hugh House (fig. 37). This handsome building originally housed the officers of the Garrison, and now contains the Duchy of Cornwall offices. Brett was clearly fascinated by the extraordinary rock formations on Peninnis Head, the island's principal showpiece, and made a number of sketches there. He also painted on St Agnes, and did preliminary work around St Mary's harbour for his main Academy picture for 1874, *Summer noon in the Scilly Isles* (unlocated).[12]

At the beginning of August they returned to Penzance, where Mary and the children remained, probably at the Star Hotel,[13] while John sailed on a small boat, the *Tyrant*, to Cowes for the race week. While in Penzance, Mary was photographed by Robert Hawkes Preston, whose studio in Market Jew Street was close to the Star. The family was reunited by August 25, and then migrated north, reaching Perranporth by the 29th. For much of September Brett worked at St Agnes, capturing perfectly the distinctive blue of the sea on this part of the coast. There were also boats to observe, particularly the colliers coming and going from what was then an important mining town, and, for Michael, the chance to play with bucket and spade on the beach.

Continuing their journey north, the family were in Tintagel by September 27, where Brett sketched King Arthur's Island. But such magnificent cliff scenery must have been wasted on small children, so they decided to press on to Bude, renowned for its expanses of fine golden brown sand. There they stayed from the second week of October until early November, most likely at the Falcon hotel, headquarters for the four-horse coaches which served the area.[14] This was a very productive period for the artist, in which he painted at least eight oil sketches. Several form a group of related studies, linked by similar views of beach, rocks, and sunset skies, which can be regarded as preparatory to his other Academy picture the next year, *Bude Sands at Sunset* (fig. 6 p.13).

1874 saw some changes in the family's life. With two growing children and a third on the way (Jasper was born in December that year), they decided to leave central London for the space and fresh air of the suburbs. They took a lease of Wimpole Lodge in St John's Road East (now St John's Avenue) Putney,[15] a new development just off Putney Hill, conveniently placed for the train into town. At the same time Brett gave up his Pump Court chambers and rented a new studio at a dentist's in Harley Street.[16] In July the family left by steamer for Guernsey, where the sketching season was spent. The following year they went to the Isle of Anglesey. But in 1876 it was time to return to Cornwall.

This year they took a house for the whole summer, rather than staying in hotels. This was Penolver Cottage at Beast (Bass) Point on the Lizard, superbly situated high on the cliffs close to the Lloyd's signal station.[17] They arrived early in July, and Brett soon revisited his old haunt Kynance Cove, painting a beautiful view of the Lizard from the Rill above Kynance on the 19th (fig. 38 and fig. 39). For the next three months he sketched, largely directly on prepared millboards, a number of local views, from Kennack sands in the east to Mullion in the north. At Mullion on September 2 he made a sketch of Mount's Bay (fig. 40) from which his large Academy picture for the following year was developed.[18] He also befriended Francis Jose, a serpentine ornament worker. His sketchbooks contain a drawing entitled 'Jose's shag',[19] an incident later recalled by

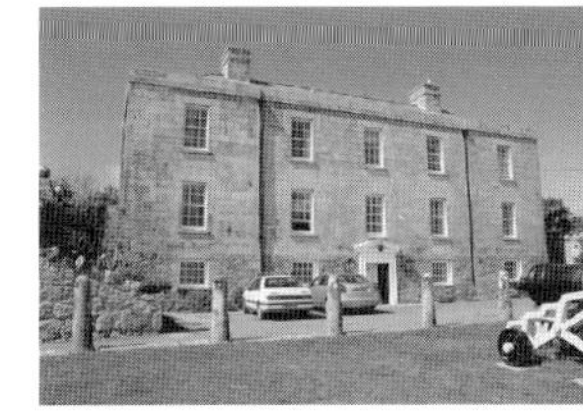

FIG. 37
Hugh House, St Mary's, Isles of Scilly
Photograph: Cécile Brett

FIG. 36
St Agnes, Scilly
1873, Oil on board
18 x 35.5cm (7 x 14ins)
Inscribed *'Scilly July 29 73'*
Private Collection

FIG. 38
The Lizard
1876, Oil on canvas
25.3 x 48.3cm (10 x 19ins)
Inscribed *'Lizard July 19 76'*
Private Collection

FIG. 40
Mount's Bay
1876, Oil on canvas
25.3 x 48.3cm (10 x 19ins)
Inscribed *'2 Sep 76'*
Private Collection

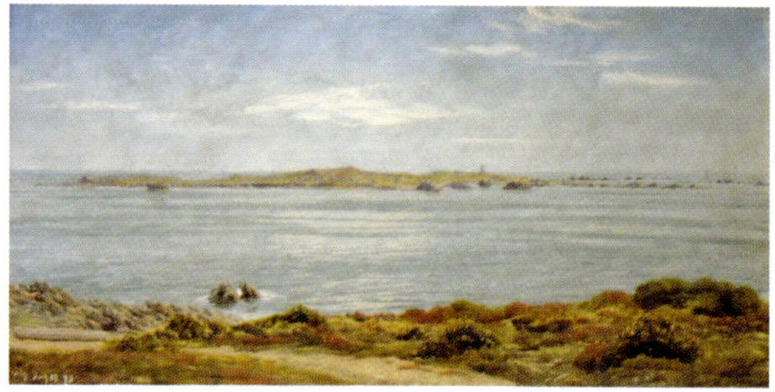

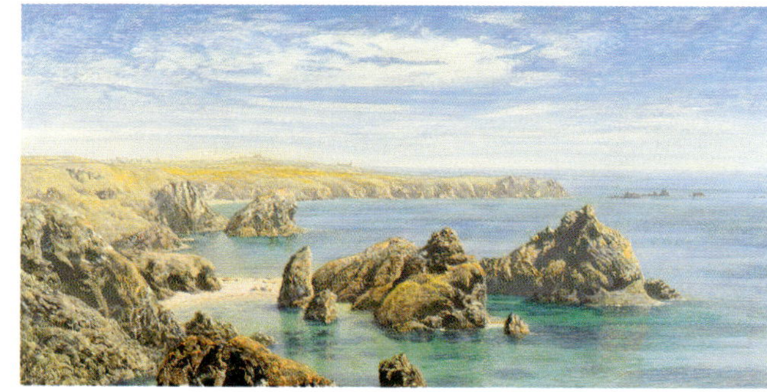

Beatrix Potter in her diary entry for April 1892: 'I was amused to enquire after Mr Brett, who is well remembered at Lizard Town, though he has not been there of late years. One old stone-cutter told us with pride that Mr Brett had sat for hours in his shed on Saturday afternoons, painting a stuffed cormorant.'[20]

The Lizard visit of 1876 was evidently a success, as Brett decided to return the following year. In the meantime there had been a further addition to the family – Alfred, born in December

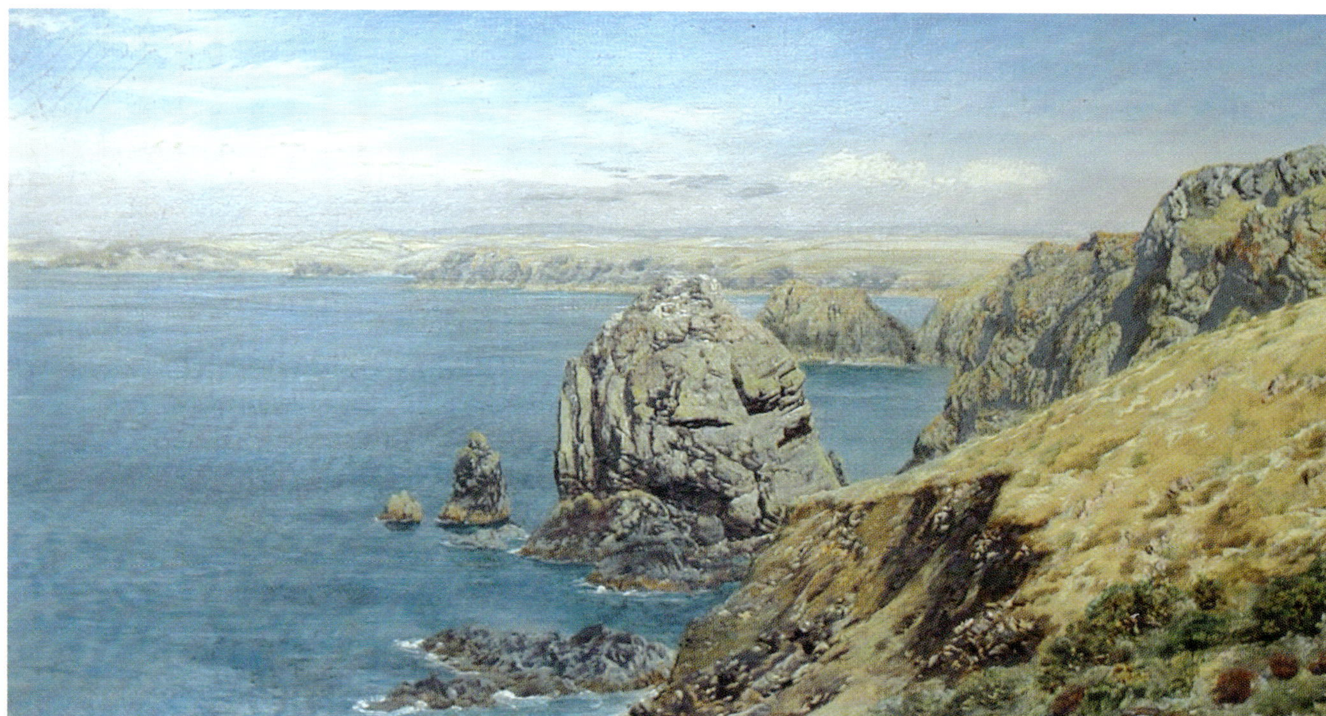

1876. Brett was also building a new house in Keswick Road, a stone's throw from Wimpole Lodge, a measure of his increasing professional success. Perhaps Penolver Cottage was not available, or too small for the enlarged family this summer. At all events they stayed at Penmenner House, a private hotel run by Thomas and Grace Rowe, who had put John and Mary up on their honeymoon. Soon after their arrival an exciting event occurred. On July 12 the Channel Fleet passed the Lizard (fig. 41), no doubt exercising in response to Russia's designs on Constantinople (war had been declared between Russia and Turkey in April). Brett sketched four of the principal warships – *Minotaur, Black Prince, Defence* and the ironclad *Thunderer* – as they passed.[21]

This season was also notable for the extensive astronomical observations Brett carried out near the Lloyd's signal station. Always an enthusiastic astronomer, he was elected a Fellow of the Royal Astronomical Society in 1871, and served on its Council in 1876–7. There was an eclipse of the moon on August 23, and throughout the autumn he kept Jupiter and Mars under close observation. He wrote up these observations in 'The physical condition of Mars', a paper published in the *RAS Monthly Notices* that December. Though these nocturnal activities must have been tiring, Brett also made a fair number of sketches on the Lizard and further afield (some Kennack sketches indicate that he spent several days working there; no doubt the children enjoyed the sandy beach). The family returned in November to their new house, bringing with them two domestic servants, one charmingly called Charity.[22]

The summers of 1878–9 were spent respectively in Devon and at Penally in Pembrokeshire. At Penally John and Mary began jointly to write the family diary – 'Memoranda of the Early Travels of our children'– which provides a detailed record of that and subsequent campaigns, and enables us to follow their movements more closely. In 1880 the family returned to Cornwall. By then two further children had arrived: Pansy, born in July 1878, and Spencer, who was five months old when they set off on August 23. The six children were accompanied by their governess, Miss Stockman, and an omnibus was hired to take them all to Paddington. As in 1873, they caught the 11.45 train for Plymouth, staying that night in the Duke of Cornwall Hotel. The following morning they continued their journey to Penzance. There they were met by a local farmer, who took them in his shaky old carriage to the tiny hamlet of Porth Gwarra, a few miles south of the Land's End. They

FIG. 39
Kynance Islands & the Lizard lights from Rill Head
Oct 10 1870, Pencil
Sketchbook 35 (Park Browse is indicated with a cross)
© National Maritime Museum, London

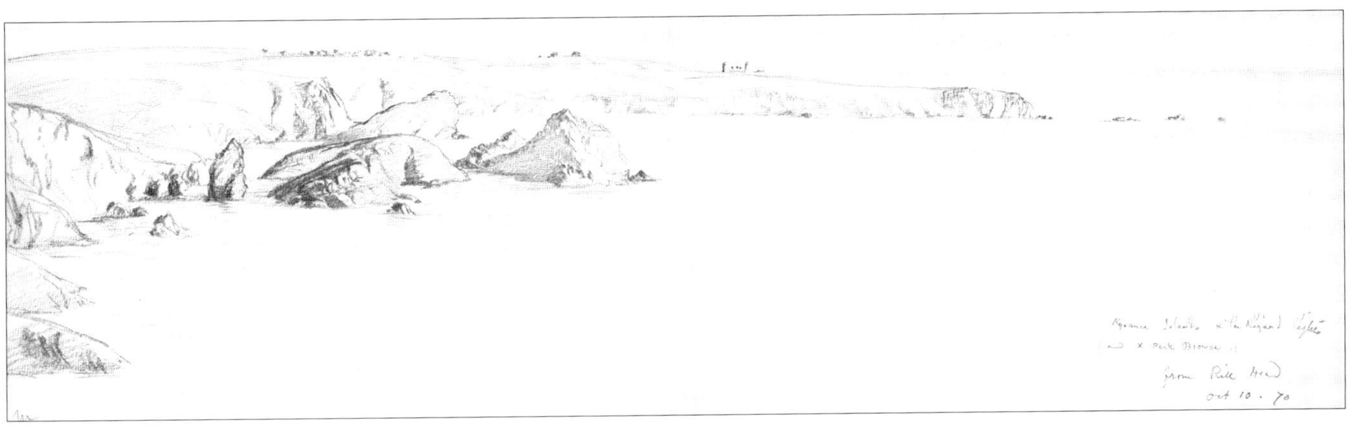

FIG. 41
Channel fleet passing the Lizard
July 12 1877, Pencil
Sketchbook 47
© National Maritime Museum, London

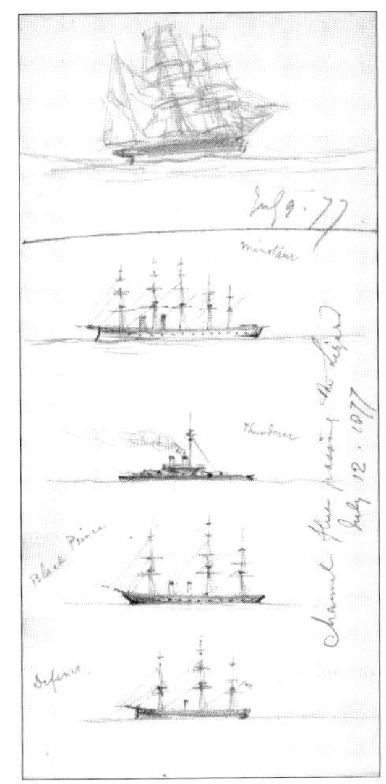

FIG. 42
The Great Western beach, Newquay, from a postcard c. 1920. Bothwicks House can be seen on the top of the cliff at the far left

FIG. 43
Golden Prospects
Signed & dated 1881.
Oil on canvas
106.68 x 213.36cm (42 x 84ins)
Nottingham Castle Museum

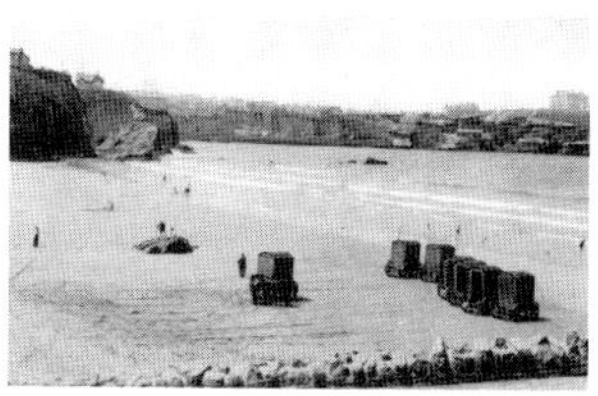

lodged in two cottages owned by a pair of fishermen, William and Matthew Jackson. Brett's first impression of the village was that it was 'like... all other Cornish hamlets – repulsive.'[23] But the gaunt granite cliffs were impressive, particularly Tol-Pedn-Penwith, a stack 'said to be 400 feet high and nearly perpendicular on the sea face. It is called the "sheer ladder" and is very frightful.'[24] He found plenty of subjects to sketch, and the season was 'tolerably fruitful', although for beauty of scenery he considered this coast 'altogether inferior to the Lizard region.'[25]

Towards the end of September the family were joined by their friend Parson Jackson, Rector of Ruan, who came over with his wife and daughters to do some sketching. But on the 30th measles appeared in the village, and both families had to beat a hasty retreat. Luckily Brett found Sea View House in Sennen, where they had stayed in 1872, unoccupied, and he was able to take it until the end of October. Some rewarding sketching was done near the Land's End, the principal result being *Golden Prospects* (fig. 43). But the weather became increasingly cold and windy, and on October 27 they left for home. On the way they stopped

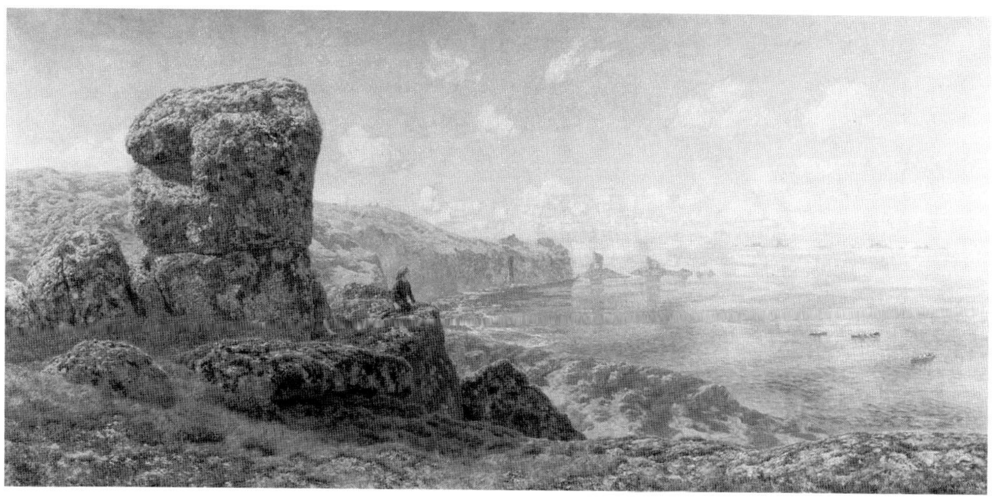

at Exeter to collect a new housemaid, Kate Turpin, who had answered their advertisement in the *Western Morning News.*

Brett's career was fast approaching its zenith. In April 1880 his *Britannia's Realm* (Tate, London) had been bought for the nation with Chantrey funds, and in February 1881 he was to be elected ARA. He was better off financially than ever before, and was seriously considering building a summer house on the coast. A Cornish site would be especially appropriate 'as we have already done a great deal to make Cornwall known and popular in our own world – and it is probable that we shall yet do much more.'[26] The top of Tol-Pedn-Penwith particularly appealed to him – 'one of the cardinal sites of England'[27] – and while at Sennen he investigated its availability and the costs involved in building a bungalow.[28] A price for the site was even agreed, 'but my solicitor soon found out that the seller really had no legal title to it, so the matter fell through.'[29]

In 1881 Brett chose Newquay for the summer campaign, and made a preliminary visit just before Easter to look for lodgings and appraise the sketching material. Newquay was still a small fishing village in those days, with barely 1,500 inhabitants.[30] Although the railway had arrived in 1876, there were only three hotels, and tourism was in its infancy. Brett managed to find a house in the centre of the town, Bothwicks, which belonged to Charles Holbrow Stanton, 'a fidgetty old bachelor',[31] and took it for four months. It was conveniently placed between Towan beach and Tolcarne Point, and close to the sea – a flight of steps led from the garden directly down to the beach.

The family left home on June 2 by the familiar route, taking Green's bus[32] to Paddington, then the train to Plymouth. A night at the Duke of Cornwall refreshed them, and they arrived at Newquay the next morning. First impressions were good. John wrote: 'as far as the sea is concerned I know no place quite equal to this for colour, clearness or steadiness of demeanour.'[33] Mary was equally delighted. 'We have found it a very healthy place... The beach is a great source of pleasure to [the children], there are such splendid pools where they can bathe and practice [sic] their swimming with perfect safety. It is also very beautiful, the sand being of a lovely fawn colour and the rocks a rich brown being... covered with seaweed and mussels.'[34]

Several of the local people were friendly and made them welcome. One was George Hicks, who had made a fortune in Peru, and built himself a house on the Beacon. Mrs Shuckford took them for a picnic at Wheal Golden, overlooking Holywell Bay, and they explored Watergate Bay and the Mawgan valley with Mr Perrin, Rector of St Mawgan. This year the children's lessons were continued on holiday, the two eldest, Michael and Daisy, receiving an hour's tuition every day from Mr Mugford, headmaster of the local school. They in turn taught Jasper and Alfred, for which they received threepence a week, while their little pupils were given a penny 'provided their marks average two for each day.'[35]

Brett had a very productive summer with the brush, painting about forty 7 x 14ins sketches ('about 30 of these saleable'), six of 10 x 19ins, and six larger finished pictures. 'Total value about 1200 which is a better season's work than usual.'[36] He was also busy with the telescope, as two major comets passed over that summer. Tebbutt's comet was visible for nearly a fortnight from June 23, and Schäberle's comet for several nights in August.

The holiday ended on September 28 in idyllic fashion. After an early dip at 6.30 in 'the grey of the morning',[37] the family spent the rest of the day on the beach. The older children frolicked in the sea, while the smaller ones bathed in lovely warm pools. Everyone dressed again 'after long scampering in a secluded part of the rocks where the sun was baking hot'.[38] It had been a thoroughly

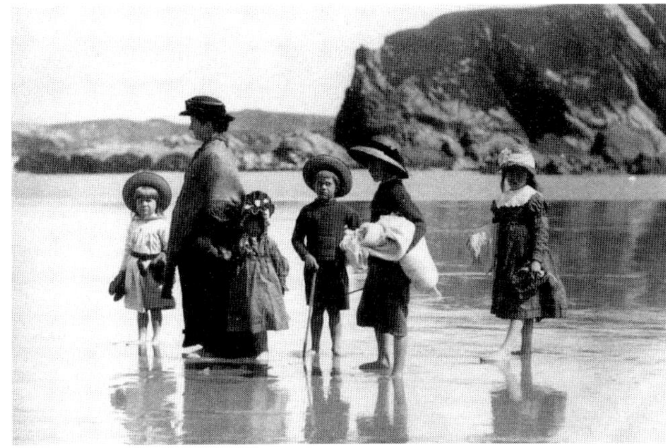

successful campaign; but there was one disappointment. Brett had spotted an ideal site for a summer house on Tolcarne Point, just to the east of Bothwicks. The land belonged to the Duchy of Cornwall, and he did all he could to negotiate a sale with the Secretary. But his offer was rejected, and he noted sadly: 'It seems as if Cornwall had decided to keep us out.'[39]

The summer house scheme received a further setback in Pembrokeshire the next year. Brett found two suitable sites near Fishguard, but 'the owner of one could not and the other would not sell.'[40] This caused him to change tack. His 'ancient proclivity for sea-faring was gradually reviving', and he admitted that 'the idea of a moving home is the one I have constantly cherished for the last twenty years or more.'[41] So he bought a boat, and a magnificent one she was. A schooner of 210 tons, 100 feet long, the *Viking* (fig. 49) was offered for sale by Lord Caledon.[42] She had previously belonged to Baroness Mayer de Rothschild, and required a crew of twelve hands to sail her. There was ample accommodation aboard for family and crew, and even a spare cabin for guests. She was an extravagance, but one which Brett, then at the height of his fame, could afford.

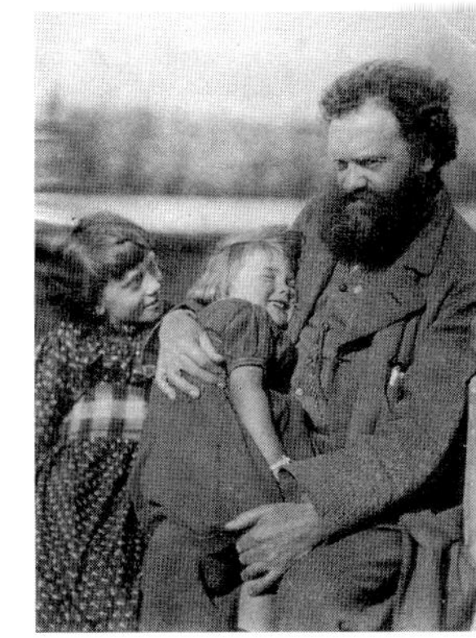

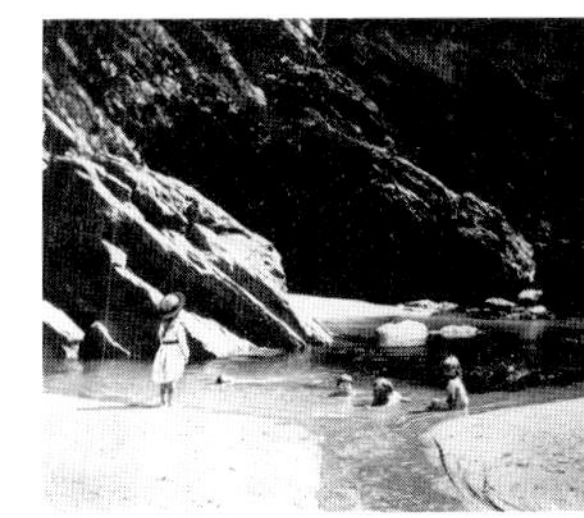

FIG. 44
On the beach at Newquay
1881, Original photograph (In the background is Crigga Head)
Private Collection

FIG. 45
Self-portrait with Daisy and Pansy at Newquay
1881, Original photograph
Private Collection

FIG. 46
The children bathing at Newquay
1881, Original photograph
Private Collection

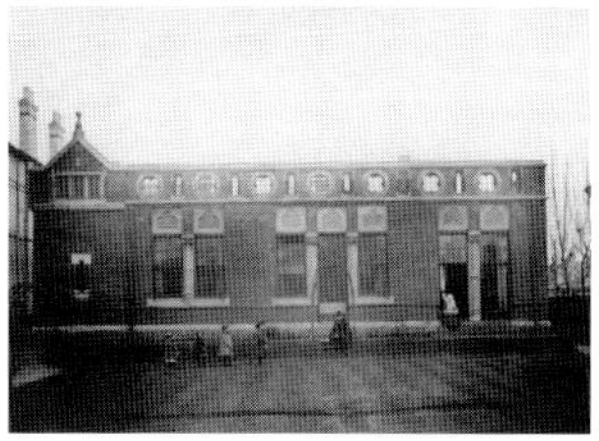

FIG. 48
Garden front of 6 Keswick Road, Putney 1879. Original photograph
Private Collection

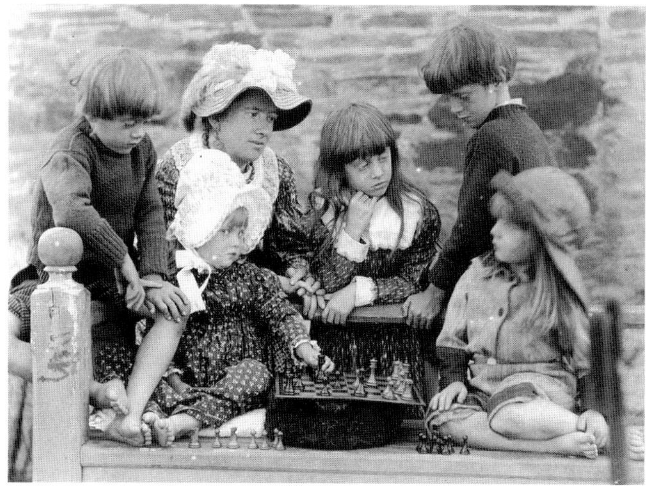

FIG. 47
A game of chess at Newquay
1881, Original photograph
Private Collection

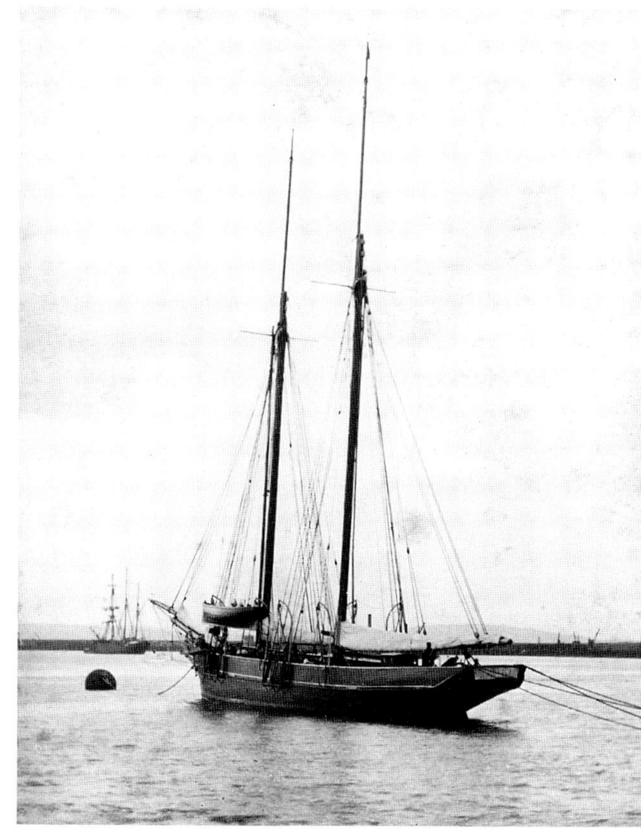

FIG. 49
The Viking
1883, Original photograph
Private Collection

The family embarked on their maiden voyage at the end of June 1883, and after a week at Plymouth, arrived at Fowey on July 10. Brett called on his friend and client Edward Atkinson, who came on board to inspect the boat.[43] The following day Brett sketched the entrance to the harbour. On the 13th they sailed along the coast, reaching Falmouth by evening. Here was another old friend, the shipping agent Howard Fox. His wife Blanche was a daughter of Charles and Eliza Orme, who had been a great source of introductions and hospitality in the old Pre-Raphaelite days. After Fox had lunched on board the *Viking*, the family 'went to his house and ravaged his superb garden. Brought off much plunder therefrom.'[44] Later Brett had a tent set up on deck, and made several sketches of the town and harbour. On the 20th the marine painter Henry Moore and his friend Mr Burnett of the yawl *Dawn* came aboard. The next day Brett repaid the compliment by visiting the *Dawn*, where he saw 'some splendid sketches of Moore's'.[45] The weather remained poor, and there was heavy rain on the 23rd. But things improved the following day, so they weighed anchor at 9.15, and with a favourable wind 'passed Lizard, going very fast'.[46] By 5pm they had rounded the Longships 5 or 6 miles distant, and at 11.45pm the Trevose light gave them their last glimpse of Cornwall. Their cruise was to take them all round the British coast, and after many adventures ended in mid-October.

Brett used the *Viking* again in 1884–5, going first to Guernsey, where the cruise was enlivened by a mutiny of the crew, and then to Oban. But by 1886 his picture sales were falling off, and it was clear that he could no longer afford to run the boat. That year he took a house for the summer in Scotland, and although

Viking was not finally sold until 1891, he never went to sea in her again. A further complication arose early in 1886. The Guildford and Kingston railway wanted to extend their line through the garden of 6 Keswick Road, which was to be compulsorily purchased. Eventually compensation of £7,500 was agreed, and by April 1887 Brett had bought an acre of land near Putney Heath to build on. That year the summer was spent on the Gower, but in 1888 much of Brett's time was occupied with the building of the new house, Daisyfield, and he decided not to travel, but to paint from pencil sketches done in previous years.

Looking through sketches made at Kynance Cove in 1870, he found one of the Lion Rock which suggested a suitable subject for a big picture he was hoping to sell to the Gallery at Sydney, NSW. He needed to refresh his memory of the scene on the spot, and seems to have tried to synchronise his visit with the dates of his earlier sketches, made between September 25 and October 10, 1870. He left London with Mary on the night train on September 26, and with a change at Gwinear Road to the newly-opened Helston branch line, was painting at Kynance the following morning. They stayed until October 6, and returned to town with eight sketches. Brett recorded that 'the expedition cost £20 for the 10 days.'[47] But it was worthwhile. From his sketches he painted *The Lion, the Lizard and the Stags* (p.123), which was eventually sold to Sydney.

By the next summer Daisyfield was finished, and the family moved in on June 21 1889. They spent a few days there before leaving on July 2 for what was to be the last Cornish expedition to involve the whole family. John, Mary, the three girls and the youngest boy, Spencer, were accompanied by Miss Barrett the governess, and the two maids. They would be joined by the three older boys when their holidays from boarding school began. Brett had taken Dennis House, Padstow for three months at six guineas a week, possibly on the recommendation of his friend the architect J.D. Sedding, who was in Padstow that year, restoring the parish church. The children were old enough now to complete the journey in a day, so the party left in Green's bus for the 10.45 train from Paddington. They changed at Bodmin Road for Wadebridge, and covered the last few miles to Padstow in 'a real Cornish bus',[48] arriving for a late supper at 10.45pm.

Dennis House, with its 18-acre farm, lay high up overlooking the Camel river, on the southern edge of Padstow, which Brett dismissed as 'a poor little godforsaken but innocent place with perhaps half a dozen coasters in harbour.'[49] But as for the house itself, its 'situation is magnificent and the air too delightful. When I awake in the morning after an absolute sleep and hear the blind flapping and the air moving round the bed the sensation is not to be forgotten. The air alone is enough to live upon.'[50] The surroundings were stimulating, the estuary being dominated by Pentire Point, 'a remarkably fine headland', and there was 'plenty of good pictorial coast towards the SW.'[51] They were also 'two miles from the open sea at Trevone, where there is capital bathing'.[52] As the weather was exceptionally fine for much of the

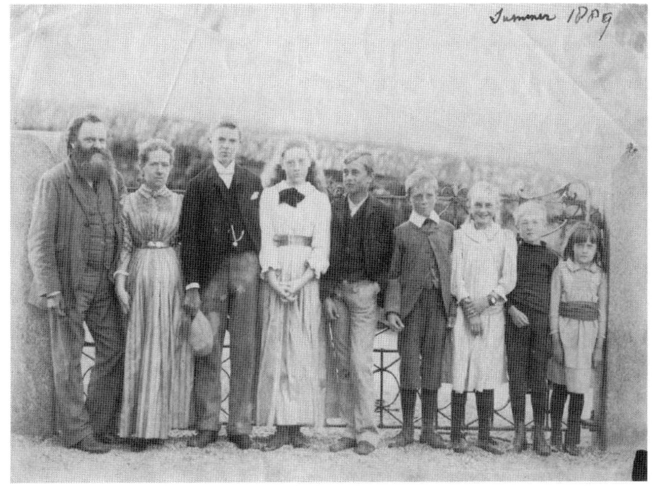

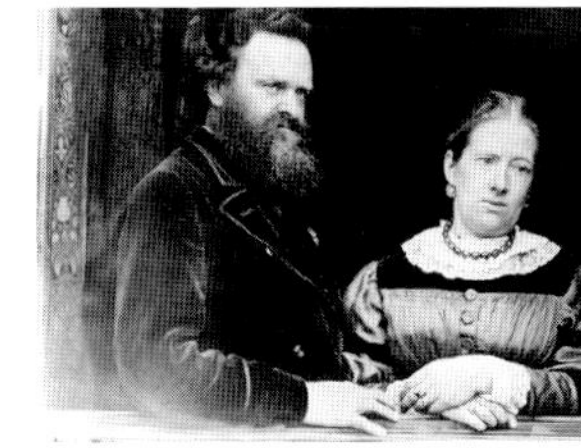

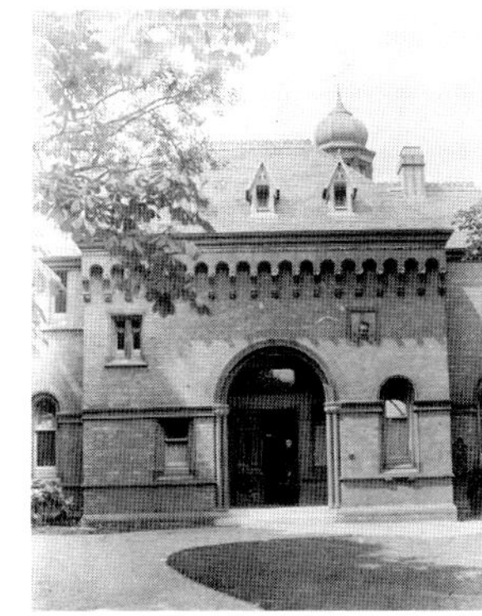

FIG. 52
The family at Dennis House, Padstow, Summer 1889, Original photograph Private Collection

FIG. 50
Self-portrait with Mary at 6 Keswick Road, Putney c.1878, Original photograph Private Collection

FIG. 51
The entrance front of Daisyfield c.1889. Original photograph. Private Collection. The family crest, 'a falcon proper, armed, jessed and belled', is set in the wall to the right of the entrance

summer, everything was in place for a successful campaign.

As usual, the family made friends among the local people. The Prideaux-Brunes were kind, inviting Michael and Daisy to tennis parties at Prideaux Place, and fishing expeditions in their boat. Dr Marley, the local medical officer, and his family entertained them, and they also got to know Mrs Millar and her son Harry at Trevone. She was the daughter of the artist Henry Bright, and ran a lodging house where Brett was to stay in later years. In August a face from the past appeared in the form of the Pre-Raphaelite Arthur Hughes, who was staying nearby at St Merryn. He and Brett had been neighbours at Maidstone back in the fifties, and Hughes was struck by the resemblance between Michael and Brett's brother Edwin at a similar age.[53] Edwin himself visited them from Fowey with Edward Atkinson, his host there. Atkinson came over again later in the summer, and bought one of Brett's sketches.

For the children there was plenty to do, with picnics and bathing at Trevone, and, in September, blackberrying. Pounds of jam were made by Daisy and Miss Barrett to supply the boarders when they returned to school. Pansy, now eleven, had inherited her father's interest in photography, and a cowshed on the farm was converted into a dark room for her; and the whole party was entertained by the amusing antics of the youngest child, Gwendolen, a bright little girl of seven. Mary considered the summer 'quite the nicest holiday [the children] have had'.[54]

For Brett himself the summer was equally successful. He recorded that 'the sketching season has been unusually good and fruitful although the materials are only second rate. I have not got one fine subject, but plenty of useful studies. A fine subject is not essential to a fine picture, so I hope to get fairly out of it.'[55] His only concern was with his right hand, which 'shakes outrageously, but the left has civilly lent it some help at times, and I am in hope it may not be found out.'[56] He added, philosophically, 'this is strictly inherited and no surprise to me.'[57] But the results of the season were very satisfactory: 27 small sketches, nine of the larger size, and four finished pictures. He had painted everything suitable from Pentire Point and the estuary to Trevose Head and beyond, and had 'a clear conviction that my sketches are better painted this year than at any previous date.'[58] When the time came to return home on October 1, he declared: 'I don't think I have ever been so sorry to conclude an expedition.'[59]

The summers of 1890–1 were spent in Scotland and Wales, but in 1892 Brett stayed at home to save money. His work was not selling, and drastic economies were required. At midsummer 1893 he gave up his Harley Street studio, and the following spring his health broke down under the strain. He was taken in hand by the well-known surgeon George Buckston Browne for a month. His hand was shaking more badly than ever. On his release from Browne's care he had a week at Mrs Millar's at Trevone to recuperate, and succeeded in painting three sketches. He was to make two further visits to Cornwall.

The first was in 1897, when, after another bout of ill-health, he went back with Alfred, Pansy and Gwendolen to the Lizard. On July 23 they took the train to Helston, where they stayed overnight before going on the following morning to Mullion. Brett approved of the Polurrian Hotel, but the weather there was very hot and enervating, so on the 27th he decided to leave for Trevone. At Mrs Millar's he 'did a few feeble sketches & bathed in sea when practicable.'[60] Mary joined them later, but the weather soon broke, and constant rain and gales caused them to return home on September 7. Eight sketches are known from this visit, and they are better than Brett made out. Five were subsequently shown at the RA, and the 7 x 14ins *Trevose Head* was bought for the Gallery at Grahamstown, South Africa. The seven-foot work

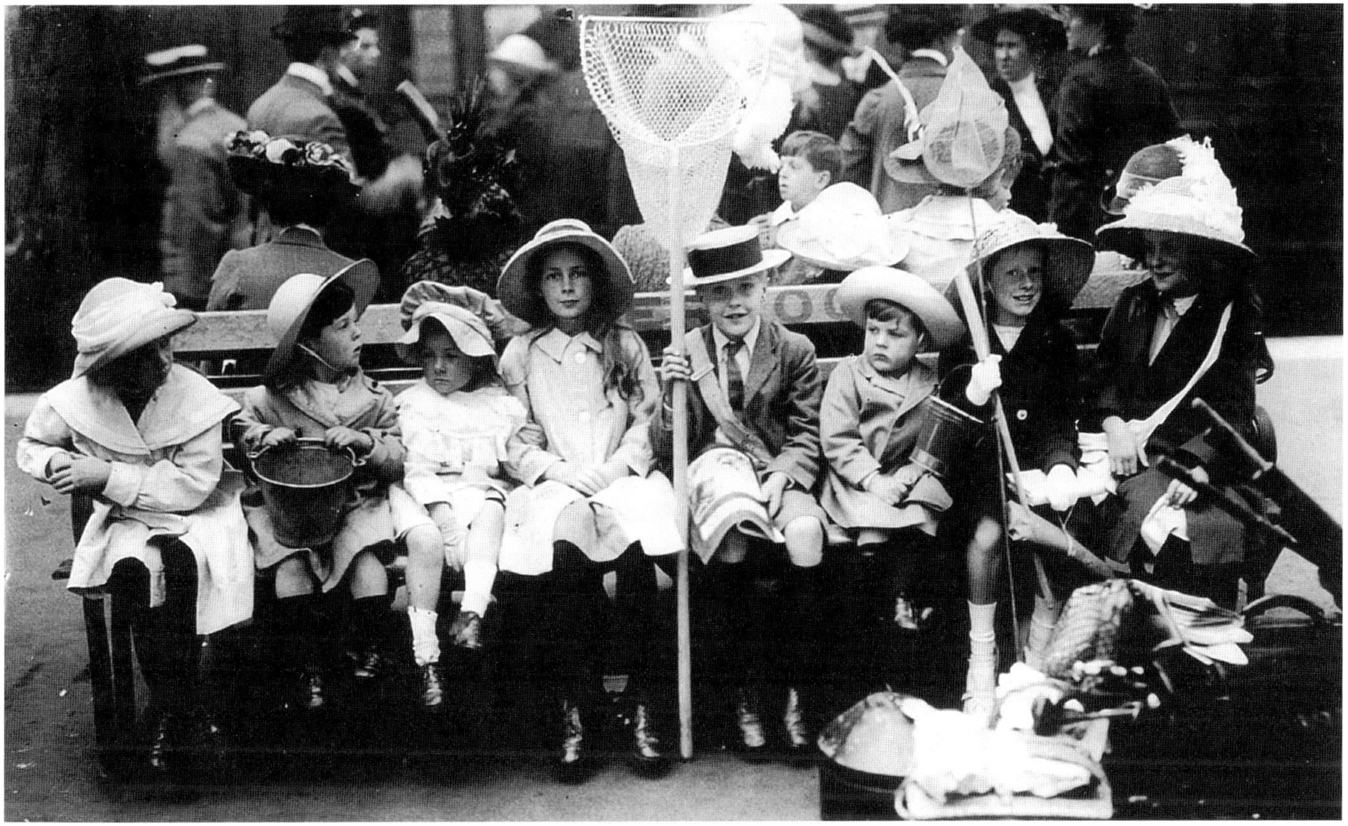

FIG. 53
At Waterloo station, on the way to Trevone, 1 August 1913
Photograph by Pansy Marshall, née Brett. A number of Brett's grandchildren are excitedly awaiting the start of their Cornish holidays.
Original photograph
Private Collection

based on this sketch (p.137) also went to the Academy, and was later sold to the Walker Art Gallery, Liverpool.

Brett's last visit to Cornwall was in 1899, when he returned to Newquay, spending some weeks in July in lodgings at 3 Harbour Terrace. He renewed his old acquaintance with George Hicks, and tried a pencil sketch or two; but his powers were clearly deserting him, and he seems to have been unable to complete any works. He returned to town at the end of the month 'after a wasted summer'.[61]

Brett's Cornish legacy is twofold. First, he left over 200 known views of the coastline from Fowey in the east to Bude in the north, painted over thirty years, in which he recorded with Ruskinian precision and Pre-Raphaelite intensity of colour its varied beauties, revelling in the diverse moods of sea and sky, and the majesty and grandeur of the cliffs. Secondly, he transmitted his love of Cornwall to his descendants, so that successive generations have continued to take family holidays there. The favourite spot has always been Trevone, where Mrs Millar kept her lodging house. There many of us have shared the delight he felt in 1889 in 'the open sea', and the 'capital bathing'.

NOTES

1 Details from JB Sketchbook 35 (National Maritime Museum).

2 See *Kilvert's Diary*, August 9 1870: 'Wharry the chemist told us he had been in Normandy, found it very uncomfortable, was mobbed, and very glad to get out of the country.'

3 Eight sketches of Swanage are contained in a wooden cabinet presented by JB to Mary in 1874 in remembrance of their happy honeymoon 'which after all was but a feeble foretaste of the greater blessedness of these later days.' (Private Collection).

4 This work, with its highly symbolic depiction of a sunlit path leading towards the horizon, was clearly of sentimental importance to John and Mary. He seems never to have tried to sell it after 1871; and she presented it to the Tate Gallery in his memory in 1902.

5 Sketchbook 35.

6 The last known sketch, a pencil portrait of the Rowes' daughter Annie (Private Collection), is dated October 19.

7 *Kilvert's Cornish Diary*, entry for July 22 1870.

8 *Kelly's Directory for Cornwall*, 1873.

9 Ibid. The population in 1871 is given as 6,965.

10 Of the 379 registered seines or pilchard businesses in Cornwall in 1870, 285 were based at St Ives (*Cornwall's Maritime Heritage* p.18). The Vicar told Kilvert that 'the smell of fish there is sometimes so terrific as to stop the church clock.' (*Cornish Diary*, July 21 1870).

11 G. Forrester Matthews pp 190–1.

12 Sketchbook 42 contains a sketch at the harbour inscribed: 'Early mid day July 22 73 (beautiful subject).'

13 Star and Commercial Hotel, 119 Market Jew St. Proprietor, George Pool (*Kelly* 1873). Sketchbook 35 contains the note: ' "Star" at Penzance best.'

14 Brochure of the Falcon Hotel.

15 See *Post Office Suburban Directory* 1876 and Wandsworth Rate Books.

16 The rent for the studio at 38 Harley Street was £80 a year (Letter from JB to his brother Arthur, dated July 6 1874, in a Private Collection).

17 This address was communicated to the Secretary of the Royal Astronomical Society on a postcard dated July 23 76 (RAS Library).

18 *Mount's Bay* (RA 1877), now at Johannesburg Art Gallery.

19 Sketchbook 47. Sketch dated Sep 28 76.

20 *The Journal of Beatrix Potter*, p.233. A shag is a small variety of cormorant.

21 Sketchbook 47. *Minotaur* was the fleet's flagship (Vice-Admiral Seymour), and *Thunderer* was commanded by Lord Charles Beresford, later a distinguished admiral (Navy List).

22 The diarist A.J. Munby records dining at 6 Keswick Road the following May, and describes how 'the parlour maid, whose name is Charity, waited outside the door during dinner; and her master clapped his hands for her as for an eastern slave.' (Hudson, p.393).

23 Early Travels, Sep 27 80.

24 Ibid.

25 Ibid. His work this year was exclusively on canvas, as he seems to have rarely used millboards after 1878.

26 Ibid, Oct 10 1880.

27 Ibid.

28 He consulted John Trounson of Penzance and Robert Tregenza of St Just, respectively architect and contractor for the Board School then under construction at Sennen (Sketchbook 53).

29 *Viking*: a history.

30 *Kelly's Directory for Cornwall* 1883.

31 Early Travels, September 28 1881.

32 William Green of Upper Richmond Road, and White Lion Yard, Putney, was a jobmaster, who supplied coaches and cabs for hire (*Post Office Suburban Directory* 1876).

33 Early Travels, September 28 1881.

34 Ibid, August 28 1881.

35 Ibid.

36 Ibid, September 28 1881.

37 Ibid. Brett used this phrase as the title of his principal RA picture the next year.

38 Ibid.

39 Ibid.

40 *Viking*: a history.

41 Ibid.

42 She was built by Camper and Nicholson in 1853, and was originally called the *Czarina*. When Lord Caledon bought her in May 1876 she was re-registered at Cowes as the *Viking*. (Details supplied by the late Peter Brett).

43 *Viking* Log, July 10 1883.

44 Ibid, July 14 1883. The Fox gardens at Rosehill were famous for their exotic plants and fruits, which included oranges, lemons and bananas, cultivated in the open.

45 Ibid, July 21 1883.

46 Ibid, July 24 1883.

47 JB Pocket Diary, October 6 1888.

48 Early Travels, July 14 1889.

49 Ibid.

50 Ibid, September 29 1889.

51 Ibid, July 14 1889.

52 Ibid.

53 JB letter to Edwin Brett, September 1 1889 (private collection). Hughes, in a letter to W.B. Scott that September, described meeting JB 'making beautiful studies about the coast among the ripples and rocks. He does one small one complete at a sitting on fine and good days – beautiful skies and lovely seas, and foreground of the pretty mermaid tresses colouring the pools or what not.' (*Bulletin of the John Rylands Library*, 1967).

54 Early Travels, September 22 1889.

55 Ibid, September 29 1889.

56 Ibid.

57 Ibid.

58 Studio Log, October 23 1889.

59 Early Travels, September 29 1889.

60 Studio Log, September 6 1897.

61 Ibid, July 29 1899.

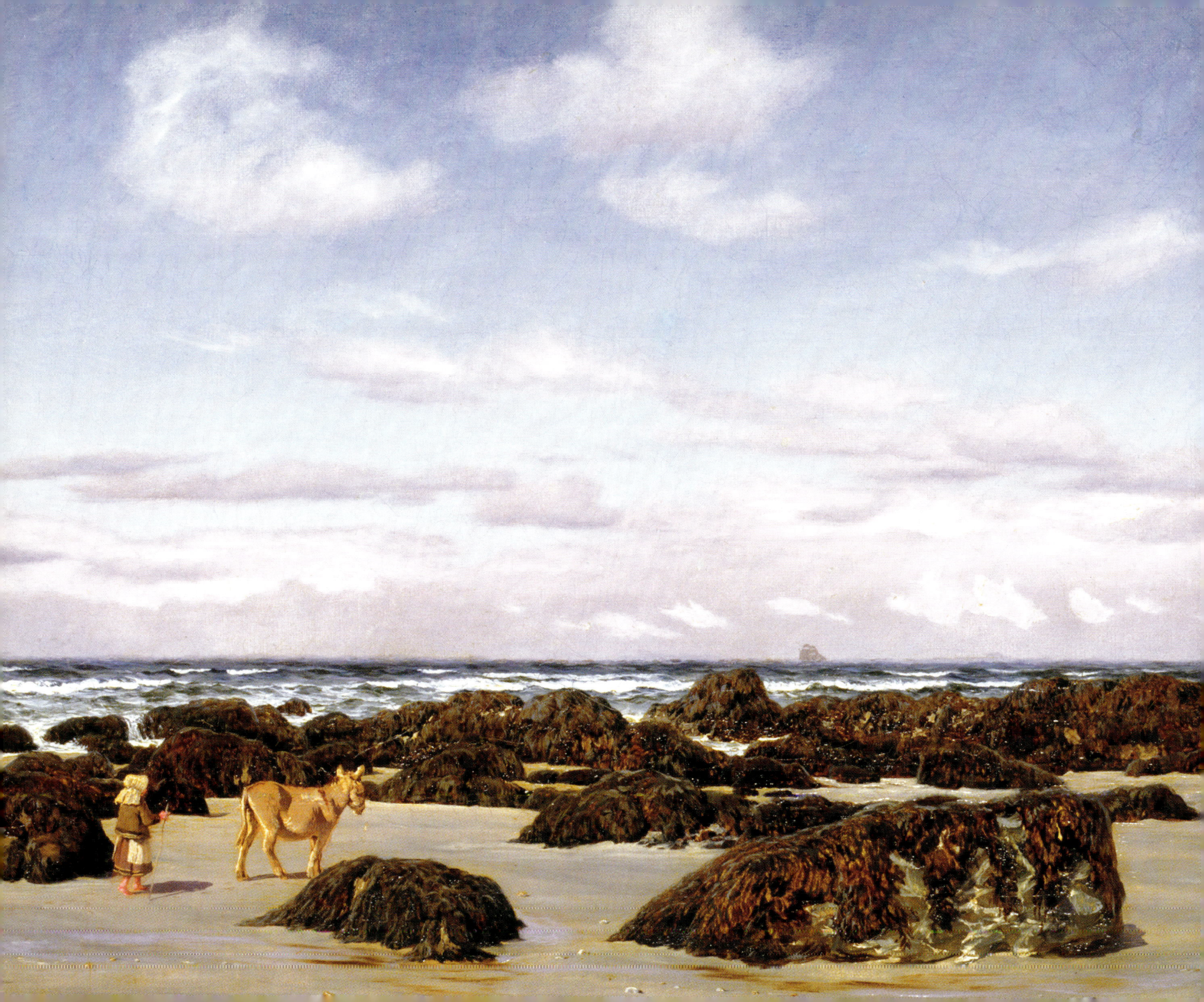

THE CORNWALL PAINTINGS

Charles Brett

OPPOSITE
View on the beach at St Agnes [detail]
1873, Oil on board
35.5 x 61.2cm (14 x 24½ins)
Inscribed '*6 Sep 73*' and
signed *John Brett*
Private Collection
Provenance: Alfred Morrison;
through the sale rooms to the
present owner

S.W. Gale, Polpeor
1870, Watercolour & bodycolour on paper, 10 x 17cm (4 x 6¾ins),
Inscribed *'SW Gale Polpier* [sic] *12 Oct 70 5.30pm'*
Private Collection
Provenance: by descent in the artist's family to the present owner

This delightful essay in blue and green is the only work from Brett's 1870 Lizard visit to have been located. It resembles two pencil sketches he had made at a similar time of day on 8 October (Sketchbook 35), matching particularly closely the sketch done at 5 pm that day, when a SW wind was blowing. By 12 October this had evidently increased to gale force, and a heavy sea is shown breaking over the Man of War rocks that lie off Polpeor Cove as Brett looked westwards towards the setting sun.

Polpeor, the little bay midway between Lizard Head and the lighthouse, was for more than a century the site of the lifeboat station, but in 1961 this was moved eastwards to the more sheltered Kilcobben Cove.

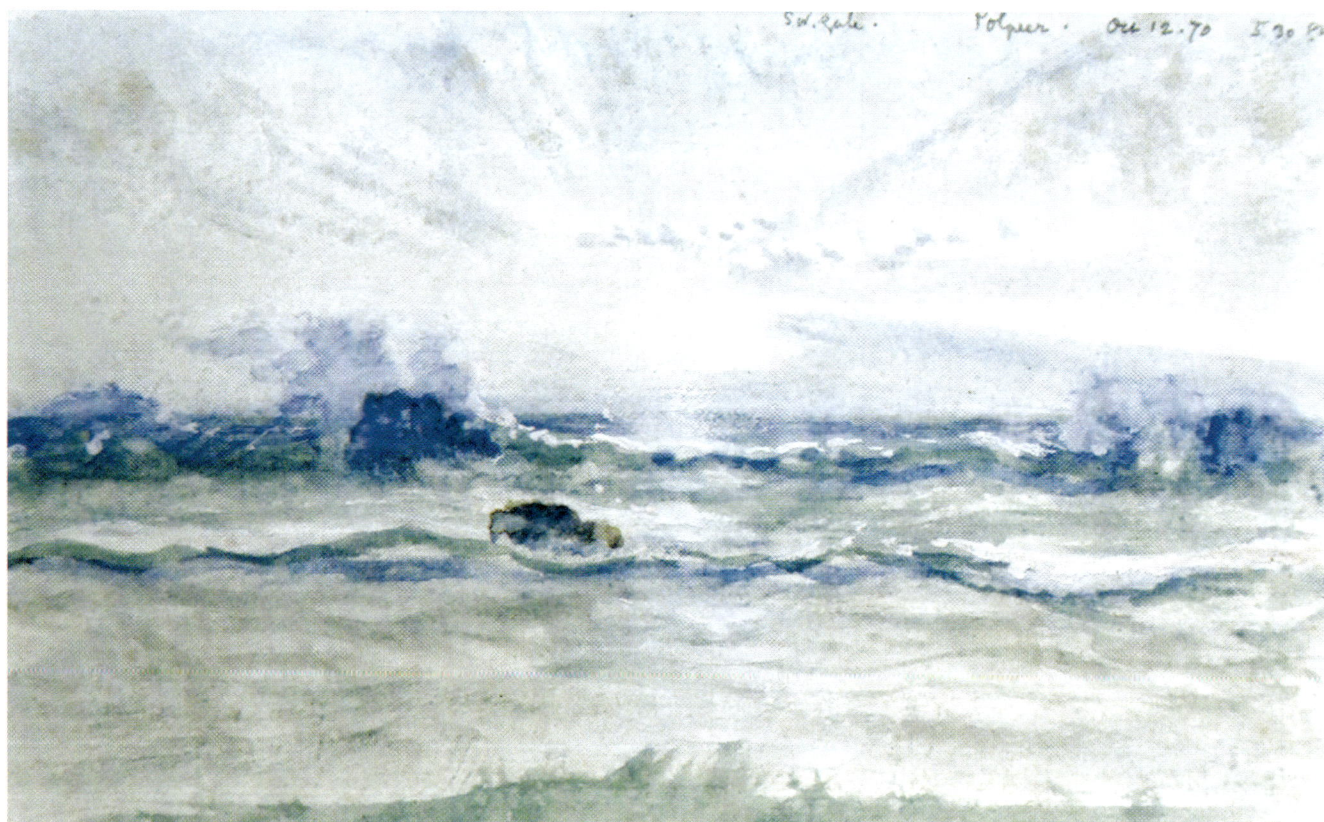

St Ives
1872, Watercolour & bodycolour on paper 11.4 x 18cm (4½ x 7ins)
Inscribed *'St Ives Sep 2 72'*
Private Collection
Provenance: by descent in the artist's family to the present owner

This is one of a number of attractive small watercolours, probably painted on sketchbook pages, that Brett produced at St Ives in 1872. The viewpoint here seems to be in the region of Barmaluz Point on the Island, looking south-east towards the Towans, or sandhills, that ring the bay between Hayle and Godrevy Point. Two St Ives luggers are seen in the bay, but the sketch is primarily a study of sea and waves, beautifully handled. The reflections on the sand as the waves break gently on the shore are particularly felicitous.

A rather similar view, executed in oil later in September (sold at Sotheby's, 22 October 1969, Lot 12), is substantially bigger, and includes a large number of craft.

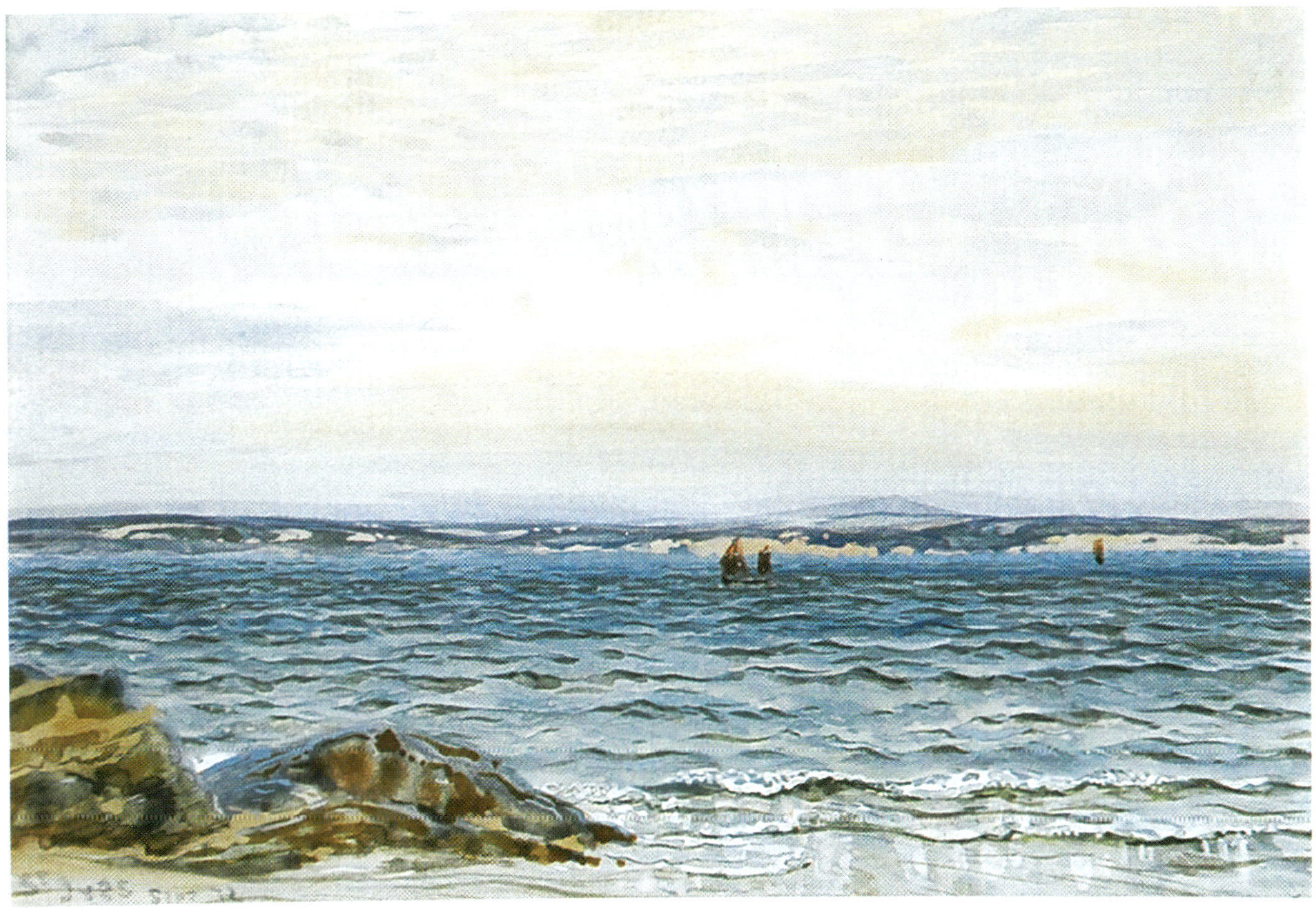

St Ives
1872, Watercolour & bodycolour on paper 10.1 x 16.5cm (4 x 6½ins)
Inscribed *'St Ives Sep 3 72'*
Private Collection
Provenance: by descent in the artist's family to the present owner

A St Ives pilchard driver, with its dinghy and two-man crew, forms the subject of this exquisite watercolour. It lies at anchor off Porthminster beach, Brett's viewpoint being from Pedn Olva, looking towards Porthminster Point. The Knill monument is visible at the top of the hill beyond the masts of the boat, and Phillack church appears on the horizon to the left.

A number of seine boats are shown drawn up on the beach. The St Ives boats were pointed fore and aft to facilitate this, and to save space in crowded harbours. The pilchard season lasted from July until November or December, and in the middle of the nineteenth century it was not uncommon for half a million fish to be caught in a single day by the St Ives fishermen. Most of the catch would eventually be exported, particularly to Italy. Towards the end of the century the shoals inexplicably began to desert the Cornish coast, and by the 1920s the St Ives fleet had largely ceased to exist.

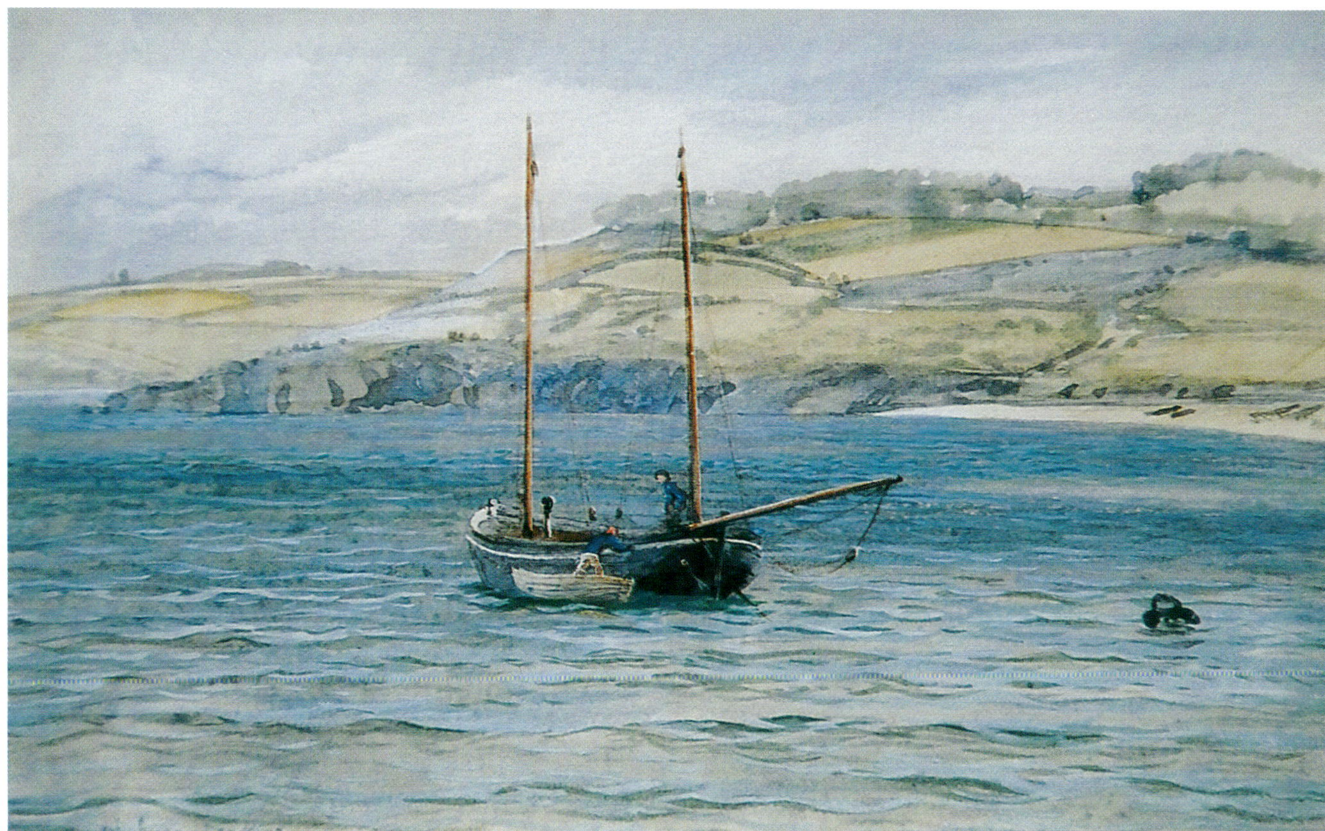

St Ives
1872, Oil on board
18 x 35.5cm (7 x 14ins)
Inscribed *'St Ives Sep 6 72'*
Private Collection
Provenance: by descent in the artist's family to the present owner

This is one of Brett's earliest oil sketches in the 7 x 14ins format he had adopted the previous year in Wales, and continued to use for the rest of his career. His viewpoint is on Porthminster beach looking towards Porthminster Point. Mary and Michael are shown, fashionably attired, on the sands, while a ketch, a lugger and a two-masted topsail schooner sail across the waters of the bay, here depicted in a lovely range of blues and greens.

The extension of the railway to St Ives was authorised by Act of Parliament the following year, and it opened in 1877. It entailed the construction of a cutting through Porthminster headland to give access to the station which was built above the beach. But in 1872 this was all in the future, and the beach remained the preserve of the fishing fleet, together with a handful of visitors.

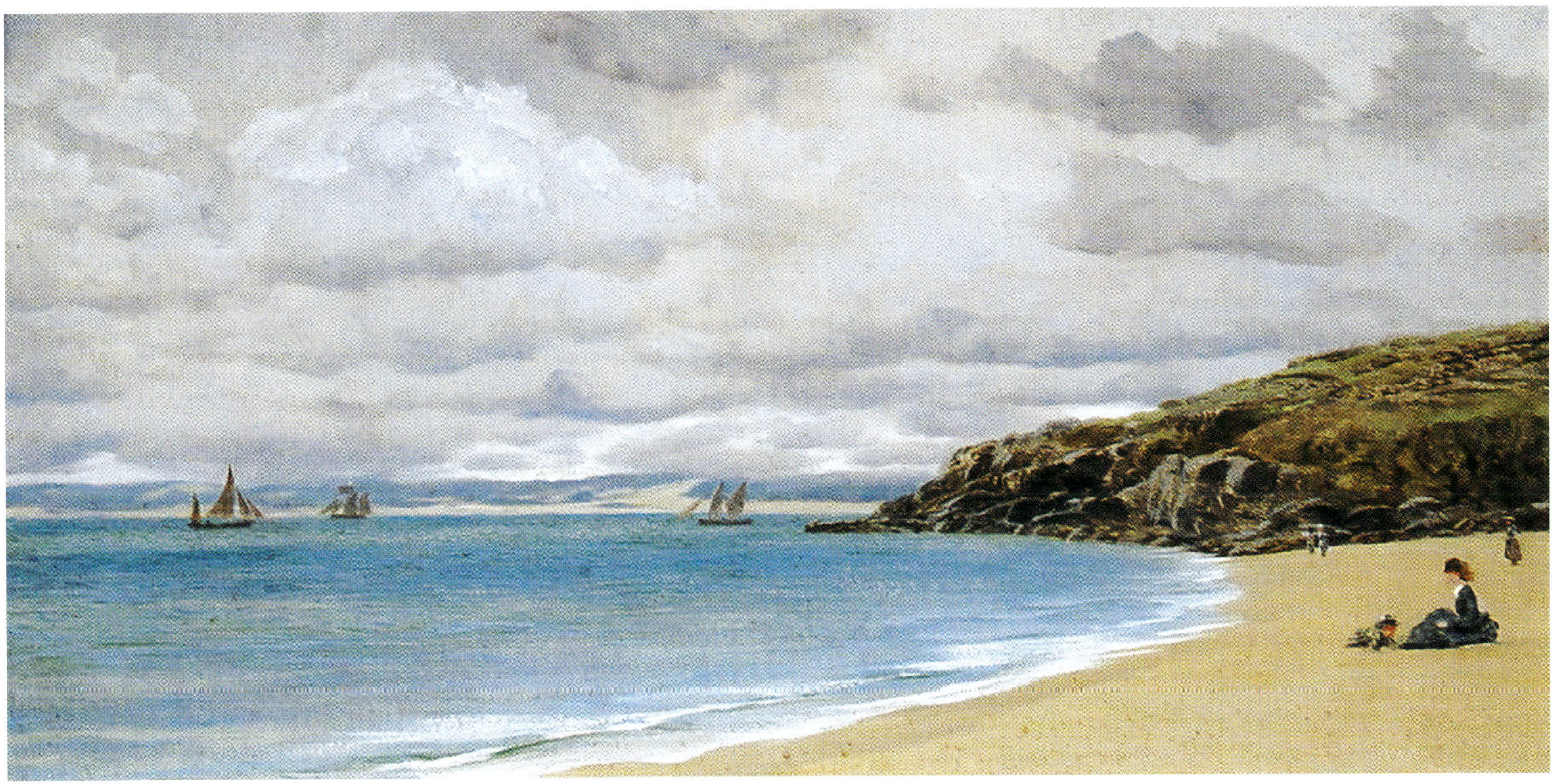

Net day at St Ives
1872. Oil on board
25.3 x 36cm (10 x 14ins)
Inscribed '*Net day at St Ives Sep 8 72*'
Private Collection
Provenance: by descent in the artist's family to the present owner

Brett began making studies of boats during his two visits to Capri in 1863–5. These led to the detailed harbour scenes in watercolour produced in Norfolk in 1868, notably the beautiful *Trawling smacks at Yarmouth* (British Museum). To an artist interested in such subjects the harbour at St Ives offered rich material, and in addition to copious sketchbook jottings, Brett painted at least five studies there in September 1872. Although unfinished, this sketch is one of the most interesting, and, like *Cape Cornwall from Whitesand Bay*, (page 69), is painted on a board of the 10 x 14ins size.

The town and harbour are here vividly portrayed at low tide from a point just west of Smeaton's pier. In the centre is the imposing tower of the fifteenth-century church of St Ia, with its four pinnacles, and behind it terraces of houses climb the hillside. There was no harbour wall in 1872, so the sand extends almost to the doors of the houses and fish cellars. Brett has clearly enjoyed depicting a variety of boats drawn up on the beach. In the left foreground are a couple of luggers, the nearer bearing the letters SS, indicating a St Ives registration. In the centre are a number of seine boats and a small blue gig, with a further pair of embryonic boats beyond, at the edge of the beach. On the left, beyond the luggers, protrudes the prow of a large merchantman. These boats brought in everything from foodstuffs to coal, the goods being unloaded on to horse-drawn carts, as Brett shows here.

Although the primary catch on a 'net day' would have been pilchard, other fish, such as mackerel and herring, were also caught. St Ives was noted for its smoked herring, or kippers, and the pall of smoke hanging over the town in this sketch no doubt emanated from the smoke houses where this process was carried out.

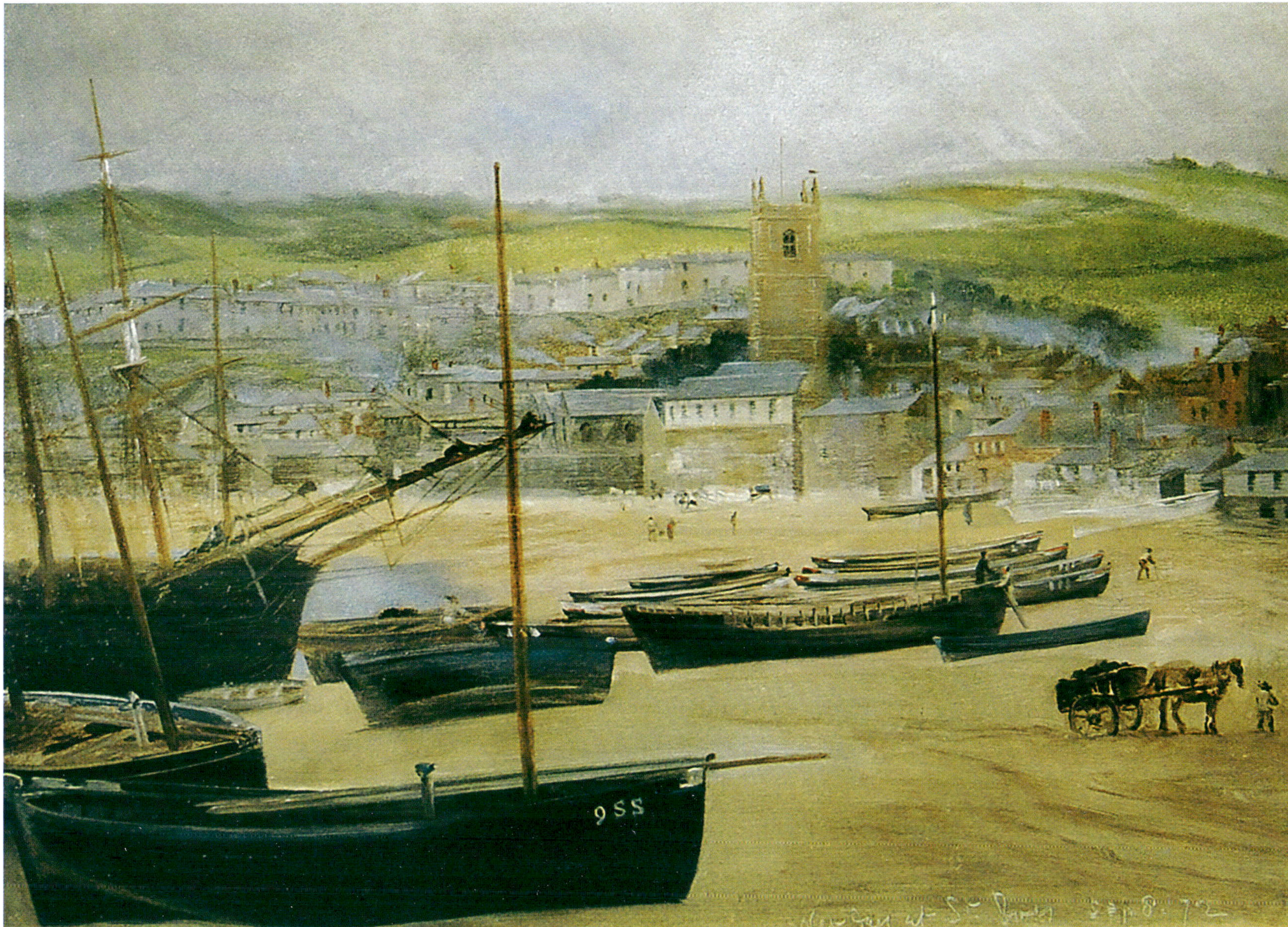
9SS

St Ives
1872, Oil on board
18 x 35.5cm (7 x 14ins)
Inscribed *'St Ives Sep 12 72'*
Private Collection
Provenance: by descent in the artist's family to the present owner

This serene study seems to relate to observations Brett had made at 3.30 on the afternoon of September 7. Sketchbook 38 contains a pencil sketch of the view, accompanied by the following notes:

> (A good distance for picture) Afternoon, sun behind spectator, clouds broken cumulus alternately cream on grey and grey on cream. the dark bits rather low and remnants of the recent S wester. To double the height of distt land they form a plain level of beautiful grey inclining to lavender... Lighthouse gleaming white Sea a clear but tender ultramarine near the land & moderately sharp lower down it is shaded into greys & greens, with gleaming Emerald over the nearer sands.

The view is of St Ives Bay seen from the harbour, looking north-east towards Godrevy Point. The Godrevy lighthouse stands out clearly in the distance, and beyond it can be seen the dark grey outline of the coast towards St Agnes Head. In the centre of the picture a lug-sailed pilchard driver is shown making its way towards Porthminster beach.

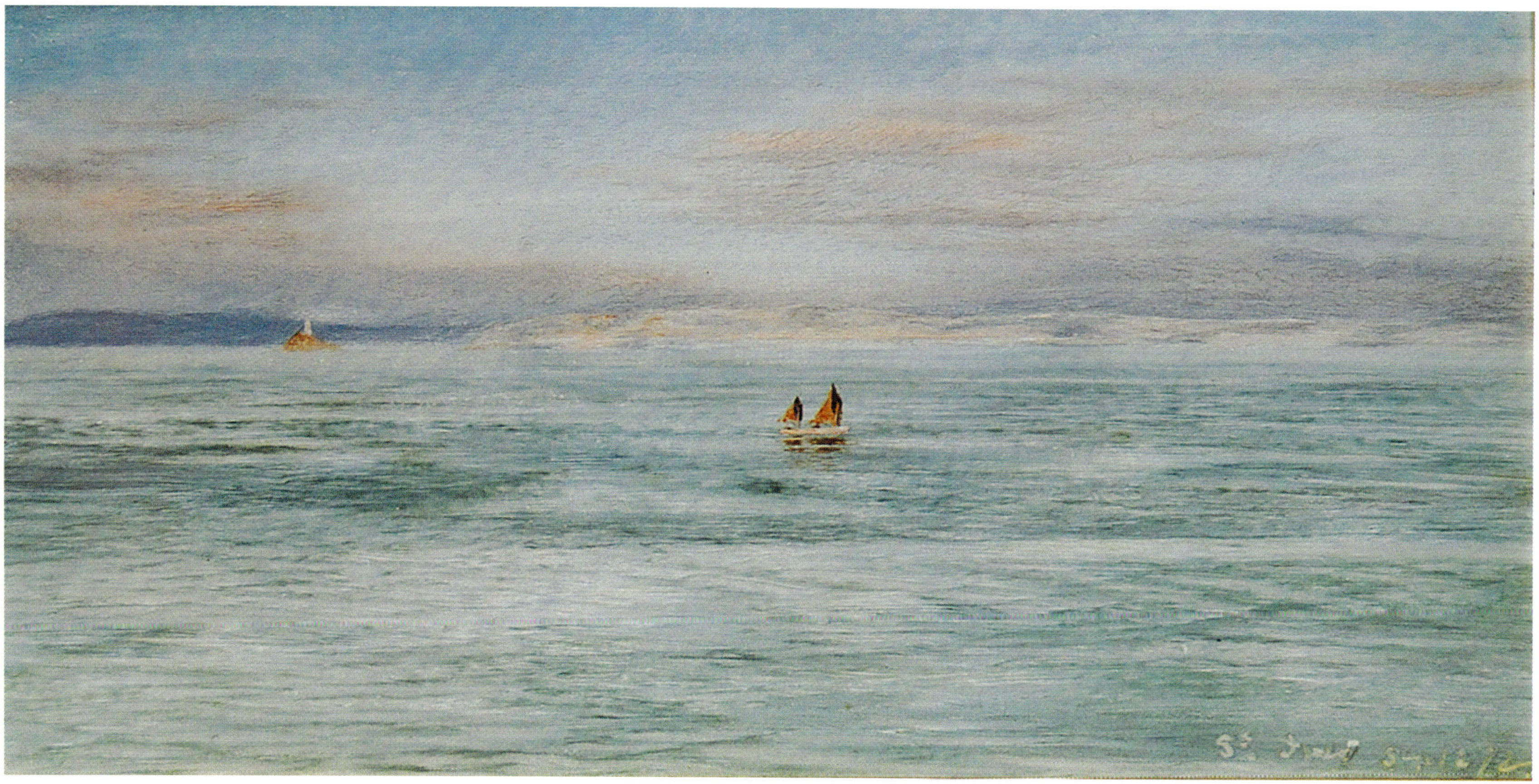

St Ives
1872, Oil on board
18 x 35.5cm (7 x 14ins)
Inscribed *'St Ives Sep 17/72'*
Private Collection
Provenance: through the sale rooms to the present owner

SUPPORTING IMAGE
St Ives
Sep 3 1872, Watercolour
4½ x 6ins
© Christie's

This is the most sophisticated and beautiful of Brett's views of the harbour at St Ives, shown here in the wider context of the bay and the surrounding coastline. It seems to have been based on a watercolour dated Sep 3 72 (sold at Christie's 21 Feb 1989, lot 76), which shows a similar view, but with the tide further up. The central feature is Smeaton's Pier, completed in 1770, with the attractive lighthouse that was added in 1831. The pier was extended between 1888 and 1890, but the original section remains to this day.

Brett's sketchbook 38 contains several pencil studies of fishermen and boats drawn on September 16 and 17, and a number of men are here depicted working on their boats in this minutely observed and beautifully composed scene. In the left foreground a man is scrubbing the bottom of a large boat, while in the centre of the picture others work on a red seine boat, and three drifters are lined up under the quay.

The contrast between the lively activity in the harbour and the ravishing view of the bay and the distant coast towards Godrevy Point is particularly skilfully handled, and the reflections of the sky in the damp sand provide another delightful touch.

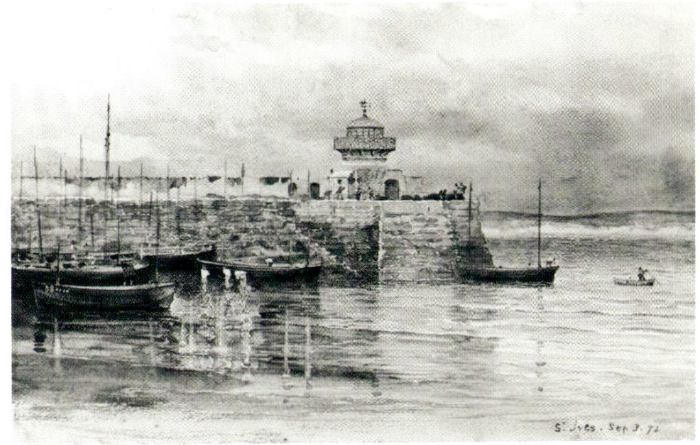

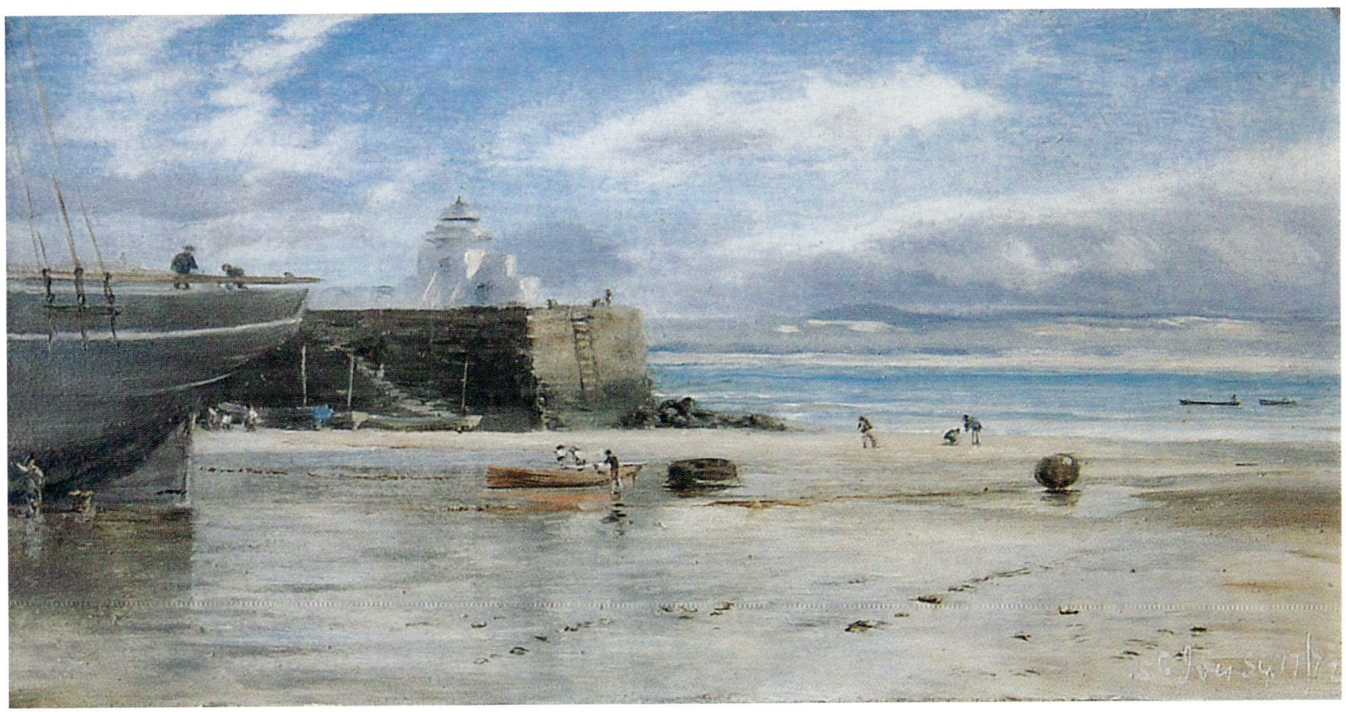

Land's End
1872, Oil on board
18 x 35.5cm (7 x 14ins)
Inscribed *'Land's End Oct 4 72'*
Private Collection
Provenance: through the sale rooms to the present owner

This is one of a group of oil sketches made in the vicinity of Land's End in October 1872, after Brett's move from St Ives to Sennen. He was clearly impressed by the granite rocks, which are hereabouts piled up in curious stacks. The diarist Kilvert had seen them two years earlier, and remarked how they were 'very strangely fantastically shaped', comparing them to 'squared baulks of timber reared up and leaning against each other.'

Brett found this unusual group on Pedn-men-du, the 'black stone head', midway between Sennen Cove and Land's End. He has used them as a foreground, or framing device, to a grand sea vista, a design often repeated in his later work (see p.72, 98–9, 101, and 102–3).

The sketch shows the view from Pedn-men-du looking due north past Bo Cowloe, the most westerly of the group of offshore Cowloe Rocks, towards the Brisons, visible in the distance to the right. Both these features later appeared in important works (see p.119, and fig 8, p.15).

All the elements in this fine sketch are beautifully handled, from the abstract shapes of the lichen-covered granite to the rich range of blues in the calm sea, and the distant mackerel driver, implicitly representing man's presence in this lovely natural scene. Together they form a highly satisfying composition, which foreshadows much of the work Brett was to do on the Cornish coast in years to come.

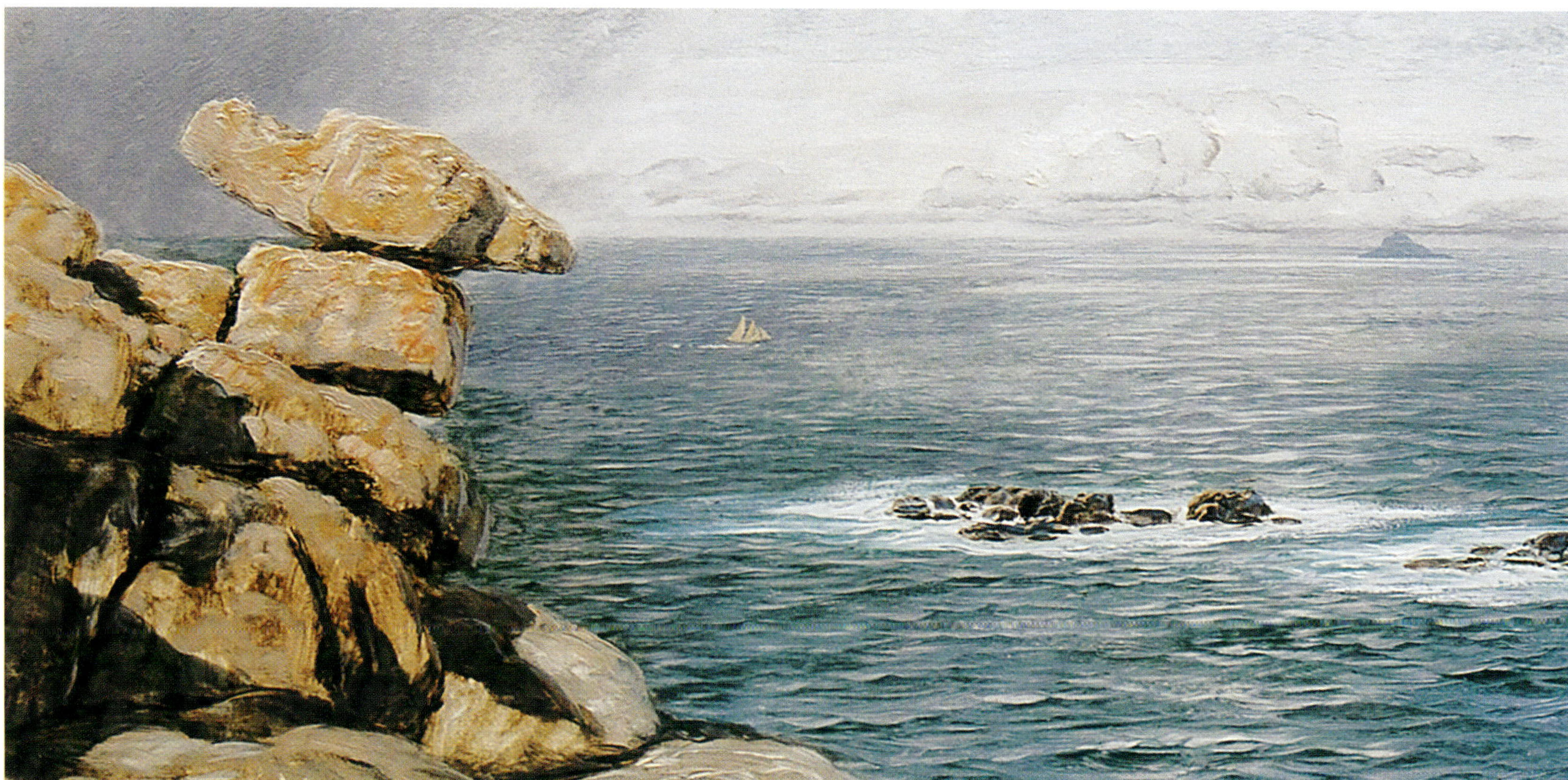

Cape Cornwall from Whitesand Bay
1872, Oil on board
25 x 36cm (10 x 14ins)
Inscribed *'Oct 24 72'*
Fitzwilliam Museum, Cambridge
Provenance: acquired by the Museum from Colnaghi, 1973

SUPPORTING IMAGE
Cape Cornwall from Whitesand Bay
Photograph: Cécile Brett

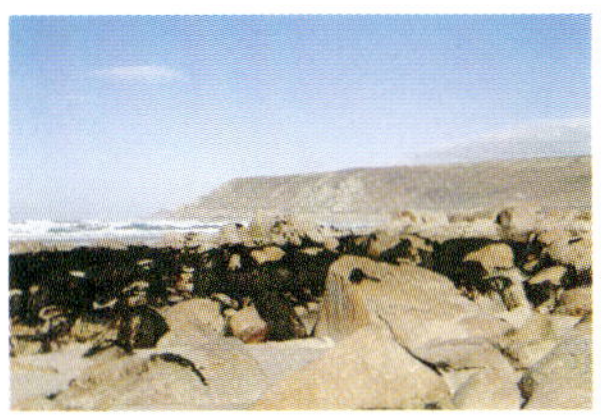

This fascinating sketch, one of several Brett painted on prepared millboards of the 10 x 14ins size in 1872, illustrates his liking for unusual rock formations and vistas. Painted from the mass of granite boulders that lie towards the north end of Whitesand Bay near Sennen Cove, it shows the view looking north to the distant Cape Cornwall. Only when Aire Point, the edge of Nanjulian cliff and Cape Cornwall itself are brought into close alignment does the curious composite outline, with its camel-like hump, emerge. Once found, the view is unmistakeable.

The same group of boulders appears in a related work, *A Morning amongst the Granite Boulders* (Fig 8, p.15), which Brett exhibited at the Academy in 1873, and which last appeared in the sale rooms in 1976. In this work Brett was looking further west, so that the picture includes the Brisons, the islands lying just off Cape Cornwall, but excludes the cape itself.

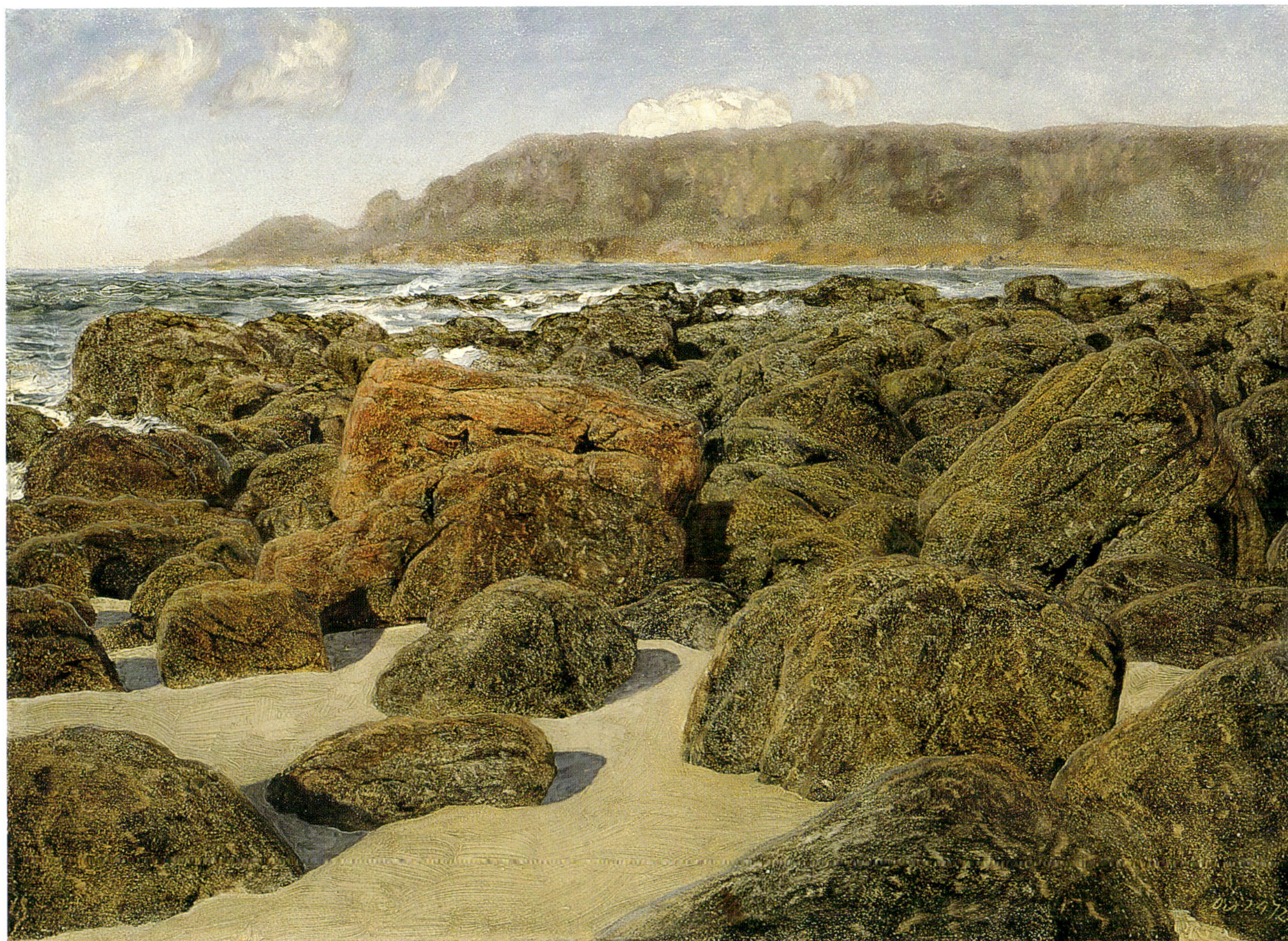

Rock study on St Agnes, Scilly Isles
1873, Oil on board
18 x 35.5cm (7 x 14ins)
Inscribed: *'Scilly July 4 73'*
Private Collection
Provenance: by descent in the artist's family to the present owner

Ever since reading Ruskin's *Modern Painters IV* in 1856 Brett had been interested in the pictorial qualities of granite rocks. Both the *Glacier of Rosenlaui* (Fig 18, p.33) and the *Val d'Aosta* (Fig 17, p.30) contain prominent examples of the stone, the latter also displaying the variegated lichens which frequently cover it. Ruskin had specifically recommended these to young artists as a suitable subject for study in his *Elements of Drawing* (1857), a book which had a powerful impact on Brett's work. The presence of this stone in spectacular profusion in the Scilly Isles may well explain his decision to take the risky passage to the Isles in 1873.

Apart from the extraordinary stone structures at Peninnis Head on St Mary's (see p.71–72), large amounts of granite boulders can also be found on St Agnes. This delightful work depicts one of these, a gigantic specimen to be seen on Wingletang Down, towards the southern end of the island. Brett has portrayed the elaborate patterns of the lichen with loving care, and has introduced a charming pair of sheep, both to give a sense of scale, and to provide a lively element in contrast with the inanimate rocks.

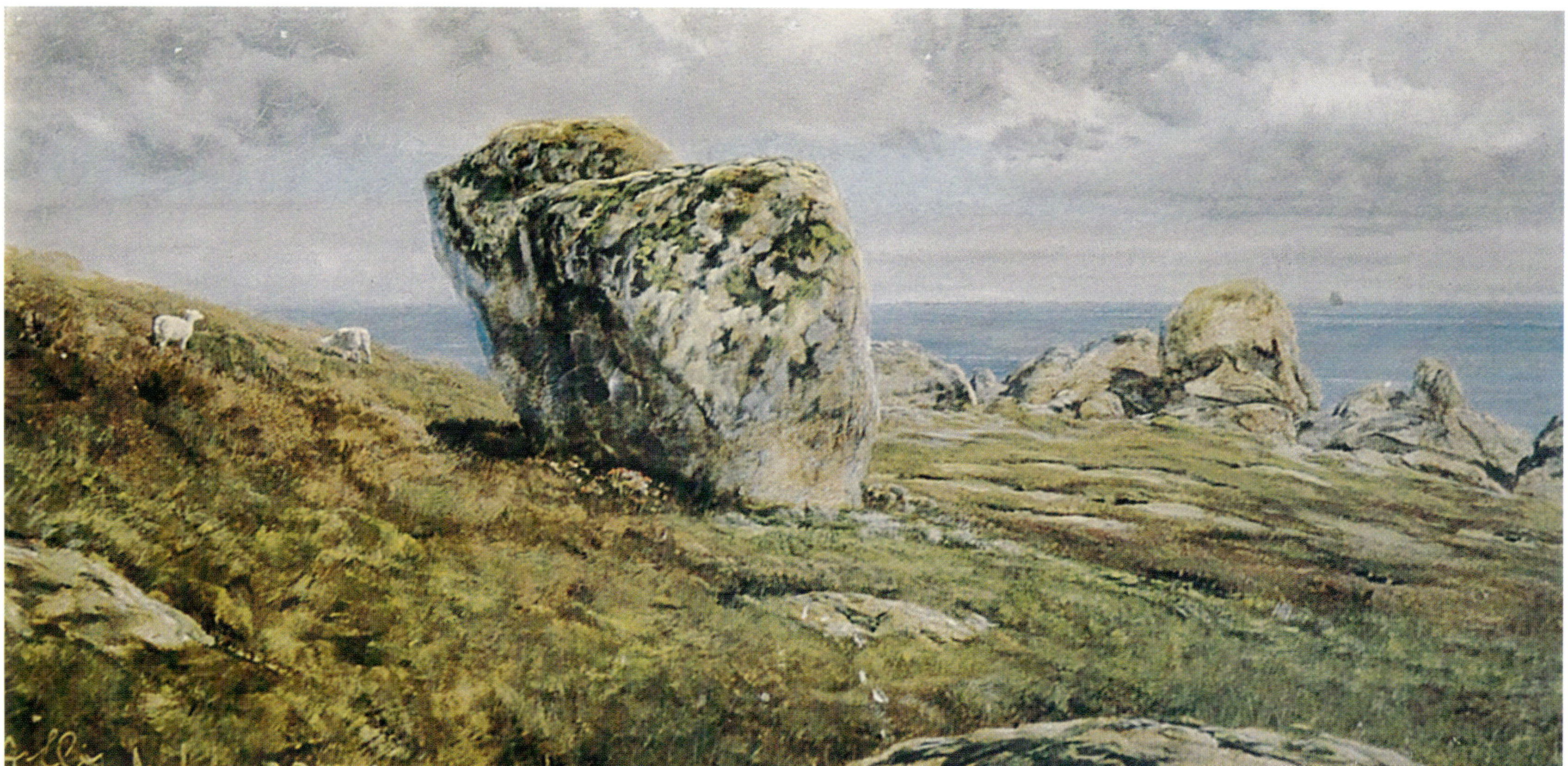

Rocks, Scilly
1873, Oil on board
35.8 x 61.2cm (14½ x 24ins)
Inscribed *'Scilly July 7 73'*
National Museums Liverpool (The Walker)
Provenance: Rev E.C. Dewick
Presented by him to the Gallery 1919

SUPPORTING IMAGE
Tooth Rock, Peninnis Head, St Mary's, Isles of Scilly
Photograph: Cécile Brett

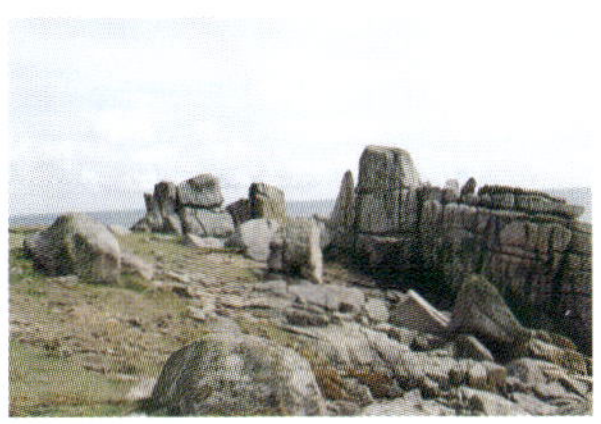

This extraordinary work ranks with Brett's 1856 *Glacier of Rosenlaui* (Fig 18, p.33) in its importance as a Ruskinian study of geology. It appears to be an almost abstract arrangement of shapes, yet it is in fact an astonishingly accurate representation of what the artist actually saw.

The vertical rock in the centre is the celebrated Tooth Rock, and this amazing conglomeration of granite forms can be found at Peninnis Head, the southernmost tip of the island of St Mary's. The surrounding area could almost belong to another planet, so bizarre is the setting. According to the antiquarian Dr Borlase, sacrificial victims were tied to the Tooth Rock in the time of the Druids, which may account for the slightly sinister atmosphere prevailing there.

Brett's picture gives no hint as to scale. In fact the rocks are of an immense size – the Tooth Rock is at least 40 feet high, and the boulder on the far left certainly 15 feet high. The view is virtually unchanged today, although the lightly-coloured rock in the centre, below the Tooth Rock, has at some point snapped and toppled over.

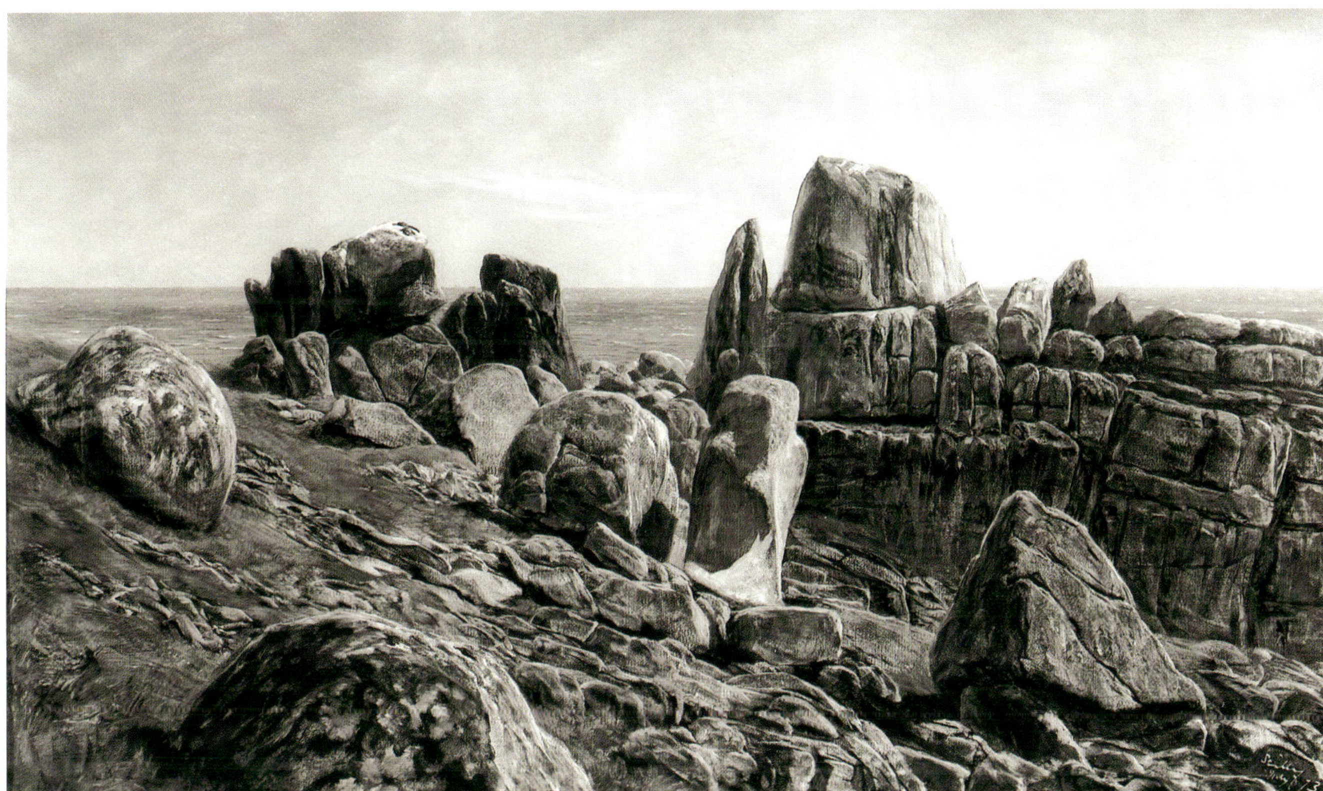

Mary Brett, Scilly
1873, Oil on board
18 x 35.5cm (7 x 14ins)
Inscribed *'Scilly July 21 73'*
Private Collection
Provenance: by descent in the artist's family to the present owner

SUPPORTING IMAGE
Mary Brett, 1873
Photograph: Robert Hawkes
Preston, Penzance
Private Collection

This charming little study depicts Mary sitting sewing on a rock at Peninnis Head, St Mary's. Brett also made a pencil sketch of her on the same day, which shows her picking flowers (Sketchbook 42).

Although this work was clearly painted quickly, it was cleverly composed. Mary sits in the shade, and the eye is led by the sunlight through the gap in the rocks to the distant brig. Brett has taken pains to convey the texture of the granite rock on the left, and the contrast between sunlight and shadow in the centre of the picture is beautifully handled. The delicate ultramarine of the sea forms the perfect backdrop to an enchanting scene.

The site is easily recognisable today. It lies immediately below the automatic lighthouse that Trinity House erected in 1911 to supersede the St Agnes light, which then became a private residence. Mary seems to be wearing the same dress and hat as in the Preston portrait photograph taken shortly afterwards in Penzance.

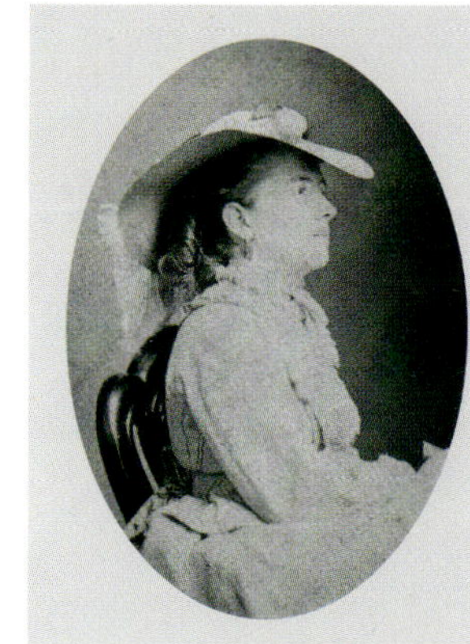

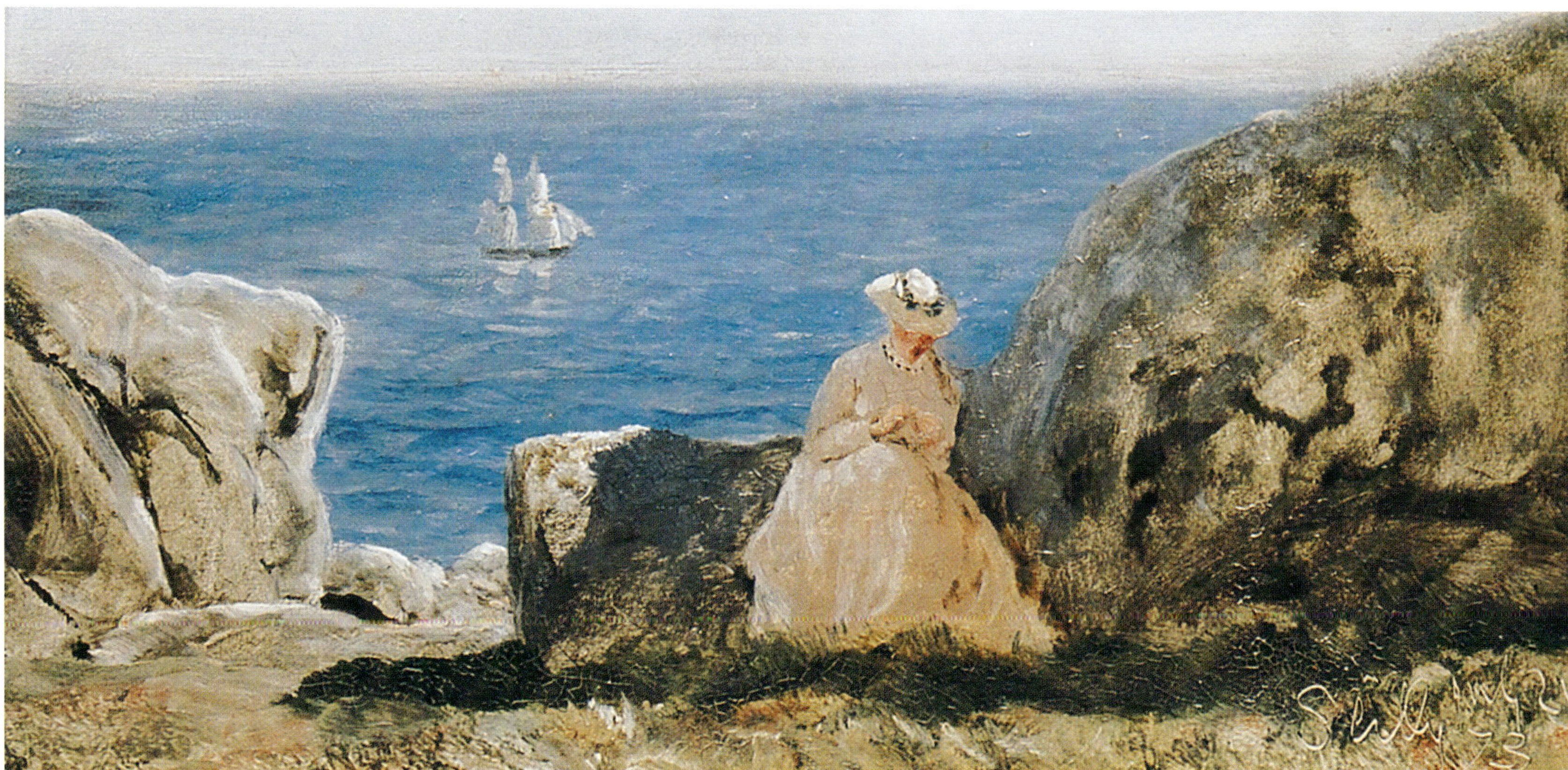

St Agnes
1873. Oil on board
18 x 35.5cm (7 x 14ins)
Inscribed *'St Agnes Sep 10 73'*
Private Collection
Provenance: through the sale rooms to the present owner

This is an acutely observed and finely painted geological study made at low tide at St Agnes. The area was in 1873 one of the great mining districts, both tin and copper being found in the granite elvan. Here Brett has emphasized the attractive veining of the quartz in the foreground rocks, contrasting this with the deep red sandstone in the distant cliffs to the north.

The scene is enlivened by a delightful group of gulls cavorting on the sand. Although birds frequently appear in Brett's larger works (see p.123 and 133), it is unusual to find such a prominent group in one of his sketches.

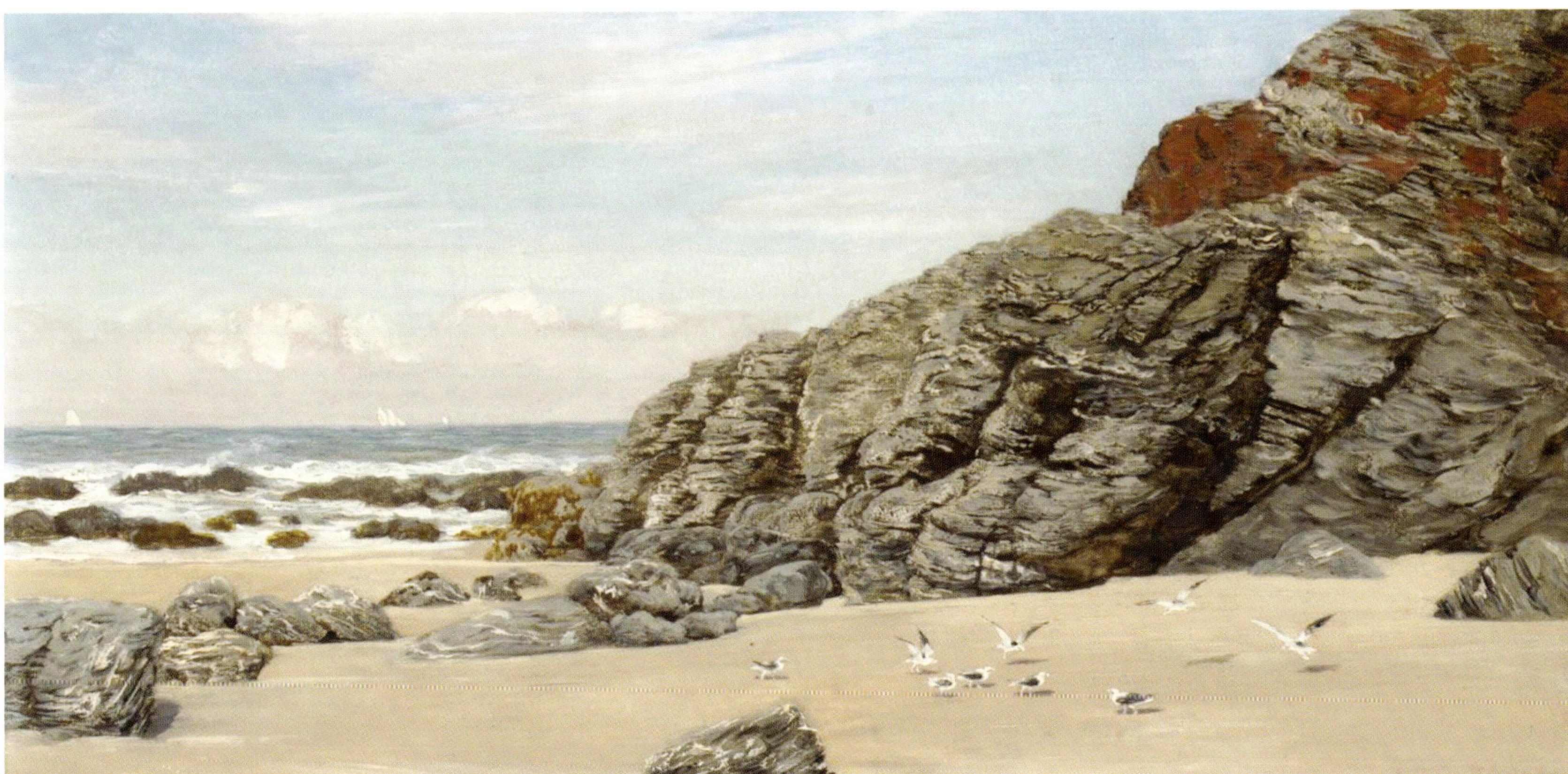

View on the beach at St Agnes
1873. Oil on board
35.5 x 61.2cm (14 x 24½ins)
Inscribed *'6 Sep 73'* and
signed *John Brett*
Private Collection
Provenance: Alfred Morrison; through the sale rooms to the present owner

This is an unusual work for Brett in that, although the rocks and sky are important elements, it is dominated by the figure of the little girl driving a donkey across the beach. It was originally sold to Alfred Morrison, the connoisseur and collector, in 1873. Morrison had met Brett in October 1864, and was his principal patron for the next fifteen years, buying more than twenty-five works in all. Among these were several Academy exhibits, including *Bonchurch Downs* and *Capri in the Evening* (1866), *Christmas Morning 1866* (1868), and *Contiguous to a melancholy ocean* (1870). Apart from *Christmas Morning*, now at the Russell-Cotes Art Gallery, Bournemouth, all are unlocated.

After Morrison's death in 1897 his widow sold the bulk of his collection at Christie's, and this work was acquired by the dealer McLean of the Haymarket. On 29 August 1899 Brett recorded in his Studio Log that McLean had sent it round for him to sign for a client. 'It is a good picture – as good as I can do, so I readily consented to sign it, and told him to call for it when dry (in about a week).'

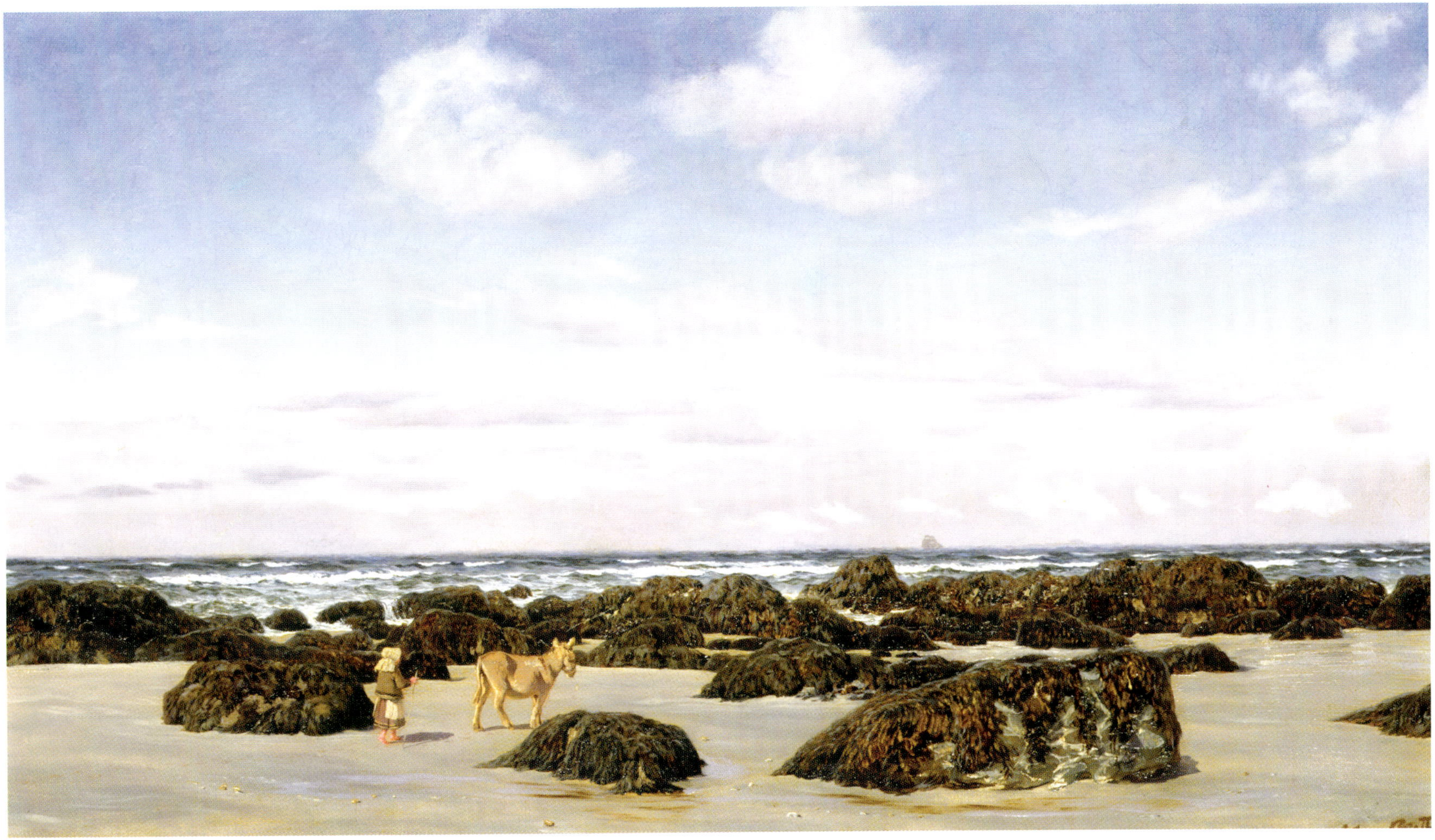

Bude
1873, Oil on board
18 x 35.5cm (7 x 14ins)
Inscribed *'Bude Oct 15 73'*
Private Collection
Provenance: by descent in the artist's family to the present owner

SUPPORTING IMAGE
Bude Oct 13 73 5.20pm
Pencil, Sketchbook 42
© National Maritime Museum, London

Brett and his family had arrived at Bude by October 13, 1873, when a period of intense activity began. By the end of the month he had completed at least eight oil sketches of the beach and its surroundings. His first recorded pencil sketch is inscribed 'Oct 13 at 5.20 pm' (Sketchbook 42), and is related very closely both to this work, painted two days later, and to *Bude Sands at Sunset* (see fig. 6 p.13), the large Academy picture he developed from his sketches early the next year.

Bude was primarily an agricultural trading port, with a canal which originally extended some thirty miles inland, down which large quantities of the brown Bude sand, highly prized as a fertilizer, were carried. To protect the canal entrance a breakwater was constructed in 1840, terminating in a large rock, Barrel Rock, surmounted by a beacon. This feature forms the focal point of several of Brett's studies, as well as the Academy work itself. Here it is viewed diagonally from the opposite side of the beach, under Summerleaze

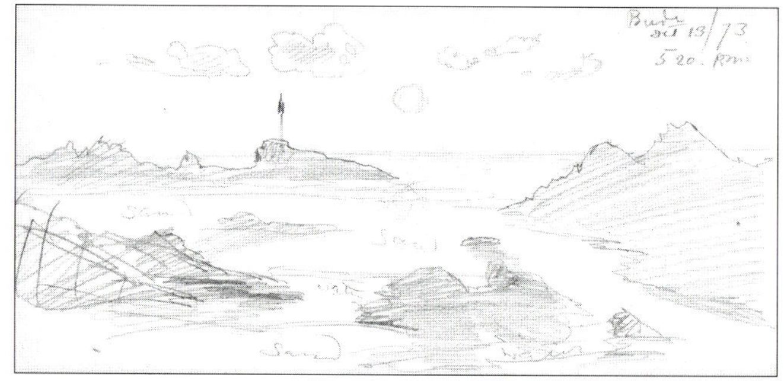

Point, looking due west towards the sunset. Even at this angle, the beach is rather wider than Brett has made it – an uncharacteristic example of artistic licence in his work. In this first oil sketch the sunset is painted in a particularly delicate and beautiful range of colours, the sea is calm, and the evening peaceful.

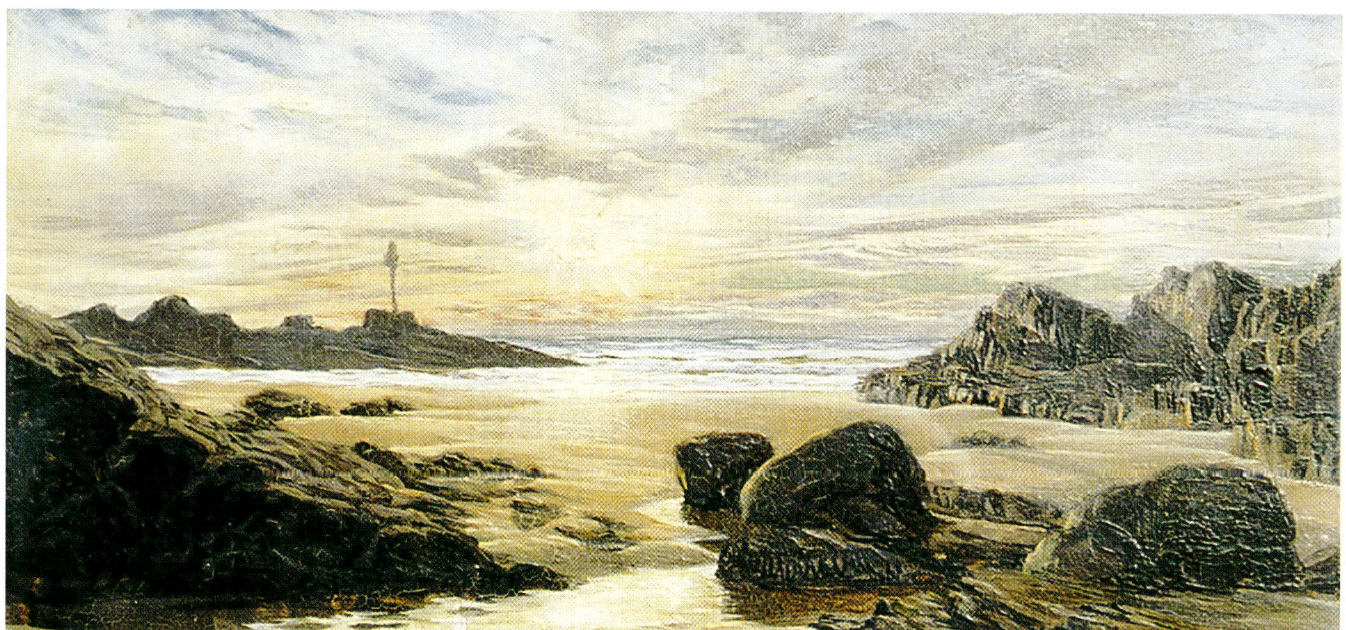

Sunset
1873, Oil on board
18 x 35.5cm (7 x 14ins)
Inscribed *'Bude Oct 21 73'*
The Maas Gallery Ltd
Provenance: Daisy Watson, née Brett

While at Bude Brett is likely to have observed some lovely sunsets. Sometimes spectacular there, they are easily viewed from the open, spacious position of the town, and particularly from the cliffs to the south. On October 21 he painted this beautiful study of a sunset from the cliffs high above a perfectly calm sea, a clear indication that a sunset was to be a central feature in the composition of his eventual Academy picture.

His viewpoint was quite likely Compass Point, immediately south of the breakwater, from which magnificent views of the coast can be obtained. On its summit is a storm tower, or coastguard shelter, which would have provided a convenient temporary studio. Alternatively, a short walk across the downs would have brought him to Efford Beacon, 300 feet above the sea, where there was a signalling station. Both these points are within easy reach of his likely base at the Falcon Hotel.

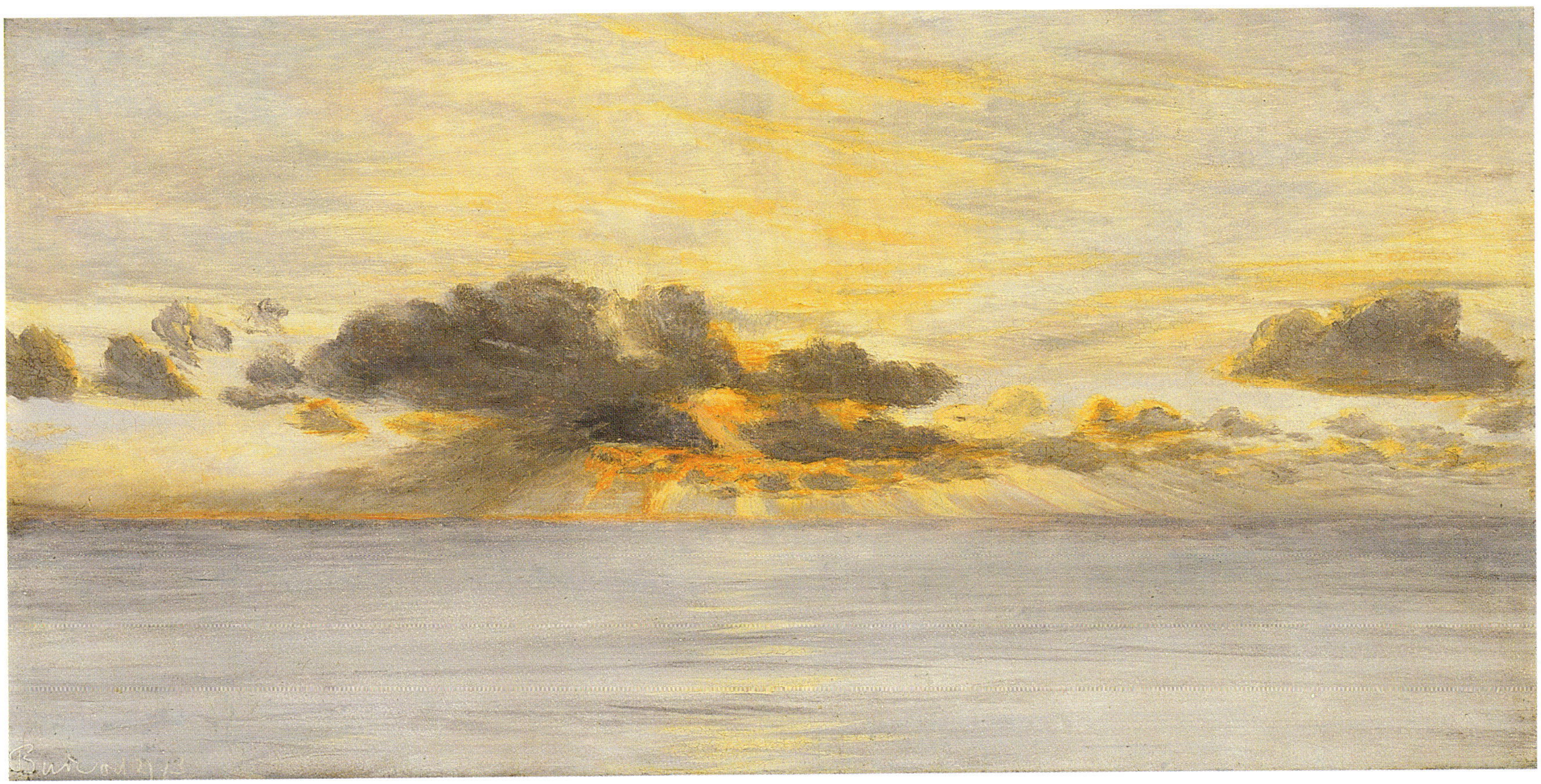

Bude
1873, Oil on board
18 x 35.5cm (7 x 14ins)
Inscribed *'Bude Oct 25 73'*
Private Collection
Provenance: by descent in the artist's family to the present owner

Here Brett experiments with a different sort of sunset scene. An exquisitely blue sky and glowing sunset colours are about to be blotted out by the approaching storm clouds. Beyond the beacon on Barrel Rock rain is falling, and the sea is disturbed.

Brett's viewpoint is similar to that in *Bude* (p.76), but somewhat further forward, towards the front of the beach, and closer to Barrel Rock. He has also added the figures of Mary and the two children, shown hurrying across the beach to avoid the impending storm. They bring an additional sense of urgency to this dramatic and evocative little sketch.

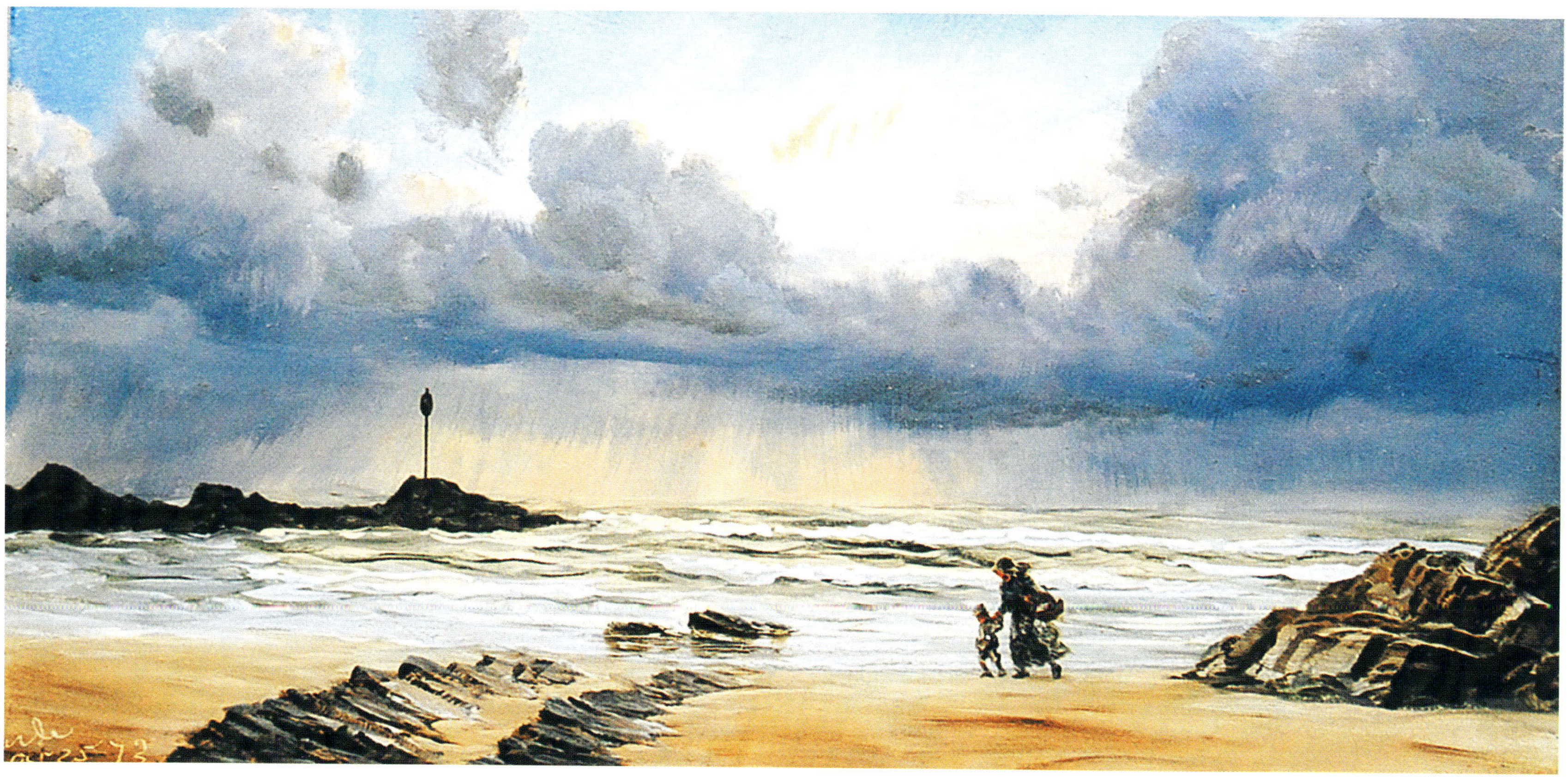

Bude
1873. Oil on board
18 x 36cm (7 x 14ins)
Inscribed *'29 Oct 73'*

Provenance: through the sale rooms to the present owner

This work differs from the other beach views of Bude in that Brett has chosen a vantage point further to the south, thereby excluding Barrel Rock from his composition. Instead he concentrates on the curious shelves of rock which stretch seaward in the distinctive brown sand. The tide is out, and he has introduced the figure of a man apparently searching for shellfish in the shallows. The sketch was also clearly painted earlier in the day, with as yet no hint of sunset in the sky.

The lone figure reappears, a little further to the left, with a basket on his back, in *Bude Sands at Sunset* (Fig 6, p.13), which although closest in design to the October 15 work (p.76), is an amalgam of different elements from all the small sketches.

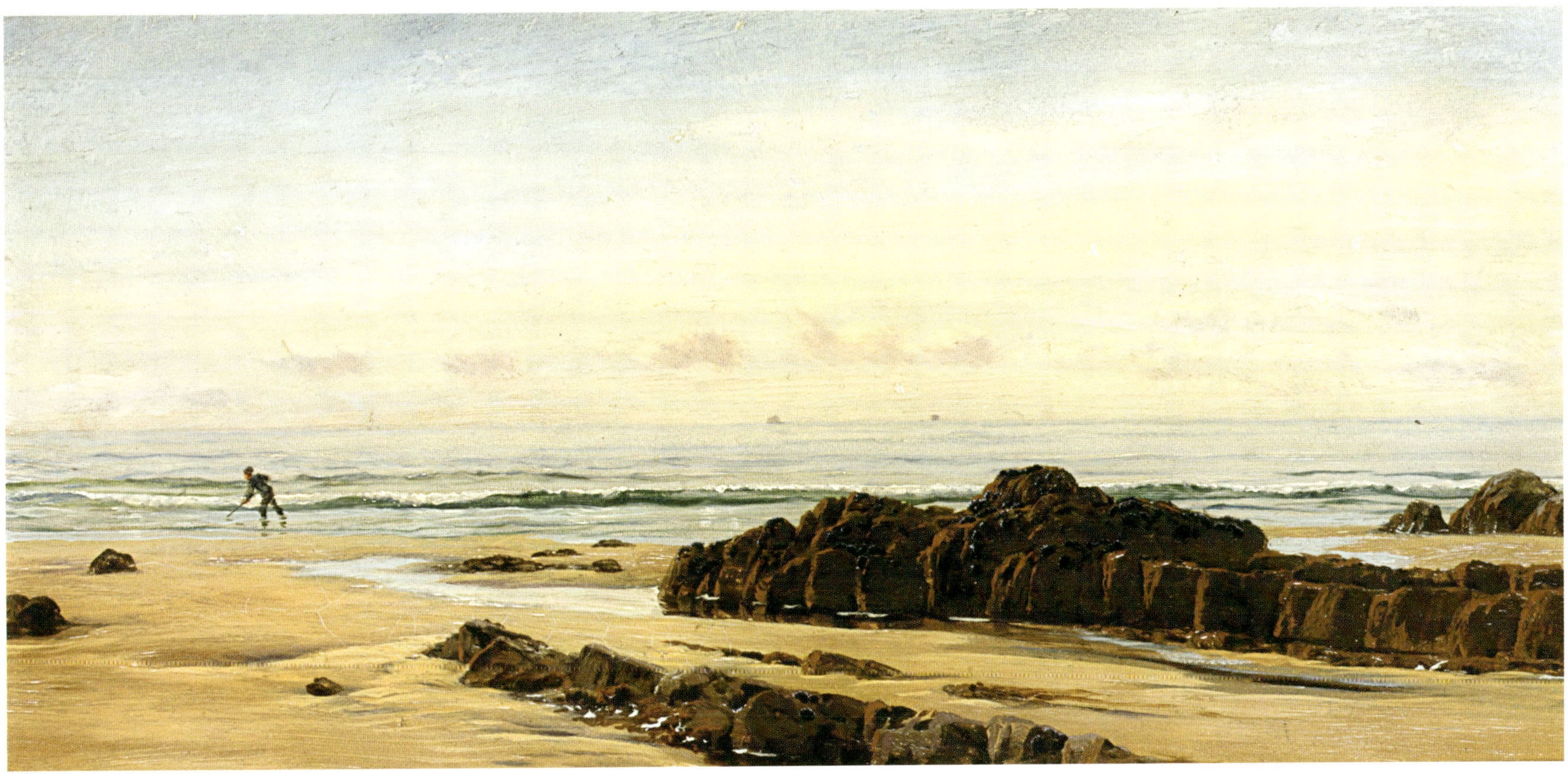

The Lizard
1876, Oil on canvas
25.3 x 48.3cm (10 x 19ins)
Inscribed *'Lizard July 19 76'*
Private Collection
Provenance: through the sale rooms to the present owner

SUPPORTING IMAGE
The Lizard from the Rill
Photograph: Cécile Brett

This fine view of the Lizard was painted on a canvas of 10 x 19ins, the larger of Brett's two standard sizes for sketches (the 7 x 14ins works were all done on board until 1879).

It was painted from the Rill, high above Kynance Cove, looking south-east towards Lizard Point, a view the artist had discovered in 1870. Brett has portrayed the celebrated group of serpentine rocks at Kynance – Steeple Rock, the Bellows, Asparagus Island, Gull Rock, and, in the middle distance, the Lion Rock – with great precision. Beyond he shows the sweep of the Lizard peninsula, with the twin towers of the eighteenth-century lighthouse visible in the centre, above Asparagus Island, and the group of offshore rocks known as the Stags on the right, in the far distance.

The view has barely changed since 1876, and as so often with Brett's work, once one has managed to find his vantage point all the details immediately fall into place. And yet, for all its photographic accuracy, this remains a romantic work of great beauty. The curious veined rocks bask in the sunshine, and the sea is painted with the brilliant Pre-Raphaelite greens and blues so characteristic of the artist.

During the following winter, Brett made a larger version of the work, adding a number of craft. Measuring 27½ x 47½ins, this picture, under the title *The Lizard Head*, was last heard of in July 1912, when it was sold at Christie's (Witt Library).

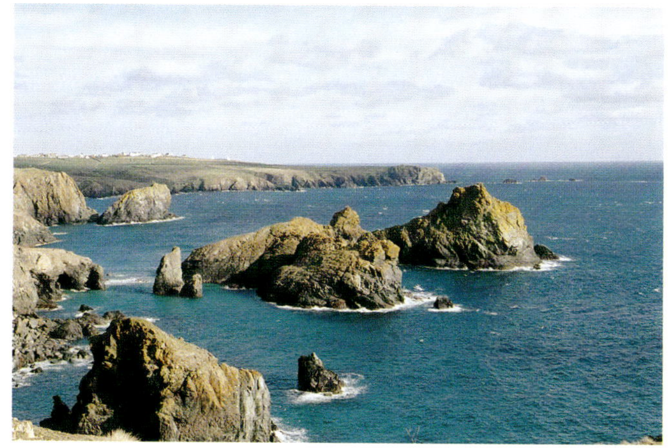

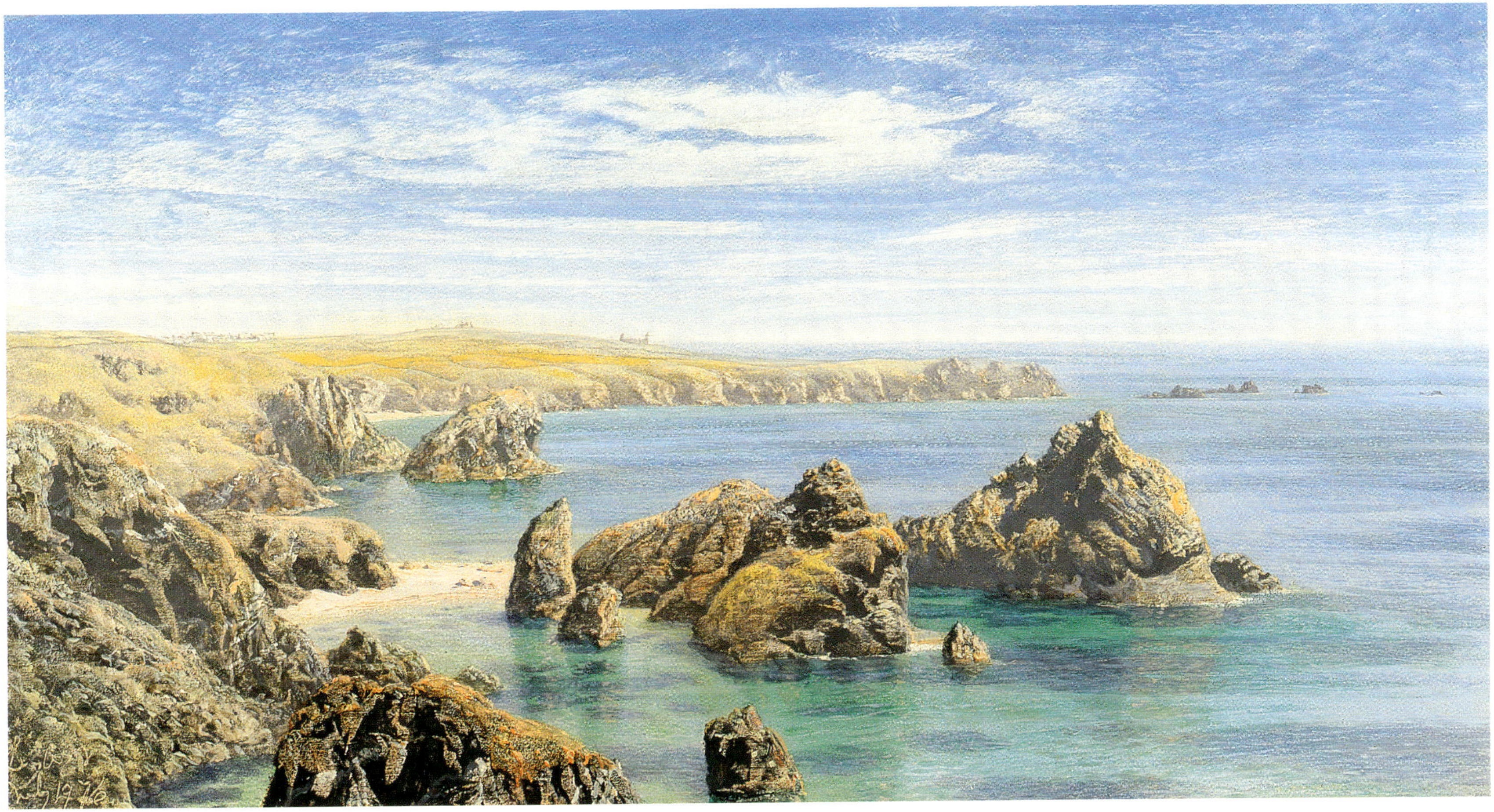

Pen Olver
1876, Oil on board
18 x 35.5cm (7 x 14ins)
Inscribed *'Penolver 29 July 76'*
and, probably in a later hand,
'John Brett'
Private Collection
Provenance: by descent
in the artist's family to
the present owner

This beautiful study shows the grandly piled headland of Pen Olver, which protects the little sandy inlet of Housel Cove on its eastern side. Brett observed a smack and other craft out in Housel Bay as he looked south-east from the western corner of the cove. Out of sight on the right were Bumble Rock, and, on the cliff top, the Lizard Lighthouse. Brett evidently found the patterns of light and shade in the grass-covered cliffs satisfying, and he set them off against the delicate turquoise of a calm summer sea.

Brett also subsequently developed this sketch into a larger work. This was given the title *Housel Bay* and measured 20 x 36ins (unlocated). While keeping its basic form unchanged, he typically refined the detail, notably by adding a gig with two men aboard about to be beached on the left-hand side of the cove (Witt Library).

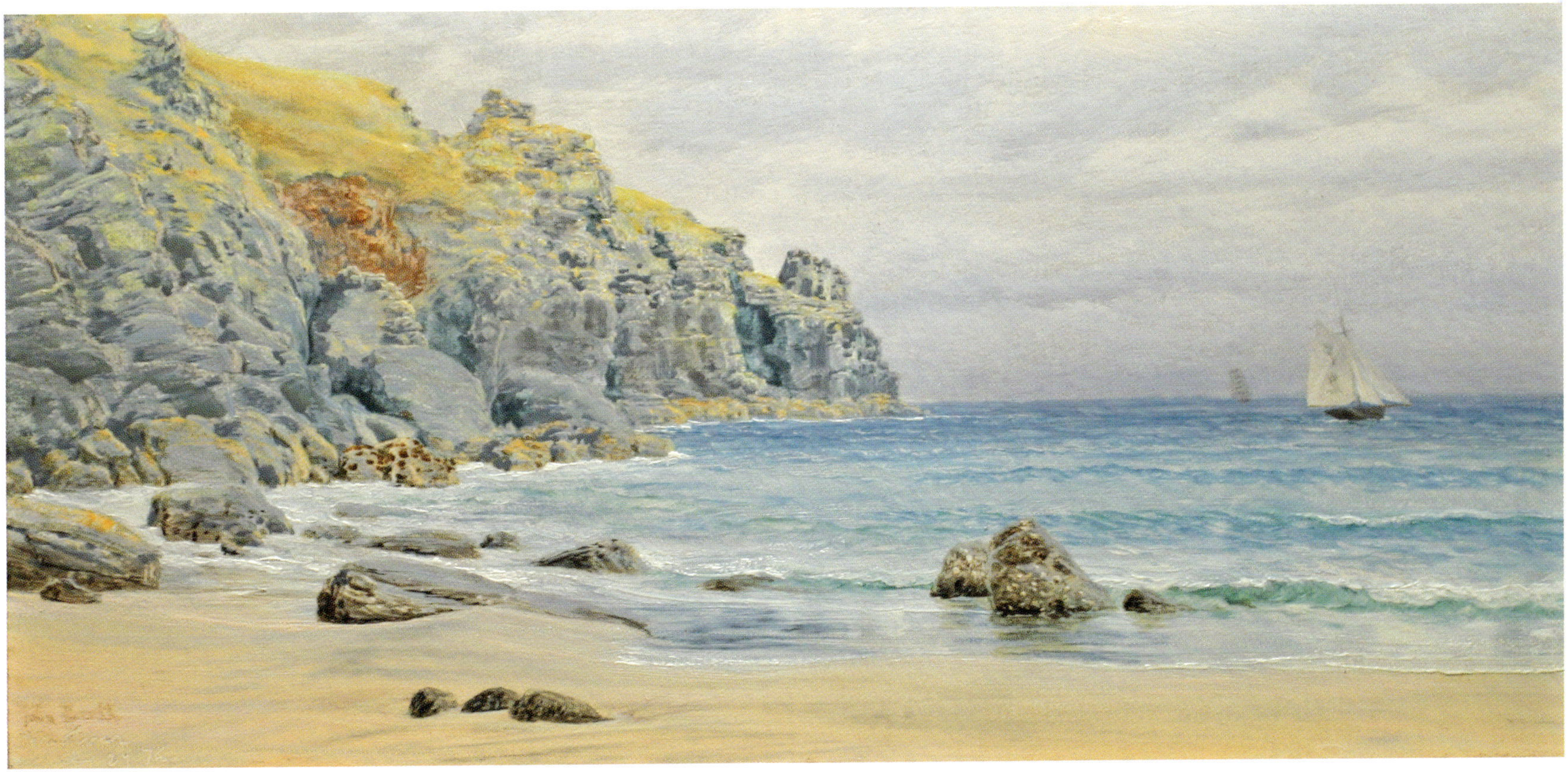

Cadgwith
1876, Oil on board
18 x 35.5cm (7 x 14ins)
Inscribed *'Cadgwith 7 Aug 76'*
Private Collection
Provenance: by descent in the artist's family to the present owner

This charming study of Cadgwith Cove was done from the centre of the shingle beach looking north-east, with the tide half-way up. Brett has emphasized the distinctive diagonal bands in the hornblende schist cliff, and immediately under the cliff he has painted the water with a rich array of colours. Elsewhere the paint has been laid on very thinly.

Cadgwith, a particularly picturesque village, has always been renowned for its crabs and lobsters. Brett has given due prominence to this tradition, showing a fisherman, boats and lobster pots on the beach, while a lugger lies moored offshore at the entrance to the cove.

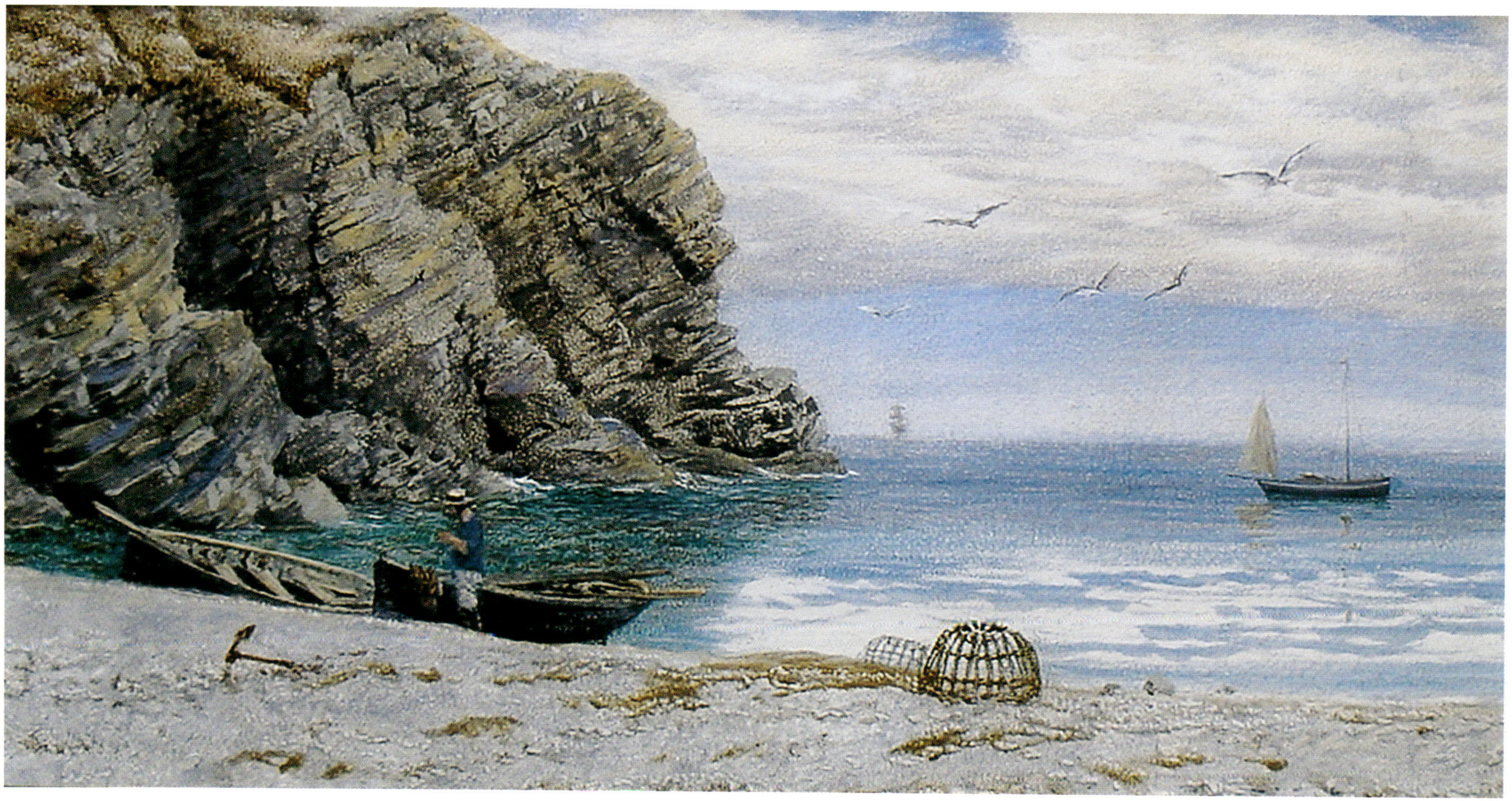

Lizard
1876, Oil on board
18 x 35.5cm (7 x 14ins)
Inscribed *'Lizard Aug 8 76'*
Private Collection
Provenance: through the sale rooms to the present owner

Painted the day after Brett's visit to Cadgwith (see p.84), this work shows the view from the southernmost point on the Lizard looking east across Polbream Cove towards Bumble Rock. The lighthouse stands on the top of these cliffs, but Brett has chosen to exclude it from view, limiting himself to a study of the variegated shapes and colours of the cliffs themselves, and the low shelf of rock known as Vellan Drang shown under the water in the foreground. Delicate greens and blues predominate, and Brett has characteristically included the white sails of a ketch in the far distance.

Little is known of the provenance of this sketch, but it could be the work entitled *Under the Lizard Light* which belonged to Brett's great patron Sir Thomas Devitt Bt, and was exhibited by him at the Whitechapel Art Gallery in 1902.

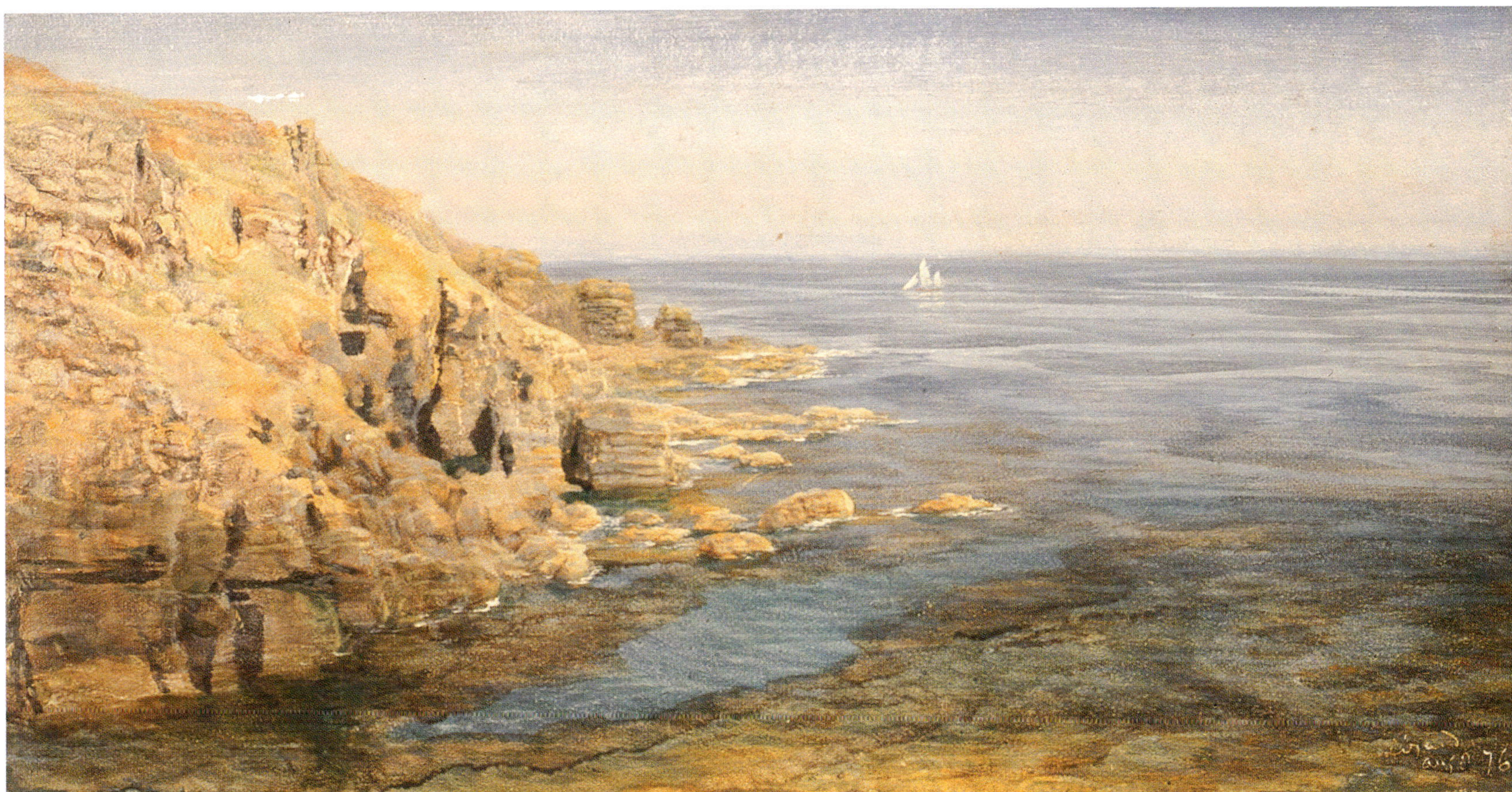

Kennack
1876, Oil on board
18 x 36cm (7 x 14ins)
Inscribed *'Kinnack Aug 22 76'*
© Sotheby's Images Ltd
Provenance: probably
J.H. Chamberlain: through the sale rooms to the present owner

SUPPORTING IMAGE
These yellow sands
1883, Oil on canvas
42 x 84ins
© Sotheby's Images Ltd

This is the earliest 7 x 14ins sketch to have been found in the distinctive frame supplied to Brett by Dolman and Son of New Compton Street. It was painted from the western part of Kennack Sands (actually 'Kinnack' in Brett's inscription), looking due east. In the middle distance the dark tongue of serpentine rock stretching seawards, known as the Caerverracks, is visible, with beyond it the headlands of Carrick Luz and Pedn Boar. On the horizon various craft are shown, including a steam vessel and a full-rigged schooner.

Kennack (literally 'rocky') is particularly interesting for its geology. In addition to Lizard serpentine, gabbro, basalt, flint, amethyst, asbestos and talc are all found there, as well as the unique Kennack gneiss. This consists of interlayered bands of pale granite and dark basalt, as illustrated here, and, even more clearly, in the work for which it formed a source, *These yellow sands* (RA 1883). Although it was clearly painted on the spot, it has proved impossible to identify the precise point from which the sketch was made, but the sand at Kennack is notoriously mobile, and the scene can vary considerably from year to year.

The work probably belonged originally to J.H. Chamberlain, the Birmingham architect who, with his partner William Martin, built Brett's house in Keswick Road, Putney, the following year.

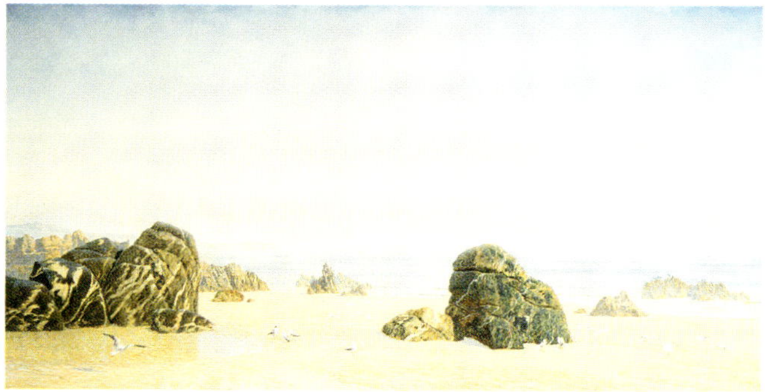

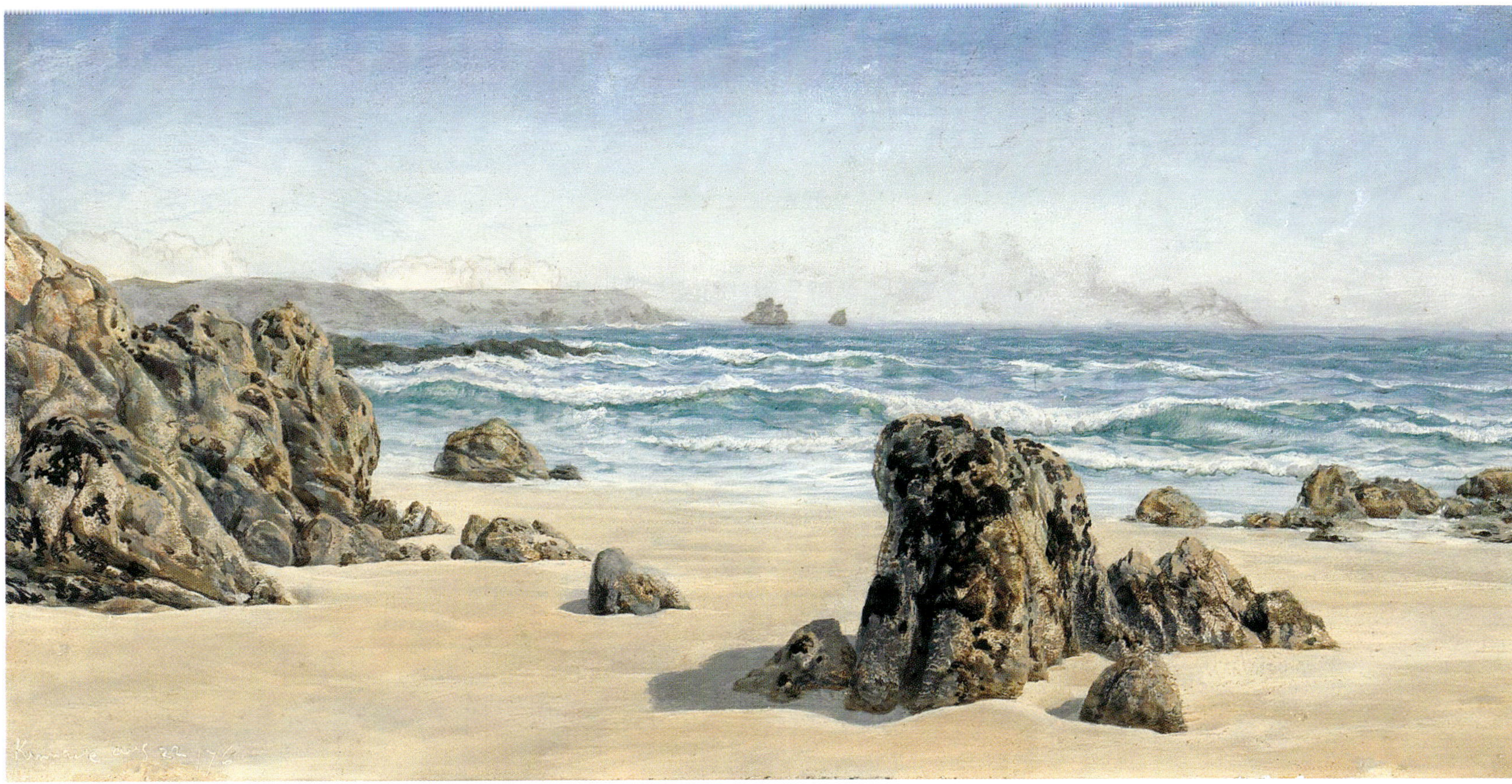

Mount's Bay
1877, Pen and ink on paper, mounted on card
11.4 x 22.8cm (4½ x 9ins)
Brighton Art Gallery & Museums
Presented by J. Bingham

SUPPORTING IMAGES
Mount's Bay
1877, Oil on canvas 42 x 84ins
© Johannesburg Art Gallery

Looking north from Higher Predannack Cliff
Photograph: Cécile Brett

When Brett expanded his Mullion sketch (fig. 40 p.48) into the seven-foot picture of Mount's Bay destined for the 1877 Academy, several additional elements were introduced. A number of boats helped to fill the expanse of the bay on the left; the hillside was enriched by undergrowth and bright yellow gorse; and finally, a group of sheep was added in the right foreground.

The work received good reviews, the Art Journal referring to Brett's 'glorious view of Mount's Bay, flecked into ever-varying sheen by the summer's sun.' Henry Blackburn also drew attention to it in his Academy Notes, writing 'in the principal portion on this wall (of the Lecture Room) is a delightful bit of English coast scenery in its sunniest aspect, lighted in the foreground with the bloom of gorse and the sparkle of a quiet summer sea.' In 1879 it was sent to the Sydney International Exhibition where it received a 'First degree of Merit Special' silver medal. It subsequently entered the collection of the Johannesburg Art Gallery.

This pen-and-ink sketch was submitted by Brett for reproduction in Blackburn's publication. Academy Notes first appeared in 1875, and the following year artists were invited to send in sketches of their works to illustrate the Notes. This was Brett's first such submission. He continued to supply sketches until 1888, after which photographic reproductions were used. Two other Brett sketches for Blackburn's illustrations have survived in Private Collections – *The Norman Archipelago* (1885), and *The Earth's shadow on the sky* (1888).

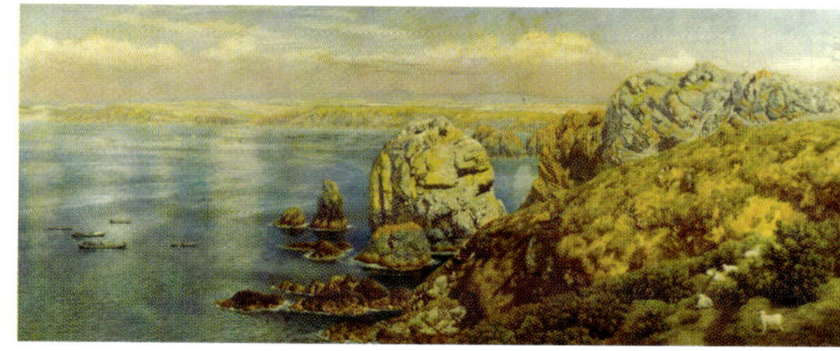

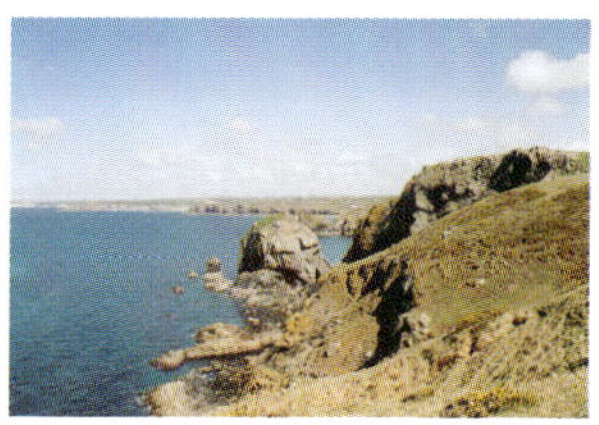

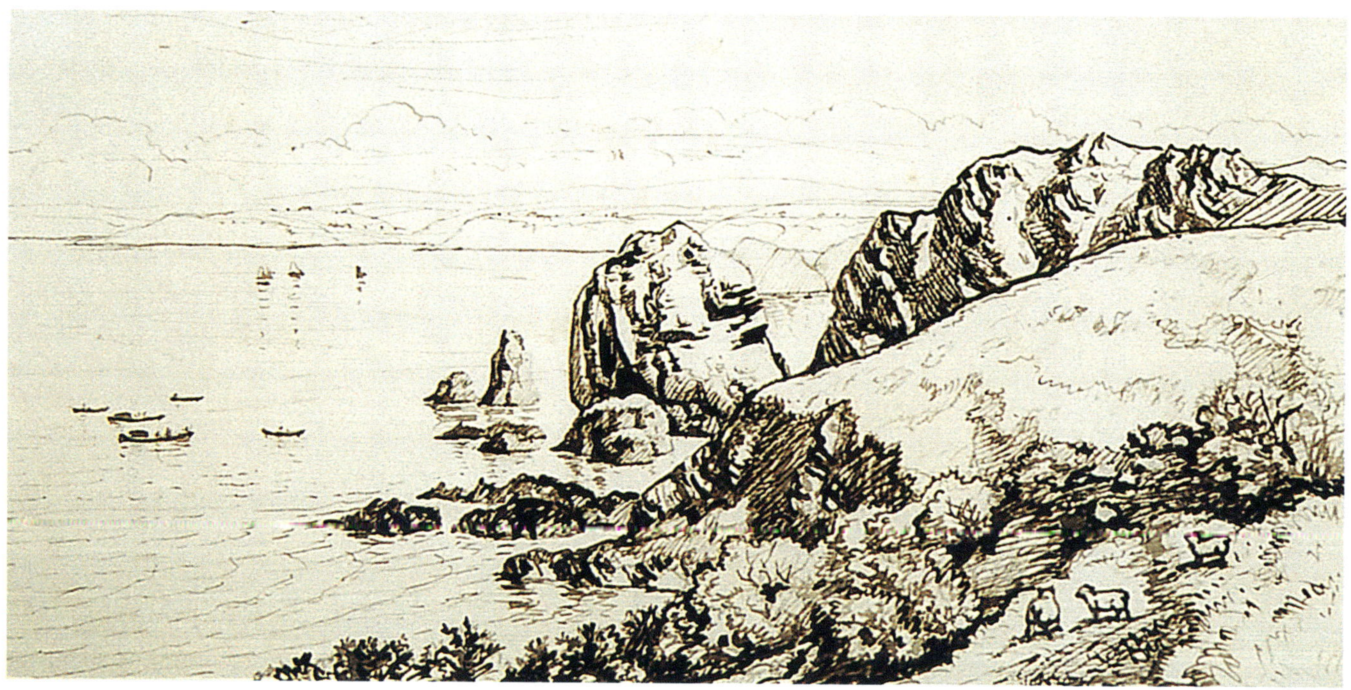

Lizard
1877, Oil on board
18 x 35.5cm (7 x 14ins)
Inscribed *'Lizard Aug 11 77'*
Private Collection
Provenance: by descent in the artist's family to the present owner

This beautiful little work, in which the thistles, ferns and sea pinks of the foreground are painted in a delightful range of colours, seems to be the prototype for a number of similar cliff-top pictures Brett produced in later years. These include *Summer on the cliffs* (1891), *The outlook from my native cliffs* (RA 1895), and *Gull Island* (RA 1899).

But it can also be seen in the context of his earlier Pre-Raphaelite work. His masterpiece, *The Stonebreaker* (1857–8), contains prominent thistles in the foreground, and elaborate foreground flowers appear also in *The Hedger* (1858–60). According to the Spectator review of the 1861 Academy Exhibition, *Champéry* apparently had a foreground of gigantic marigolds. Although this work has disappeared, a drawing in Sketchbook 8 which almost certainly relates to it shows 'a mass of marigolds & rununculus'. All these compositions in turn probably reflect the influence of Dürer's detailed foregrounds, to which Ruskin had drawn attention in *The Elements of Drawing* (1857).

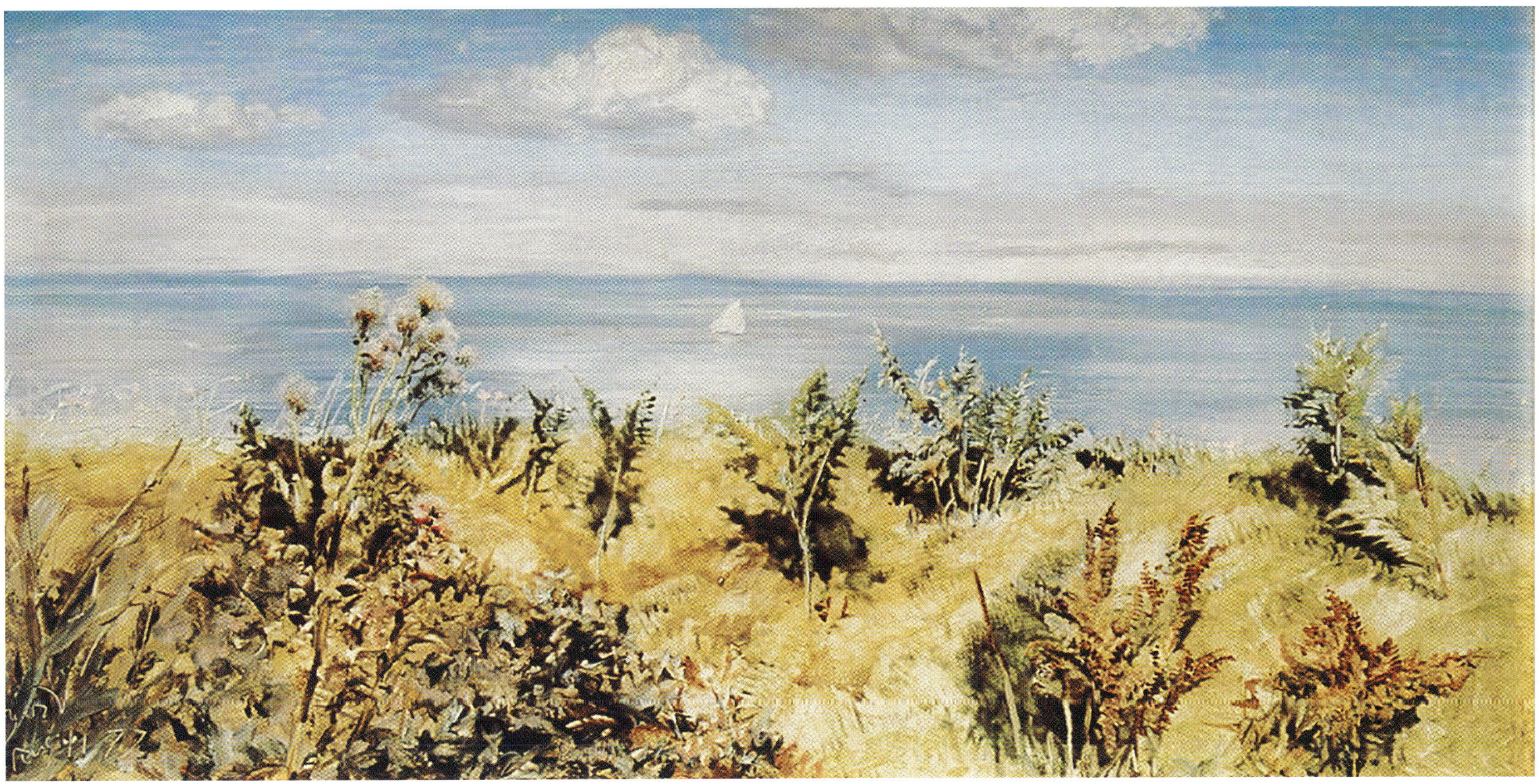

Housel
1877, Oil on board
18 x 35.5cm (7 x 14ins)
Inscribed *'Housel Sep 28 77'*
Private Collection
Provenance: by descent in the artist's family to the present owner

This delightful little sketch shows Mary sitting on the beach at Housel Cove, while Michael plays among the rocks. As in *Mary Brett, Scilly* (p.72), Mary is occupied with sewing or embroidery of some sort – perhaps making a garment for herself or one of the children. Housel, which lies immediately east of the Lizard Lighthouse, was the closest beach to Lizard Town, and offered safe bathing, being entirely free from dangerous under-currents.

Unusually Brett has almost completely excluded the sea from his view. He has concentrated on the fascinating way in which the rectangular blocks of hornblende schist are piled up to create castellated walls of rock. These are interspersed with dark caves, producing dramatic contrasts of light and shade.

At this date Brett was still occasionally introducing members of his family into his sketches. After 1879 this becomes increasingly rare, as he turned to photography as a better way of recording their activities. Many of his photographs have survived, providing a vivid picture of the family's life; but none has greater charm than this little work.

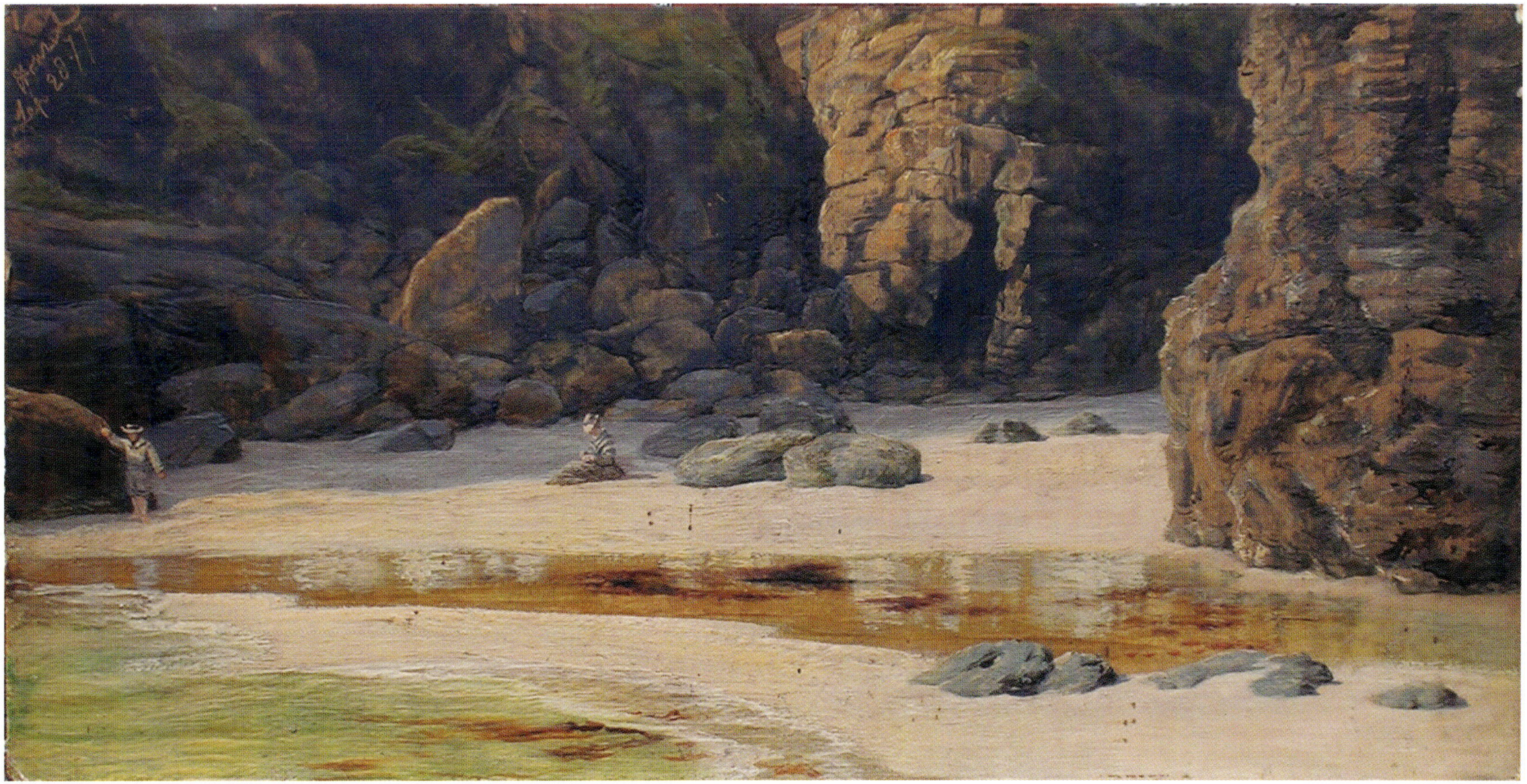

Shipping off the coast
1877, Oil on canvas
38 x 76cm (15 x 30ins)
Inscribed *'Oct 1877'*
Private Collection
Provenance: Sir Alfred Hickman Bt; then through the sale rooms to the present owner

This picture was painted on the Lizard in October 1877, and appears to be related to the sketch dated July 25 77, now in the Ashmolean Museum, Oxford. It shows a similar view looking directly out to sea from Kennack Sands, although in this work the tide is much further up, and Brett has added a prominently placed brig, two schooners, and other craft on the horizon.

It belonged originally to Sir Alfred Hickman Bt, 'the Iron King of South Staffordshire,' a major Brett patron. Hickman, the Black Country's leading pig-iron manufacturer and a Conservative MP, bought at least ten works from Brett, for about £2,500 in all, over a period of twenty years. Several were large Academy pictures, which adorned his walls at Wightwick Hall, near Wolverhampton, or his town house in Kensington Palace Gardens. Of Hickman's acquisitions this work seems to have been the first, and the most modest in size.

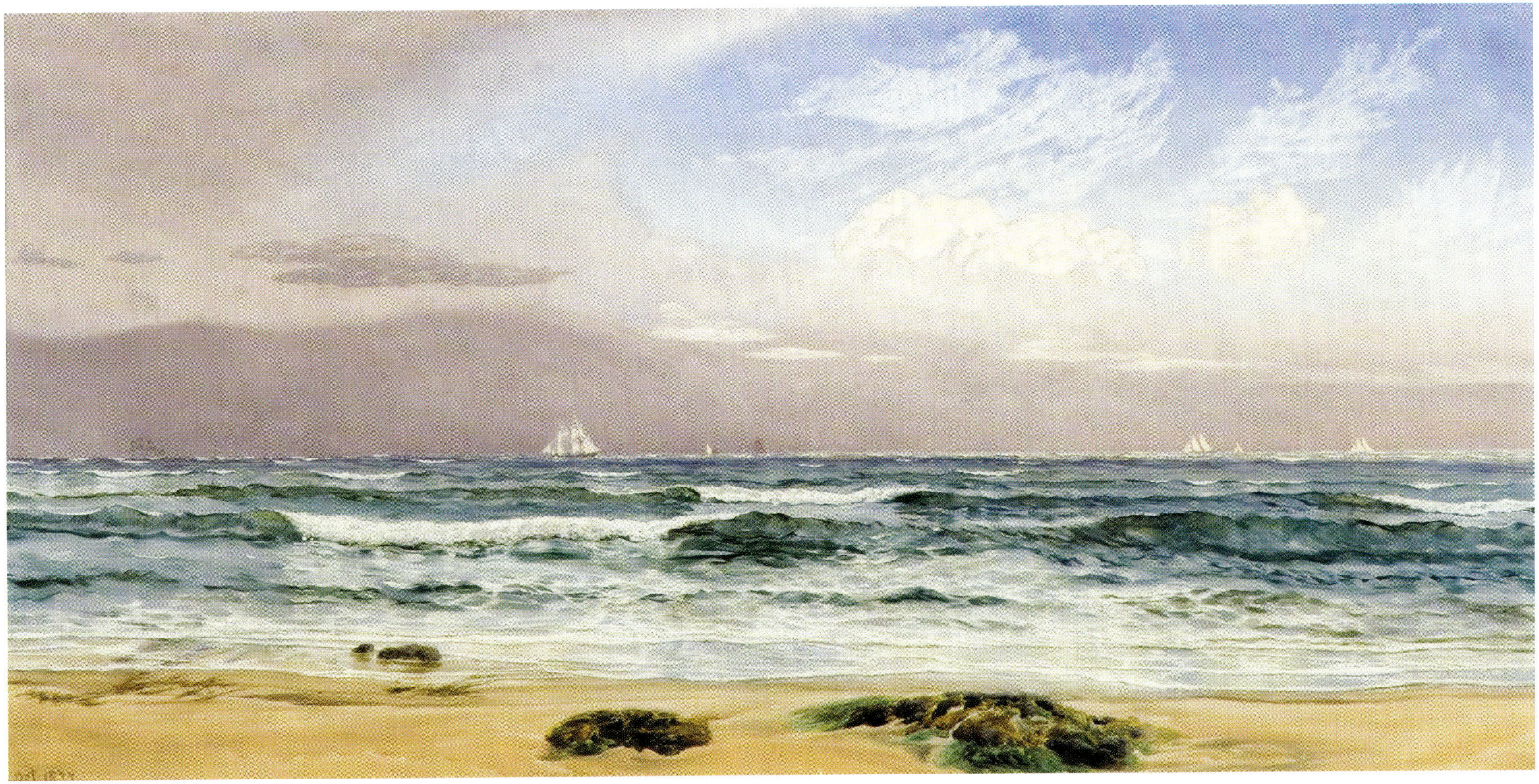

Coast scene with calm sea
1877, Oil on canvas
30.5 x 61cm (12 x 24ins)
Signed and dated *'1877'*;
inscribed on an old label
attached to the stretcher:
*'1885/Janry 16th/no 39/
Alfred Morrison Esq/Coast scene
with calm sea/by J Brett 1877'*
© Sotheby's Images Ltd
Provenance: Alfred Morrison;
through the sale rooms to the
present owner

This beautiful view of Parn Voose Cove, east of the Lizard, seems to have been partly derived from a pencil sketch Brett had made on Sep 26 1870 (Sketchbook 35). The angle and height of the viewpoint suggest that this was supplemented by observations from a boat. The picture focuses on the prominent piece of cliff known as the Balk in the centre, the entrance to Church Cove lying between this and the nearer cliff. Above the cove is a daymark in the form of a Celtic cross, and on the right, at the north end of the cove, the feature known as the Chair.

Brett's original pencil drawing is accompanied by colour notes, some of which were used in working up the picture in his studio:

> Low cliffs rich sepia colour covered with green mould … a texture like velveteen. Clear terre vert sea below, … the clefts of the rocks take rich green reflections from the sea. Veins in rocks of pale terre vert warmed with sunlight. The earth's crust a warm pinkish umber.

The picture was sold to Brett's patron Alfred Morrison. He is known to have owned another work of the same date and approximately the same size, *Breakers on Kennack Strand*, and both may have been commissioned at the same time. The date Jan 16 1885 and the number 39 on the stretcher possibly indicate that Morrison lent it for an exhibition that year.

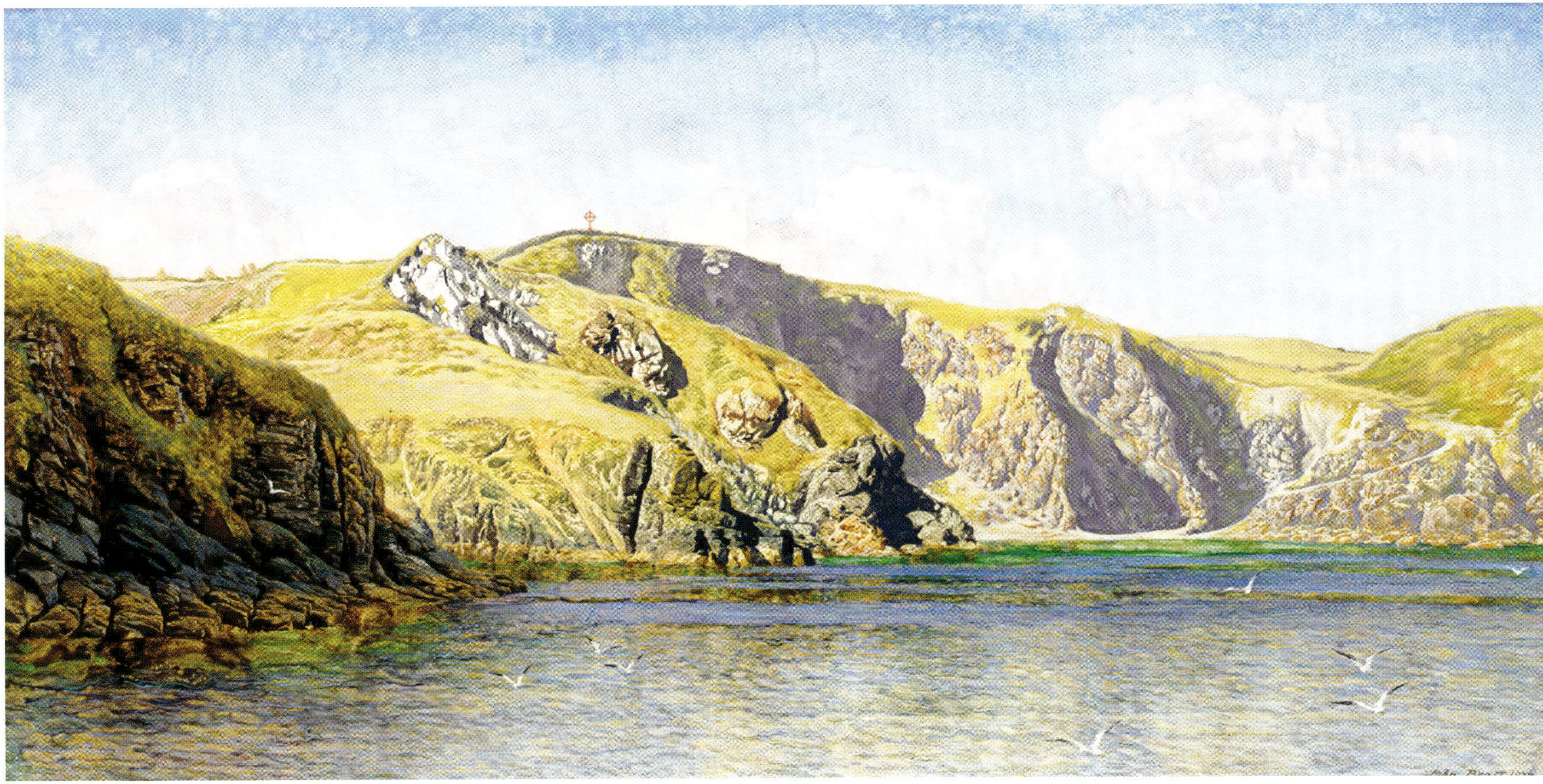

Parn Voose Cove
1877, Oil on board
18 x 35.5cm (7 x 14ins)
Inscribed on an old label verso *'Daisy Watson'*
Private Collection
Provenance: through the sale rooms to the present owner

Brett returned to Parn Voose Cove (literally 'the fortified cove') in 1877. This is clear from two pencil drawings dated Sep 7 77 in Sketchbook 46, which seem to relate to this sketch. In the intervening years since his original 1870 sketch of the cove (see p.95) several things had changed. The daymark on the cliff had been taken away, and the shape of the Balk significantly altered as the result of quarrying, involving the removal of quantities of serpentine rock. From Brett's high vantage point on the cliffs the tower of Grade church was visible, and it can be made out on the horizon in the centre of the picture.

The old church, too dilapidated to repair, had been demolished and replaced by a new building in 1862 by the Rector, Rev Frederick Jackson, who was both patron of the living and the incumbent. An enthusiastic amateur artist, he was a good friend of the Bretts, as the 'Early Travels' reveal.

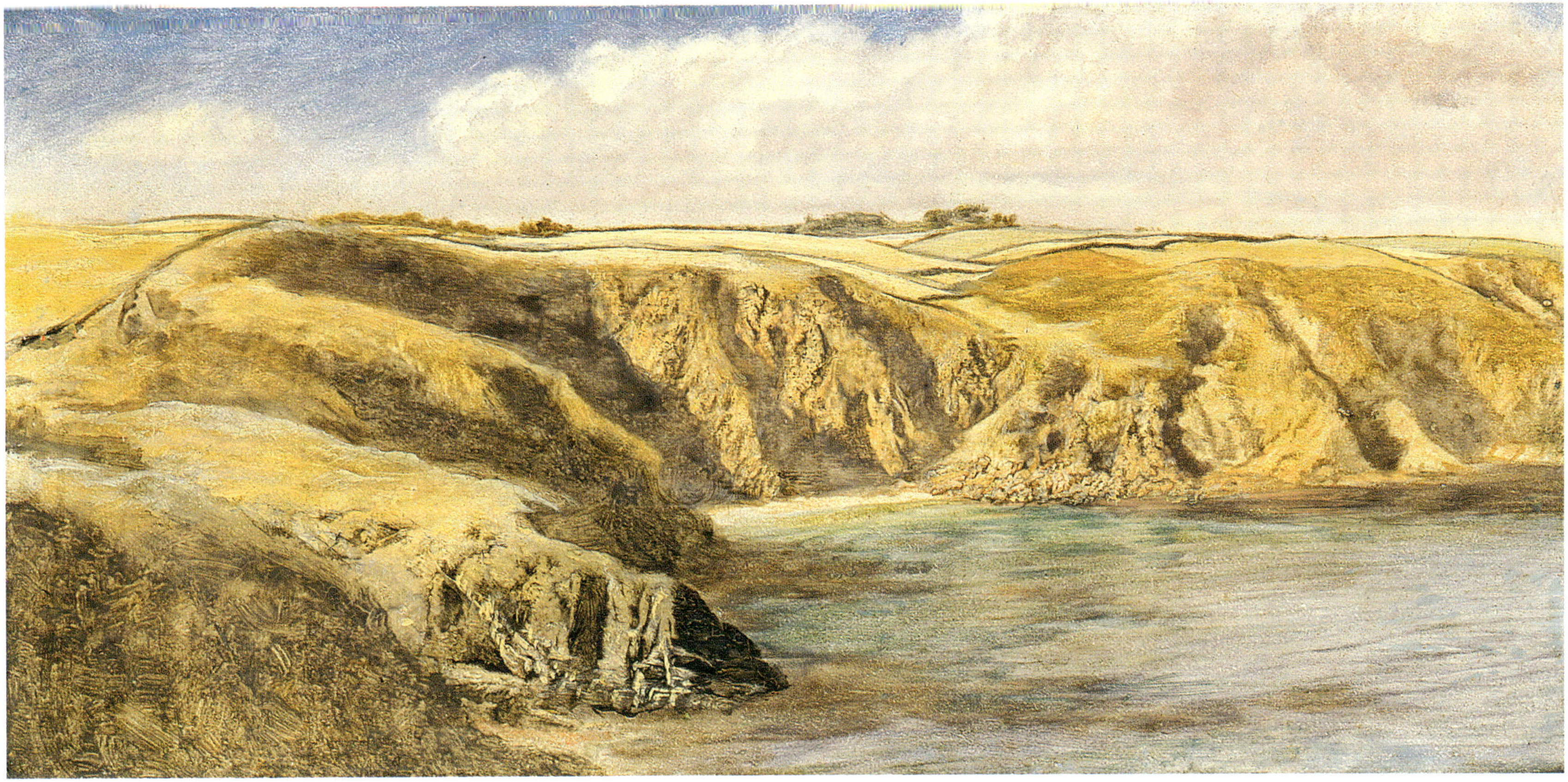

Carthillon Cliffs
1878, Oil on canvas
45.7 x 91.4cms (18 x 36ins)
Inscribed *'John Brett 1878'*
© Royal Holloway College
Provenance: William Lee; acquired for the College at his sale at Christie's 26 May 1883

SUPPORTING IMAGE
Kynance Cove from Caerthillian Cliffs
Photograph: Cécile Brett

This work was based on a pencil sketch dated Sep 18 77 (Sketchbook 52). It shows the view from the downs above Caerthillian Cove, about half a mile from Lizard Town, looking north-west towards Kynance Cove. Typically, Brett has selected a group of granite boulders on the cliff top as his focal point. The eye is led past these rocks towards Gull Rock and Asparagus Island in the centre of the picture, and Rill Head in the further distance. The Lion Rock is hidden from view behind the principal foreground boulder. As in *Mount's Bay* (p.88), Brett has introduced sheep in the right foreground, and a couple of fishing smacks float effortlessly on the calm water.

The work was commissioned by William Lee, who owned at least five Bretts. On his death in 1883 his pictures were sold at Christie's, and this work was bought for 260 guineas by George Martin on behalf of his brother-in-law, Thomas Holloway. Holloway had made a fortune from pills and ointments, and founded the Royal Holloway College for Women at Egham in 1879 in memory of his wife. In 1881 he started to form an art collection as a gift to the College, and spent the huge sum of £83,000 on pictures in two years, using Martin as advisor and agent. The 77 works he bought remain at the College, a rare surviving example of a major Victorian collection.

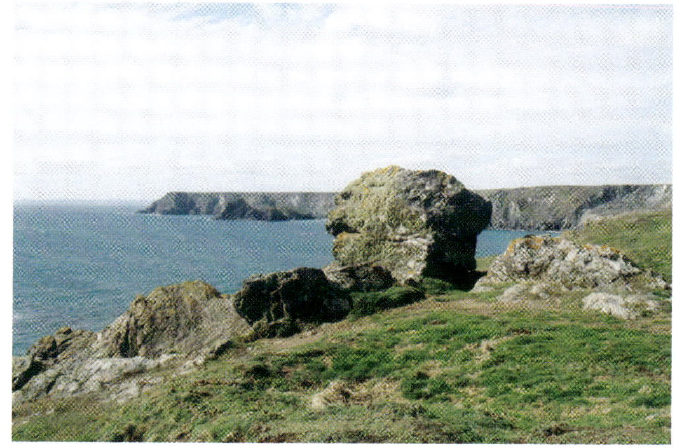

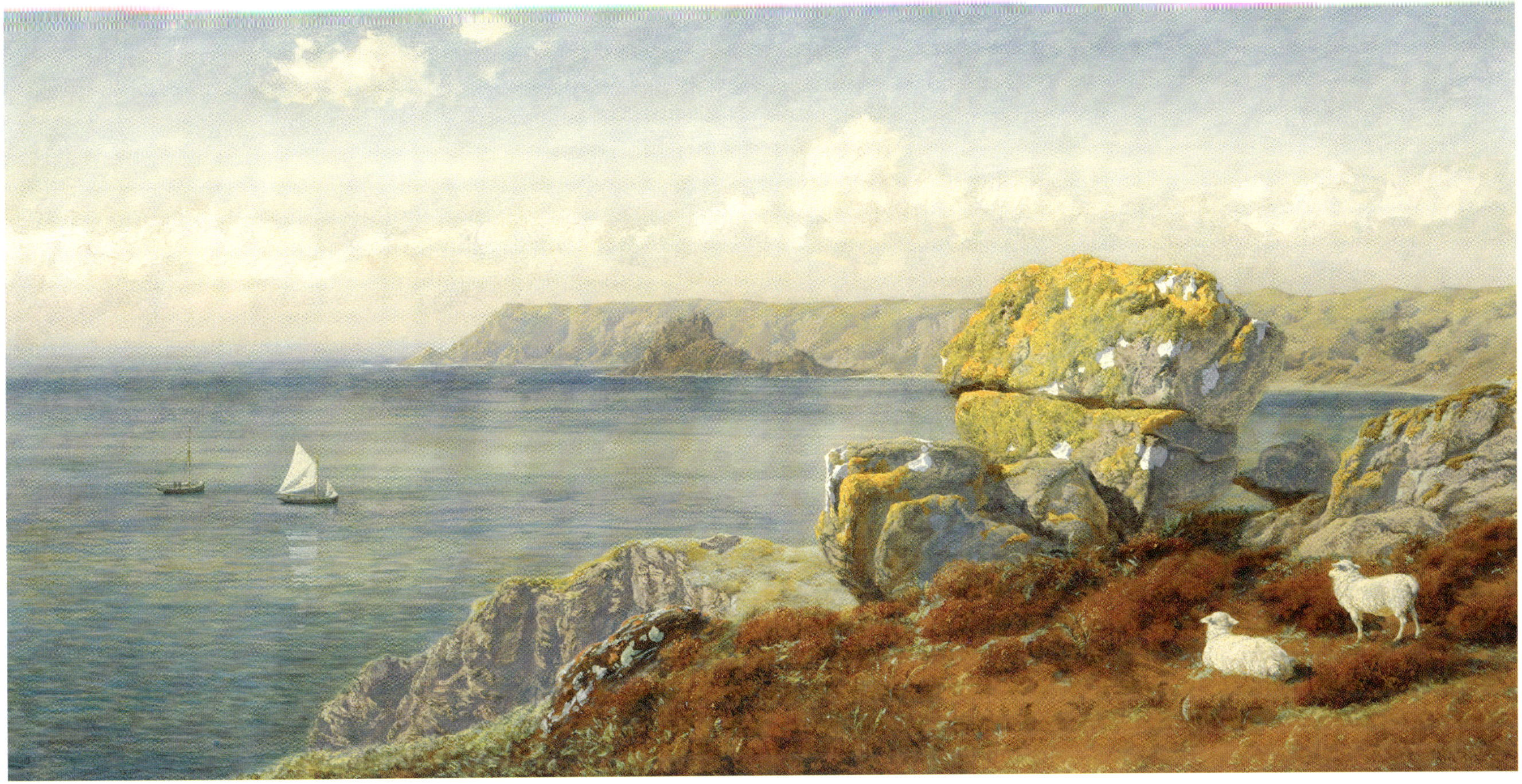

Summer mists off Tol Pedn
1880, Oil on canvas
18 x 35.5cm (7 x 14ins)
Inscribed *'Tol Pedn Aug 27 80'*
© Royal Exchange Gallery
Provenance: Albert Michael Apr 11 1881; through the sale rooms to the present owners

This masterly sketch was the first Brett painted after his arrival at Porth Gwarra near Land's End on 24 August 1880. The vantage point is Tol-Pedn-Penwith ('the holed headland in Penwith'), looking eastwards towards Polostoc Zawn ('the fisherman's cap'). The headland gets its name from a thirty-foot-wide chasm, known as 'the Funnel', that drops from the top of the cliff down to the sea.

Brett's position was precarious, as this chasm lay immediately behind him as he painted. Working from such an exposed position would have been possible only on a calm day with little wind, and August 27 must have been just such a day, with a sea mist adding to the feeling of repose. The rocks are painted with great precision, and in the foreground Brett has introduced a lyrical note by his emphasis on the colourful sea pinks and the gorgeous orange lichen which decorates the granite. In the centre of the picture a beautifully observed Mousehole lugger provides a focal point for a work in which a perfect balance between geological, botanical and meteorological elements has been achieved. The artist is shown here at the height of his powers.

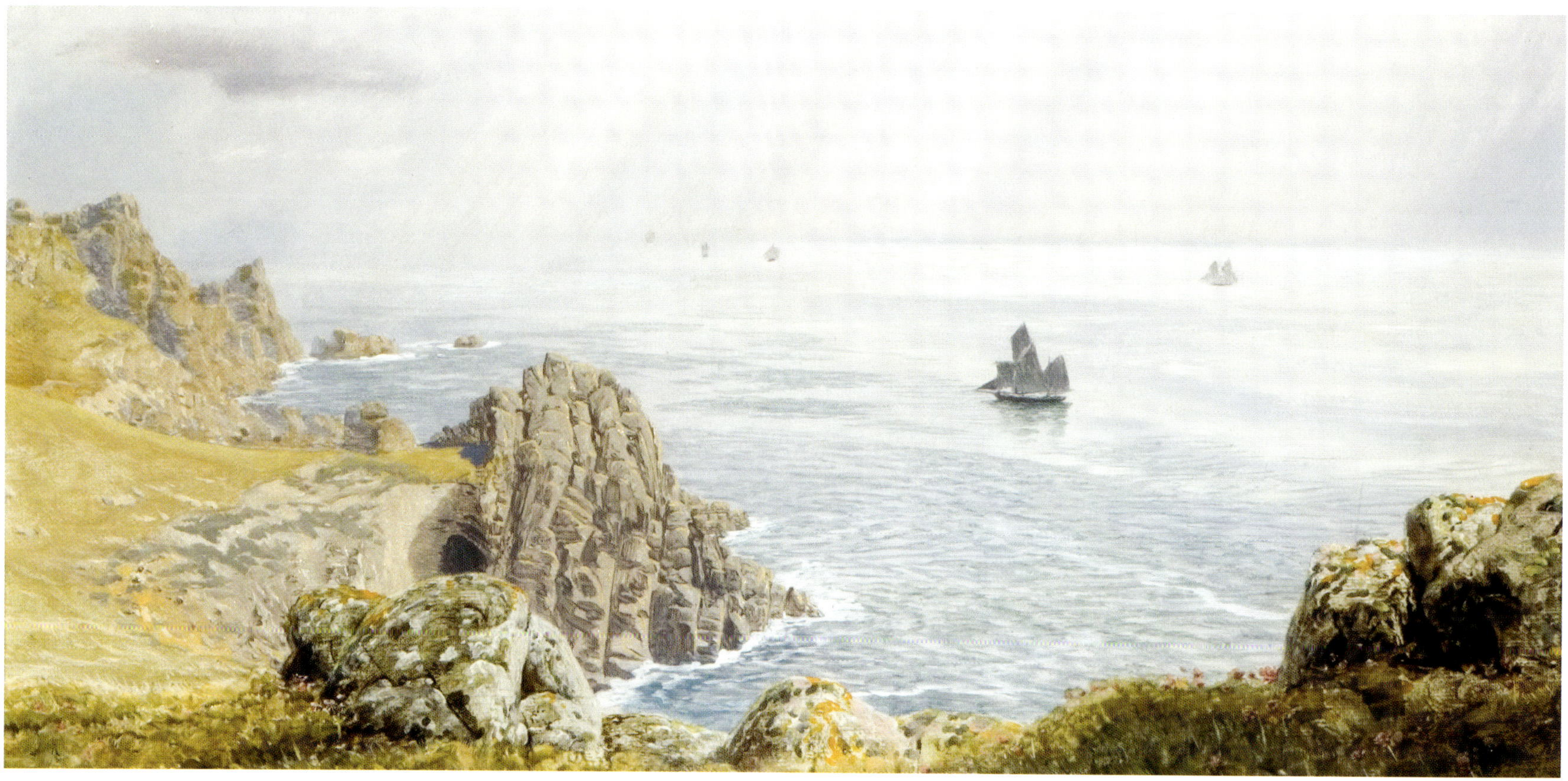

Porth Curnow
1880, Oil on canvas
25.3 x 48.3cm (10 x 19ins)
Inscribed *'Porth Curnow Sep 8 80'*
Private Collection
Provenance: Sir T.L. Devitt Bt;
by descent to the present owner

This exquisite view of Treryn Dinas was painted from a point high up on Treen Cliff, overlooking Porthcurno Bay. The tide is out, and the famous cliff castle, with its jagged outline, is seen across an expanse of wet sand, with a serene vista of sea and sky beyond. As so often with Brett, the view is framed by a group of unusually shaped rocks in the right foreground. The viewpoint is only accessible after a climb strenuous enough, even when unencumbered by painting equipment, to demonstrate the artist's determination to find and record the most dramatic views on this rugged bit of coast, whatever the cost in time and energy.

The existence of a pencil sketch of the view, dated Aug 31 80 (Sketchbook 53), suggests that the work was not painted entirely on the spot, but took several days to reach its final, elaborately finished state. Another of the works originally in Sir Thomas Devitt's collection, it cost him £85, a high price for a relatively small work, and a measure of its worth in Brett's eyes.

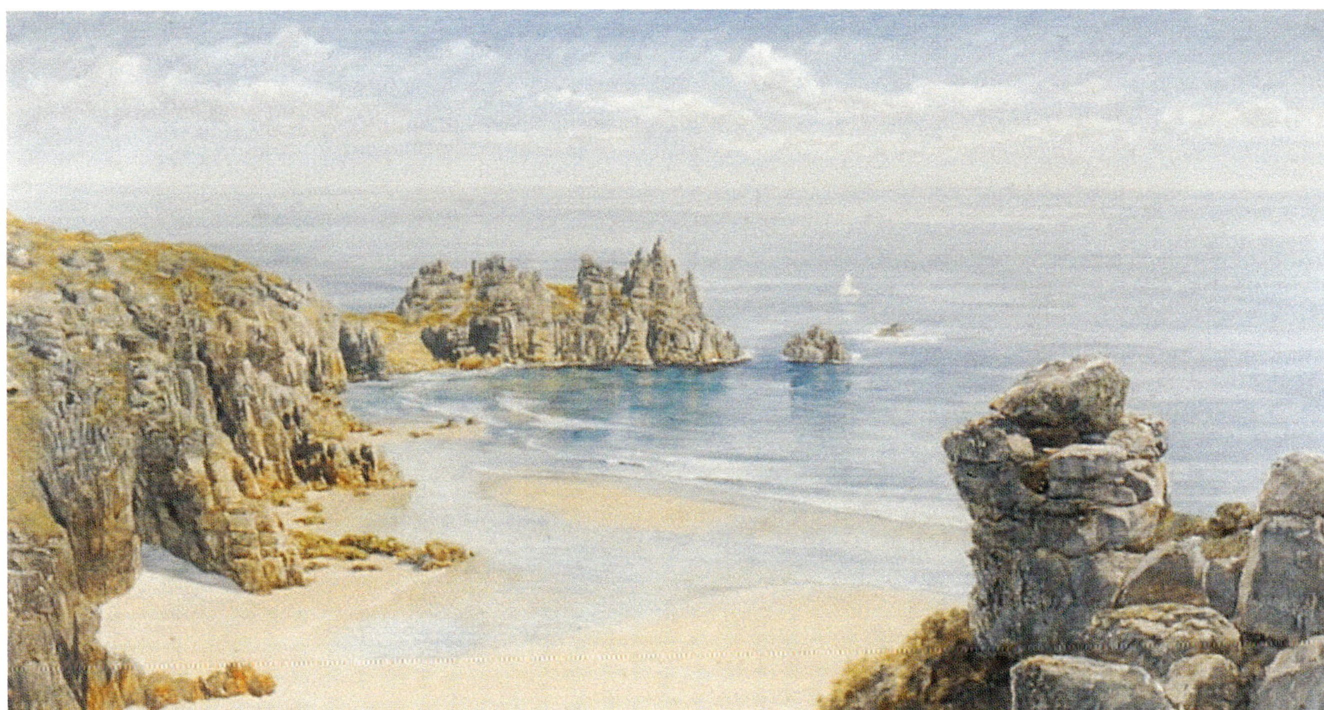

Porth Gwarra
1880, Oil on canvas
18 x 35.5cm (7 x 14ins)
Inscribed *'Porth Gwarra Sep 13 80'*

Provenance: W. Child Clark; his Bequest 1929

This sketch concentrates on the group of granite boulders Brett had used as his foreground in the sketch of Treryn Dinas finished five days earlier (p.101). Here they are shown from a slightly different angle. Their strange shapes and unusual grouping may have reminded the artist of some of the rock formations he had observed earlier in the Scilly Isles (see p.70–71). Here, too, the scale is ambiguous, although in this instance the boulders are relatively small.

The rocks are shown against a background of calm sea with a few distant craft, and, on the left, the two rocks which lie off the Treryn Dinas promontory, Great Goular and Horrace.

Although this group of boulders is still easily identifiable today, it is now covered by scrub and gorse. In the nineteenth century rabbits used to keep the coastline clear of undergrowth; but since the elimination of the rabbit population by myxomatosis, it has started to regain its hold.

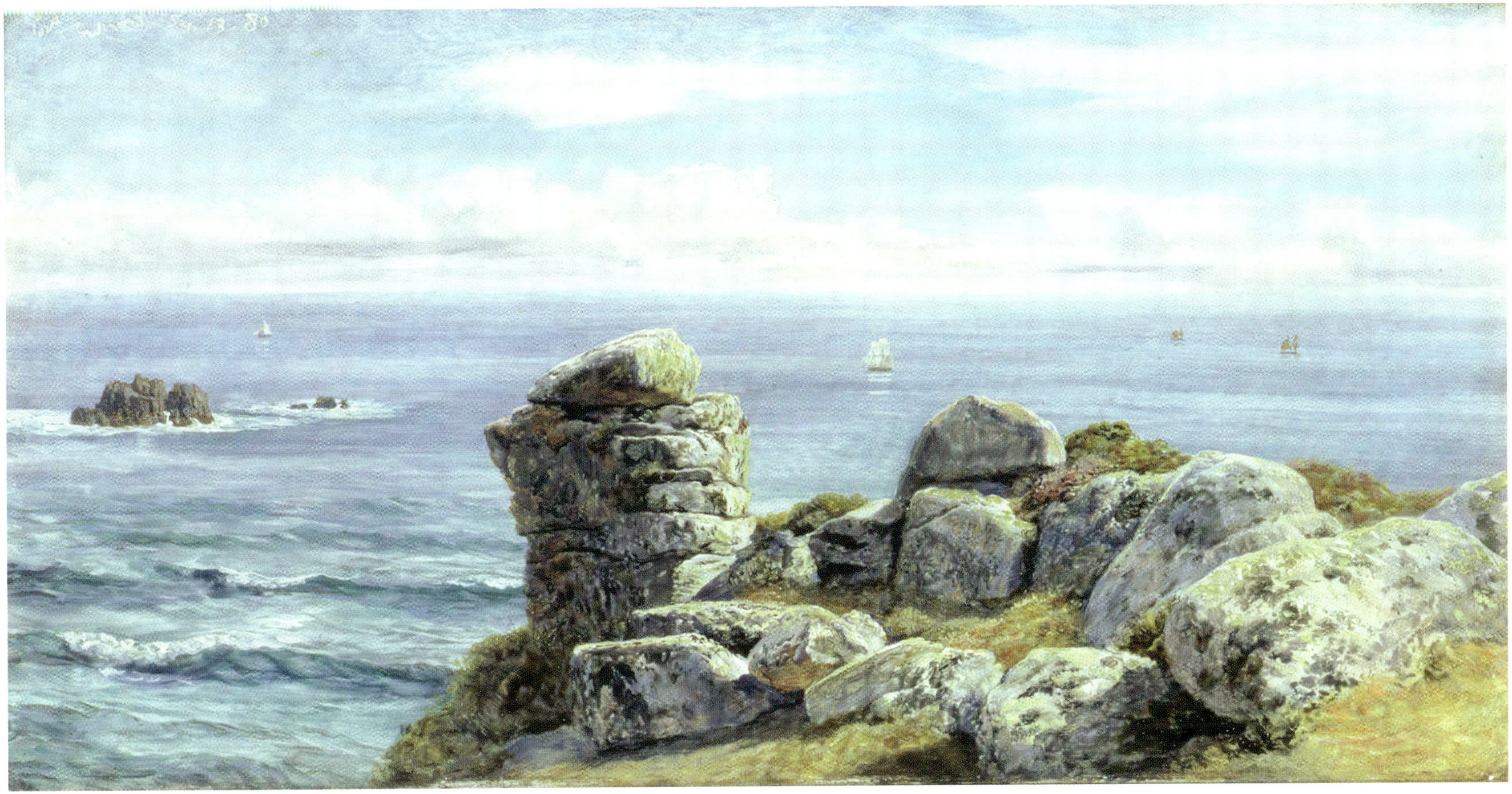

South of Cyclops
1880, Oil on canvas
18 x 35.5cm (7 x 14ins)
Inscribed *'South of Cyclops Sep 28 80'*
Private Collection
Provenance: by descent in the artist's family to the present owner

Brett's entry for September 27 1880 in the 'Early Travels' describes the headlands around Porth Gwarra as 'examples of cracked granite, very gaunt and hideous in form and often like ruins of cyclopean masonry.' This explains the rather curious title he gave this sketch, as the view is from a point just south-east of Tol-Pedn-Penwith, the most impressive of these headlands, looking east. In the distance is Polostoc Zawn ('the Fisherman's Cap'), which had also appeared in *Summer mists off Tol Pedn* (p.100), but here Brett's viewpoint was much closer to the water line, and the angle totally different.

It is also a very grey day, with a bank of threatening cloud towards the horizon. This gives a completely new aspect to the scene. The sea is now a deep grey-green, flecked with foam, and the granite rocks, carved by the sea into complex patterns, are projected dramatically against the angry sky.

The view very closely resembles a pencil drawing of September 27 (Sketchbook 53). This, together with its refinement of detail, prompts the conclusion that the sketch was largely painted in Brett's lodgings.

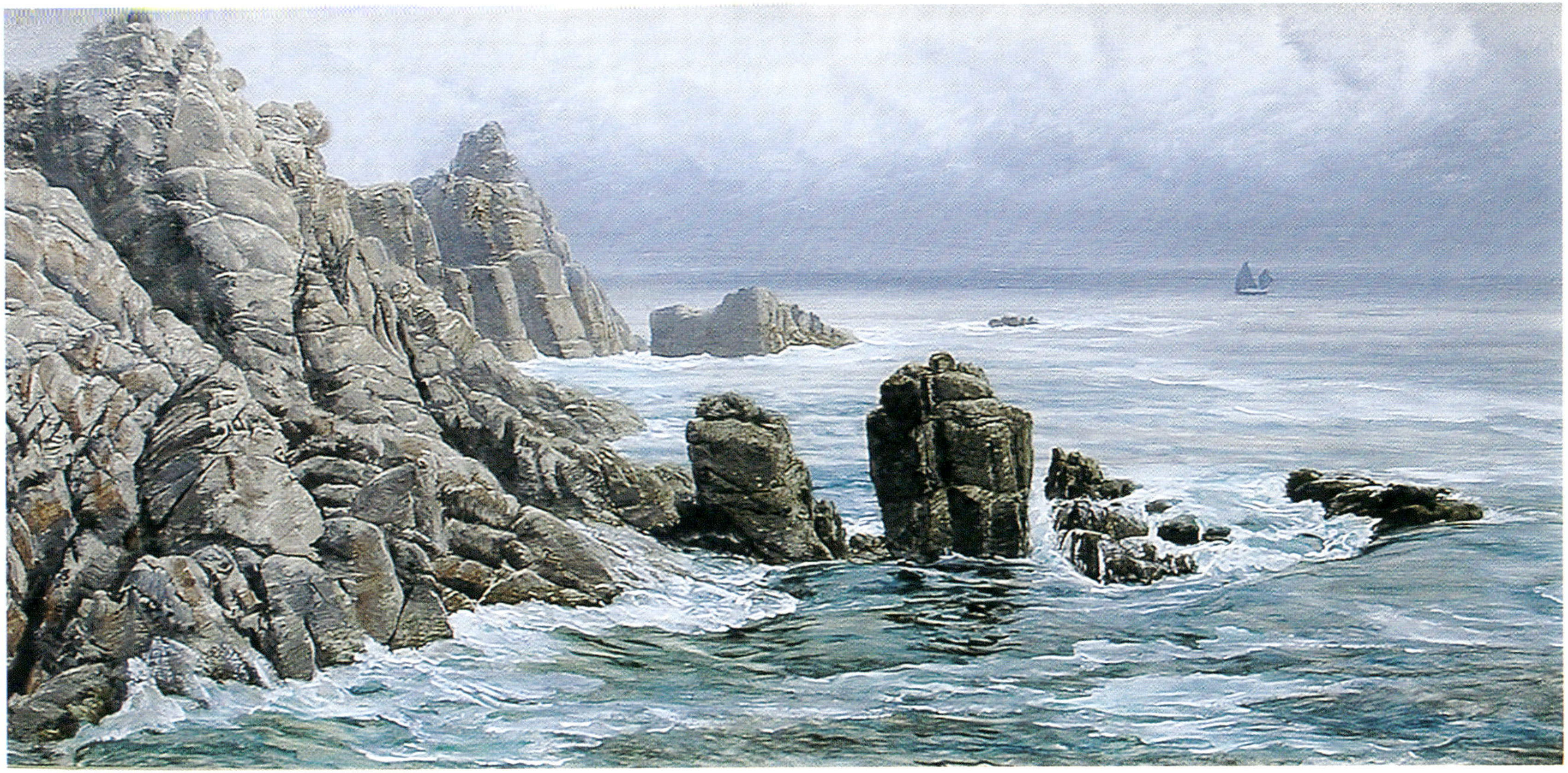

The black east wind
1880, Oil on canvas
18 x 35.5cm (7 x 14ins)
Inscribed *'The black east wind Oct 16 80'*
© Russell-Cotes Art Gallery & Museum, Bournemouth/ Bridgeman Art Library
Provenance: W. Child Clark; his Bequest 1929

SUPPORTING IMAGE
Jasper at Land's End
Photograph: John Brett
Private Collection

Measles drove the family out of Porth Gwarra on September 30, and the remaining weeks of the 1880 campaign were spent at Sennen, close to Land's End. Brett typically chose the group of boulders shown in this sketch as a foreground to a vista which includes the Land's End itself, and the distant Longships Lighthouse. This is the second, taller structure, which had replaced the earlier lighthouse he had painted in 1872–3 (see fig.35 p.45).

The 'black east wind' of the title seems to have dogged Brett's time at Sennen. On October 10 he wrote in the 'Early Travels', 'this is a truly autumnal Sunday – a strong north easterly wind which has prevailed generally since we came here some ten days ago makes the outlook dreary in the extreme, and the cold showers... disincline one to leave the house.' And a fortnight later Mary reported that 'the weather has been bitterly cold, a strong east wind has been blowing nearly all the week. There have been only one or two days that Daddie could work out of doors.'

This evidence, and the existence of a photograph showing Brett's second son Jasper sitting on the foreground boulders, suggest that this brooding, atmospheric work was largely painted indoors. It would certainly have been very difficult for Brett to portray the rocks and their variegated lichens in such minute detail on the spot in the teeth of a gale, with the constant threat of a drenching.

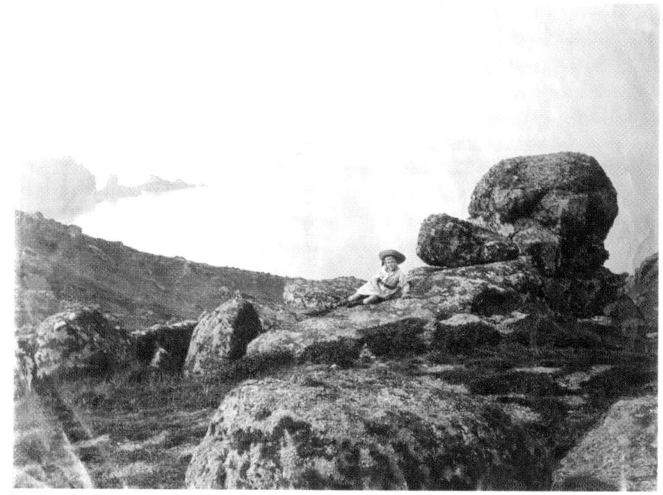

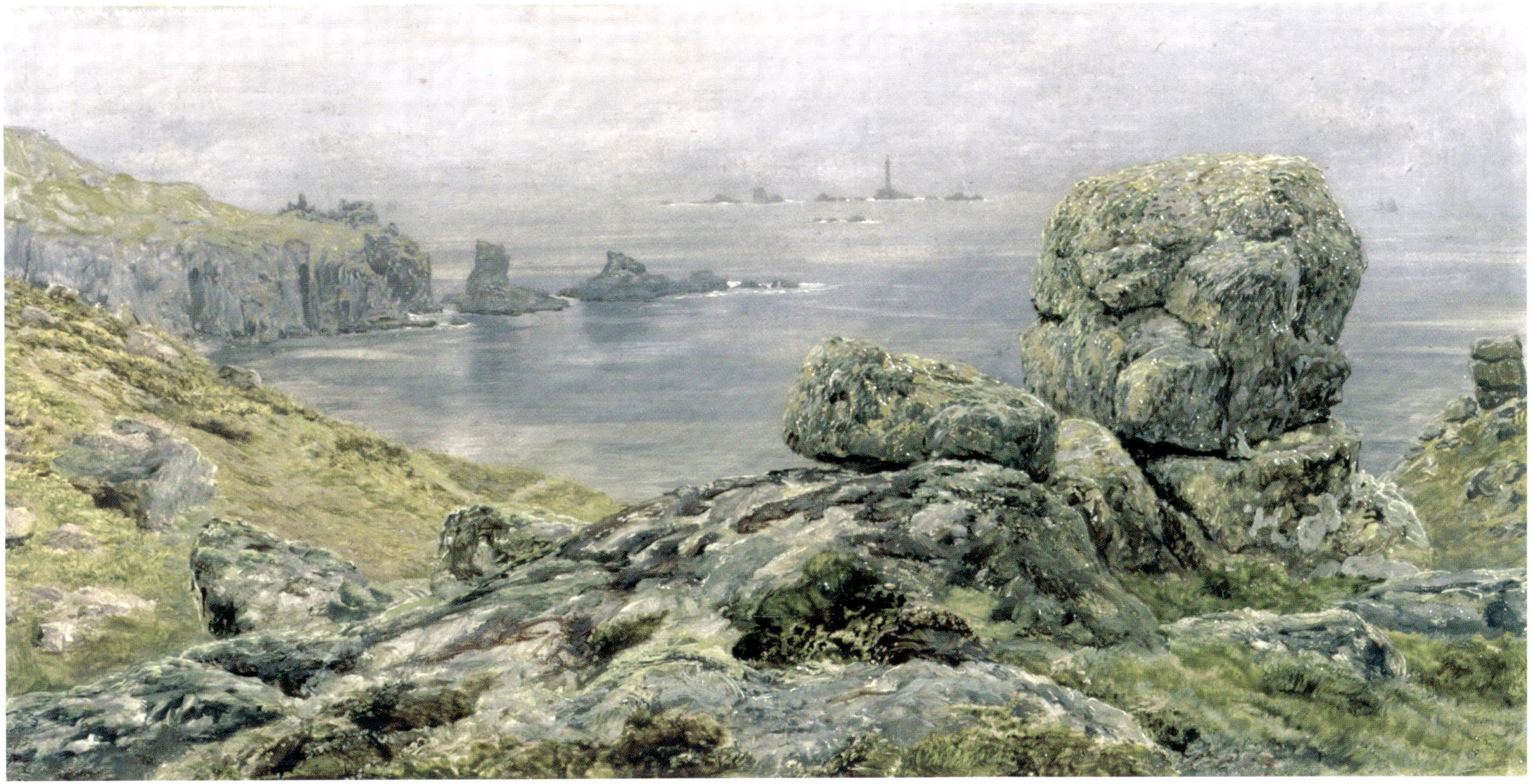

Golden Prospects
1881, Oil on canvas
106.68 x 213.36cm (42 x 84ins)
Signed and dated *'John Brett 1881'*

Provenance: T.A. Rogers; his sale Christie's 18 April 1913, lot 52. Acquired by the museum 1913

SUPPORTING IMAGES

Michael and Jasper at Land's End
Photograph: John Brett
Private Collection

Jasper on the roof
of 6 Keswick Road
Photograph: John Brett
Private Collection

This beautiful work, with its transparent symbolism, is derived from a number of sources, and is closely related to *The black east wind* (p.106–7). Brett decided to use the same group of lichen-covered rocks as in the earlier work, but showed them in profile, from a point a little further north, providing a more oblique view of Land's End and the Longships. He also considerably exaggerated their size. A 15 x 30ins picture, inscribed *Land's End Oct 25 80* (sold at Sotheby's 1 April 1980, lot 84) shows this view, and was clearly the study for *Golden Prospects*. It includes the figure of Brett's son Michael, sitting just below the principal boulder, gazing far out to sea.

At the same time Brett photographed Michael in the same pose, accompanied by his brother Jasper, also wearing a hat, leaning up against the boulder. Although Michael's pose was retained for the final work, Brett was not so happy with Jasper, and later took another photograph of him, this time on the flat roof of 6 Keswick Road. In this he is hatless, his arms are folded behind his back, and his legs are differently placed. Brett incorporated this pose into *Golden Prospects*, which formed one of his two entries for the 1881 Academy. There it was well received, the Art Journal praising 'a view from rocks, painted with microscopic fidelity, over a lovely violet-tinted sea.' The geologist T.G. Bonney, writing for the magazine *Nature*, found the 'miniature tor of granite' in the foreground 'a wonderfully truthful study: form, structure, texture of the rock, and the crisp crusting of dry lichens perfectly rendered.' He ended his note: 'Those who in anyway equal Mr Brett in his love for the

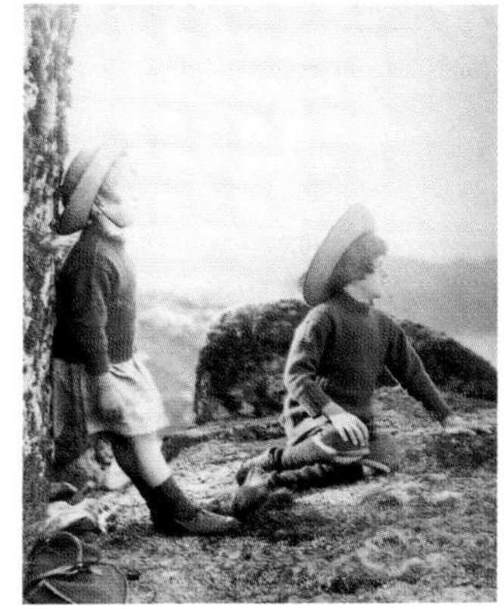

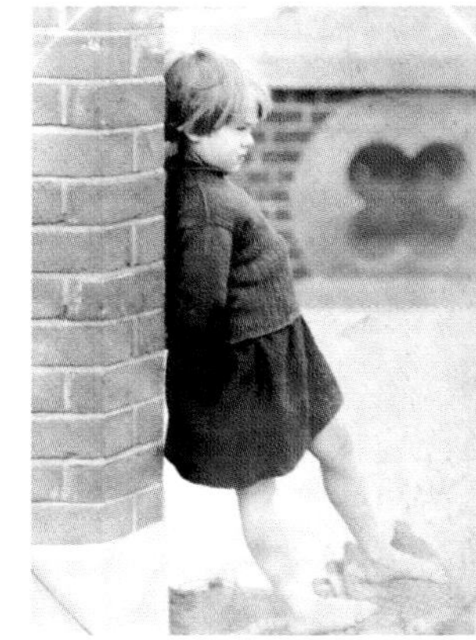

Cornish coast will find it hard to tear themselves away from this picture of one of its grandest scenes.'

The work soon sold for £1,200, the largest sum Brett ever received for a picture (only equalled by *The Grey of the Morning* the following year). This was no doubt partly due to the success of *Britannia's Realm* of 1880, its purchase for the nation by the Chantrey Bequest, and Brett's subsequent election as ARA. But *Golden Prospects* is unquestionably a very beautiful work in its own right, full of the poetry and tender sentiment that critics have sometimes found lacking in Brett's largest pictures.

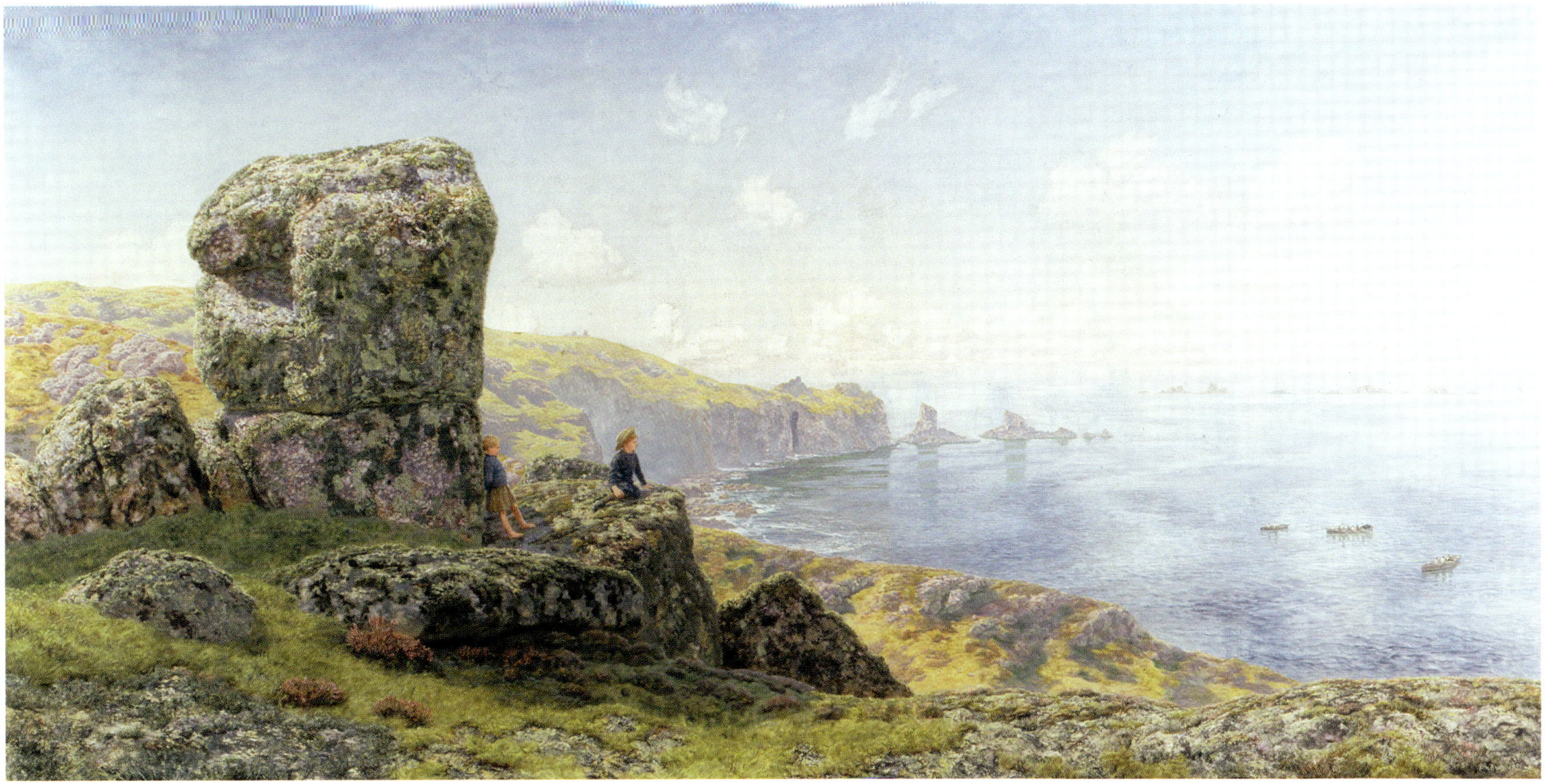

Trevose Head
1881, Oil on canvas
17.78 x 35.56cm (7 x 14ins)
Inscribed *'Trevose Head June 7 81'*
© Manchester Art Gallery
Provenance: Horsfall Museum transfer 1918

SUPPORTING IMAGE
North Westerly Rain
1881, Oil on canvas
18 x 35.5cm (7 x 14ins)
Inscribed *'North Westerly Rain June 6 81'*
Private Collection

Three days after his arrival in Newquay on June 3, 1881, Brett painted *North Westerly Rain,* a sketch depicting an approaching rainstorm. The following day he made his way north to Porthcothan, some ten miles from Newquay. The rain had apparently eased off, but the wind was clearly still blowing hard, sending the clouds rapidly across the sky, and whipping up the white horses.

Brett chose a point on the cliffs immediately above and to the west of Porthcothan beach, and painted the view looking north. The free-standing rock just to the right of centre is Will's Rock, and the coastline then sweeps round to the left, past Treyarnon and Constantine bays to Trevose Head. The Trevose light is visible, gleaming white, in the far distance to the right of Dinas Head.

A lugger is ploughing through the distinctly choppy waters, and Brett has given us a vivid impression of a blustery, invigorating day. His handling of the sea is particularly striking, reminiscent in some ways of his friend Henry Moore's work, and employs a subtle range of colours.

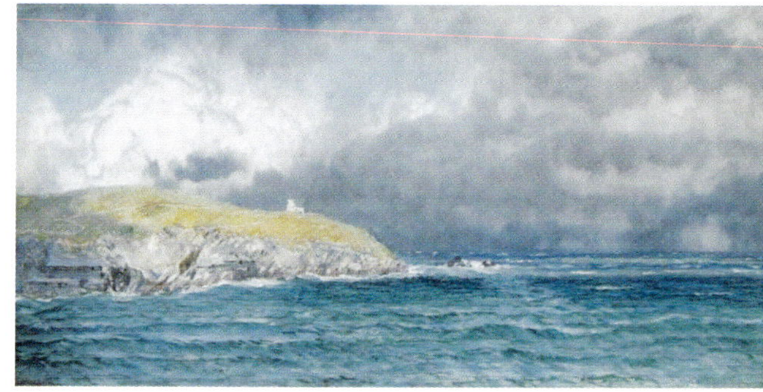

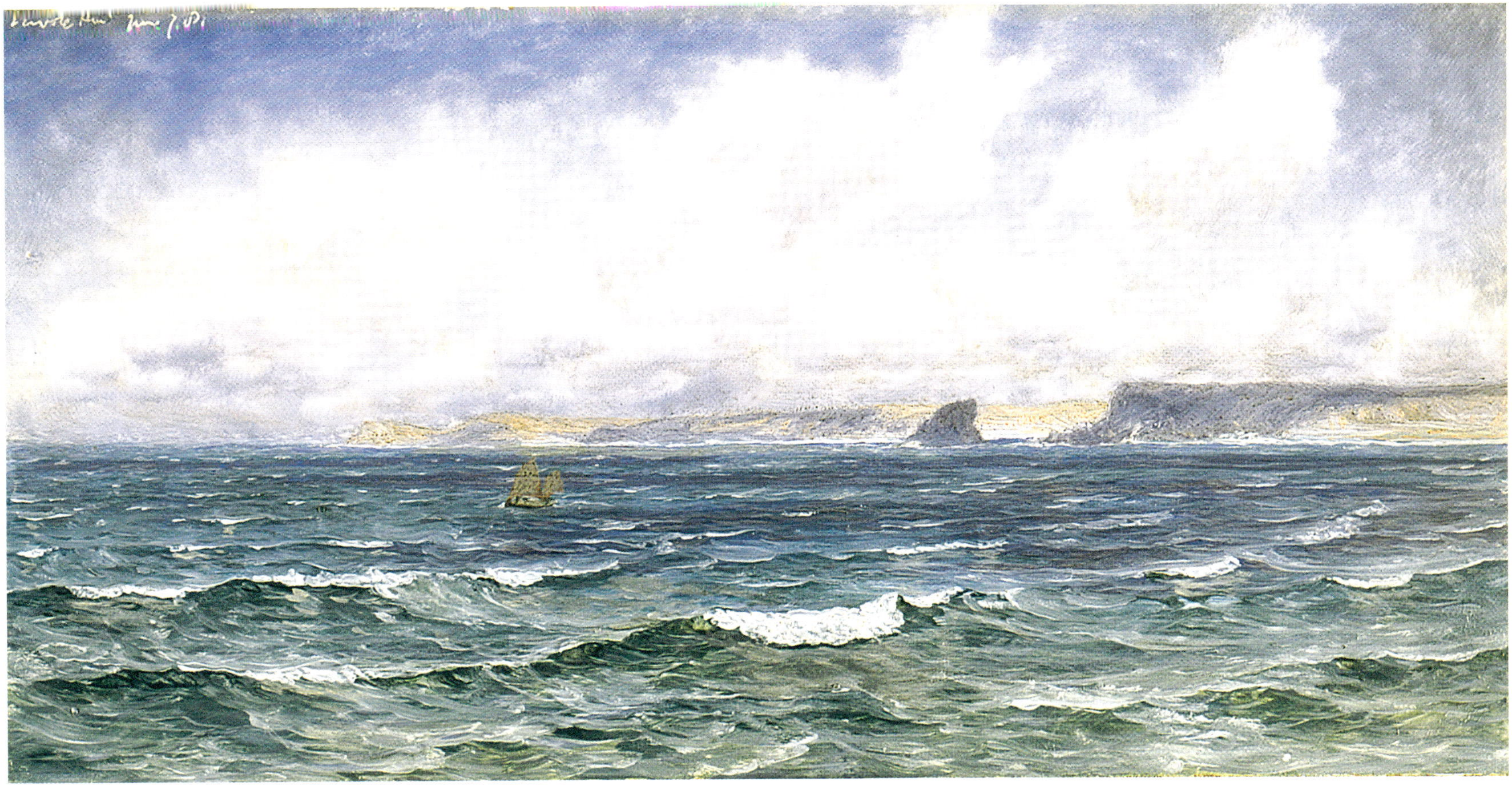

Crigga Pools
1881, Oil on canvas
18 x 35.5cm (7 x 14ins)
Inscribed *'Crigga Pools June 26 81'* and on an old label attached to the reverse, *'This sketch 14 by 7 inches dated June 26 1881 is certified at Dowdeswell's/John Brett'*

Provenance: through the sale rooms to the present owner

Crigga Head lies towards the north-easterly end of the succession of fine sandy beaches for which Newquay is renowned. At its foot is a large cluster of rocks among which, at low tide, are pools ideal for children to paddle and play in. They were a favourite attraction for the Brett children in 1881.

In this delightful sketch Brett has focused on one of the larger Crigga rocks, which is just as Mary described them in the 'Early Travels', 'a rich brown, being... covered with seaweed and mussels.' He also shows the sand 'of a lovely fawn colour,' and some of the pools reflecting the blue sky. The tide is out, and he has characteristically included a distant vessel, making its way towards the harbour. It is a hazy summer day, and everything seems at peace. Even ten years later it would probably have been impossible for Brett to paint such a view undisturbed by holidaymakers.

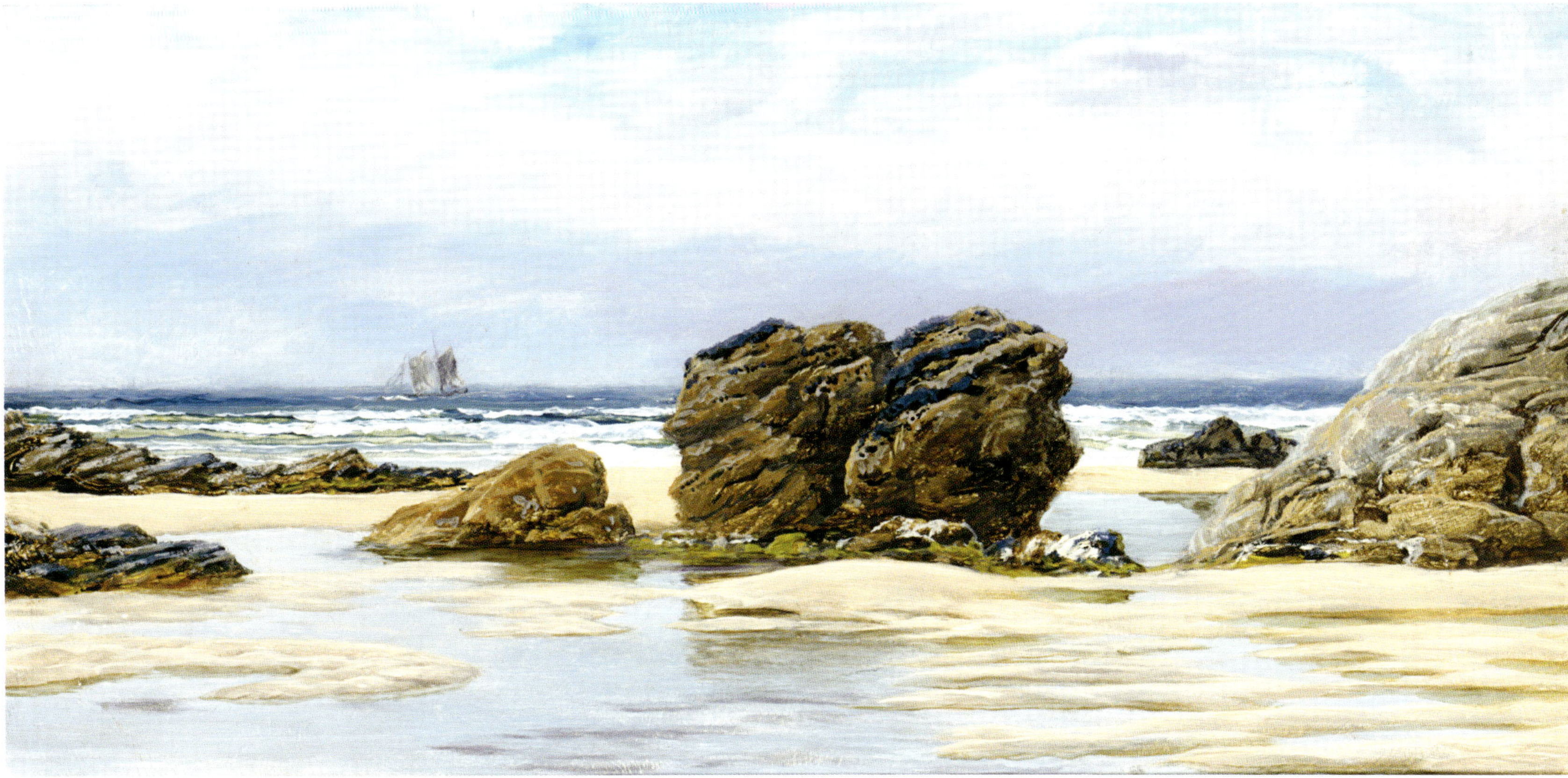

Spring Tide
1881, Oil on canvas
25.5 x 48cm (10 x 19ins)
Inscribed '*Spring Tide July 14 81*'
© Sotheby's Images Ltd
Provenance: through the sale rooms to the present owner

SUPPORTING IMAGE
The Grey of the Morning
Pencil sketch from *Blackburn's Academy Notes*, 1882

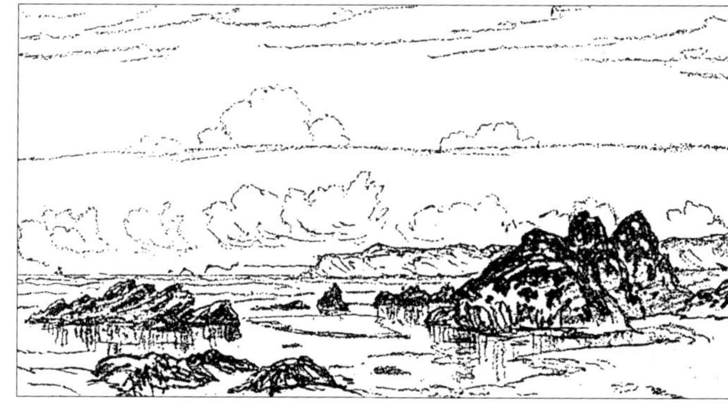

Spring tides, the highest tides of the month, occur on the days shortly after the new and full moon. Here Brett has painted a beautiful view of the aftermath of such a tide at Newquay. The sea has receded, leaving pools of water among the rocks, which are covered in mussels, and in the foreground, at the high water mark, attractive green and yellow seaweed.

The group of rocks known as the Bothwick Rocks lies between Towan beach and Killacourt Cove, and immediately below Bothwicks House, where Brett and his family spent the summer. They are the only rocks on the Newquay beaches to be adorned by this distinctive seaweed covering, and so are easily recognisable. Brett was painting from a point under the cliffs looking north-east towards Park Head, with Trevose Head in the far distance.

It is likely that this sketch was one of the sources for his Academy picture the next year, *The Grey of the Morning*. His Studio log states that this seven-foot work, painted in the winter of 1881–2, and sold in May 1882 to the major Cornish landowner, C.H.T. Hawkins, was based on 'studies at Newquay last year'. Although unlocated since the sale of the famous McCulloch collection at Christie's in 1913, it is known from an illustration supplied by Brett for Blackburn's Academy Notes. From this it seems clear that *Spring Tide* is one of the studies to which Brett was referring.

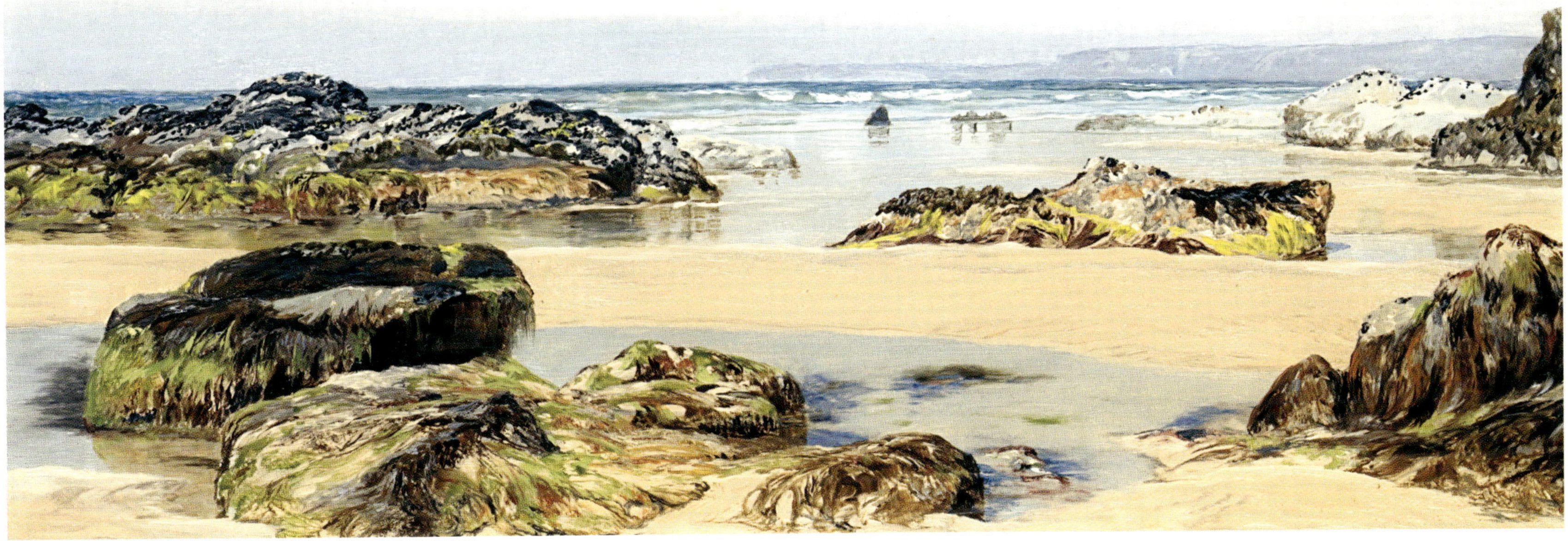

Towan Head
1881. Oil on canvas
18 x 35.5cm (7 x 14ins)
Inscribed *'Towyn Head July 20 81'* and on the reverse *'Towan Head from Pentire/Fredk Pennington Esqre MP/17 Hyde Park Terrace/from J Brett/38 Harley St May 4 82'*
Private Collection
Provenance: F. Pennington MP; through the sale rooms to the present owner

This fine sketch shows Towan Head, which marks the western end of Newquay Bay, seen from East Pentire Head. Brett actually inscribed the work *'Towyn Head'*, unconsciously using the Welsh form of the word, which means 'a round hill' or 'a sand hill.' But on the label attached to the reverse *'Towan'* is used.

The carefully observed inlet in the foreground forms part of Lewinnick Cove, and beyond it, hidden from sight, lies the sandy expanse of Fistral Bay. At that date Towan Head was completely free from building, and was merely covered in springy green turf. The Headland Hotel, which now dominates the scene, was not built until 1900.

Brett thought highly of this work as, in a letter to T.C. Horsfall of Manchester in July 1882, he mentions its owner *'Mr Pennington MP'* as having 'two of the best of my last series'. Frederick Pennington of 17 Hyde Park Terrace was Liberal MP for Stockport 1874–85, and was probably responsible for attaching the label to the front of the picture, which erroneously accords Brett the status of RA.

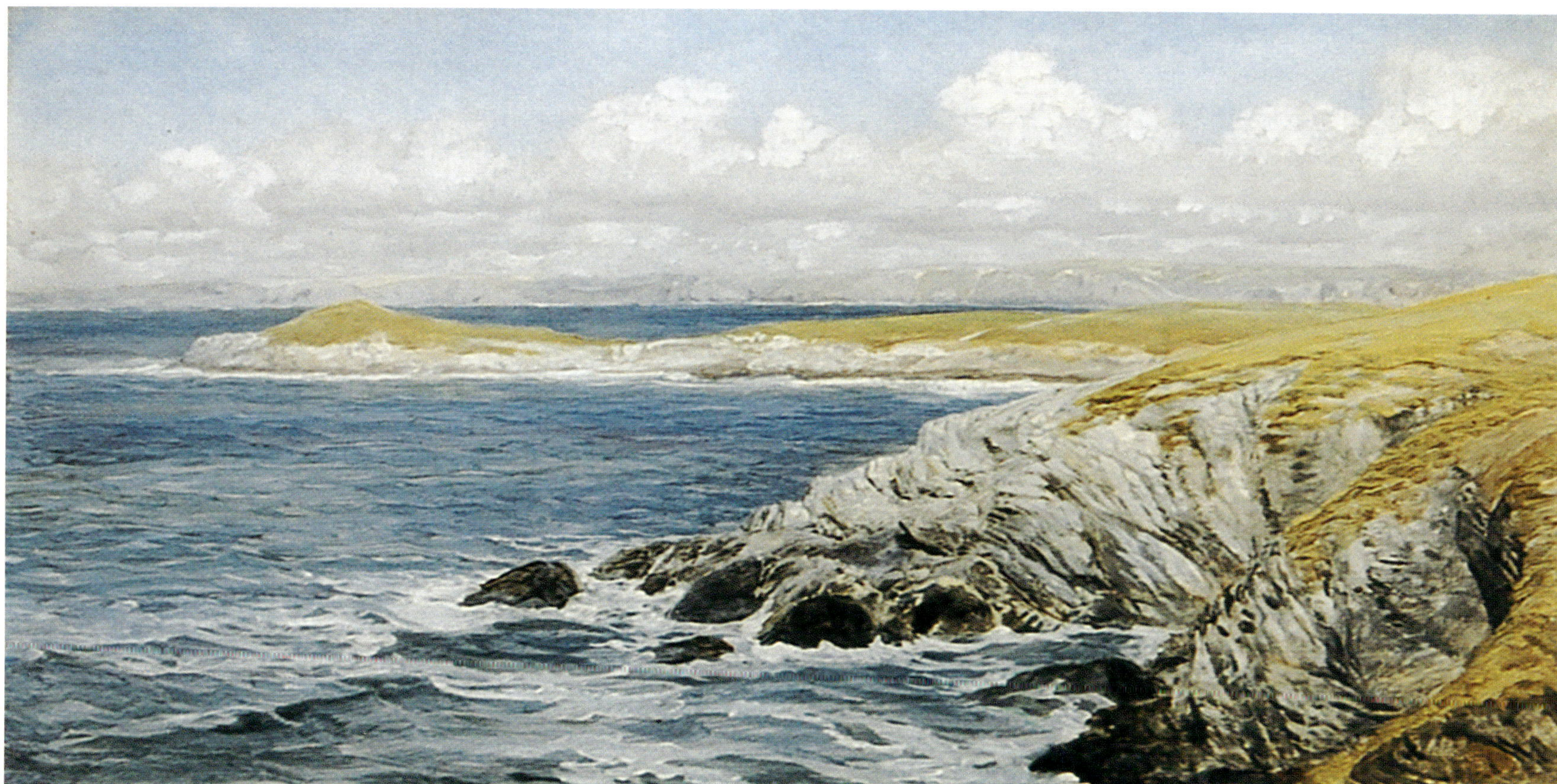

Tea Caves
1881, Oil on canvas
18 x 35.5cm (7 x 14ins)
Inscribed *'Tea Caves 13 Aug 81'*
Private Collection
Provenance: through the sale rooms to the present owner

This interesting and dramatic sketch was made on Towan Head looking south-east from a point on the cliffs above Beacon Cove. The Huer's Hut is visible on the cliff top, seen from the opposite side to the view shown in *North Westerly Rain*, (p.110) .

It is a bright but windy day, and the foaming tide crashes powerfully into the jagged coast, which contains the entrances to a number of caves. These are known as the Tea Caverns, in which consignments of smuggled tea were secreted in the days when tea was an expensive commodity. Only accessible at low tide, some of the caves extend as far as fifty yards into the headland, and must have been an ideal hiding place for contraband goods.

Brett's feeling for the texture of the cliffs here illustrates the lasting influence Ruskin's teaching had on his work.

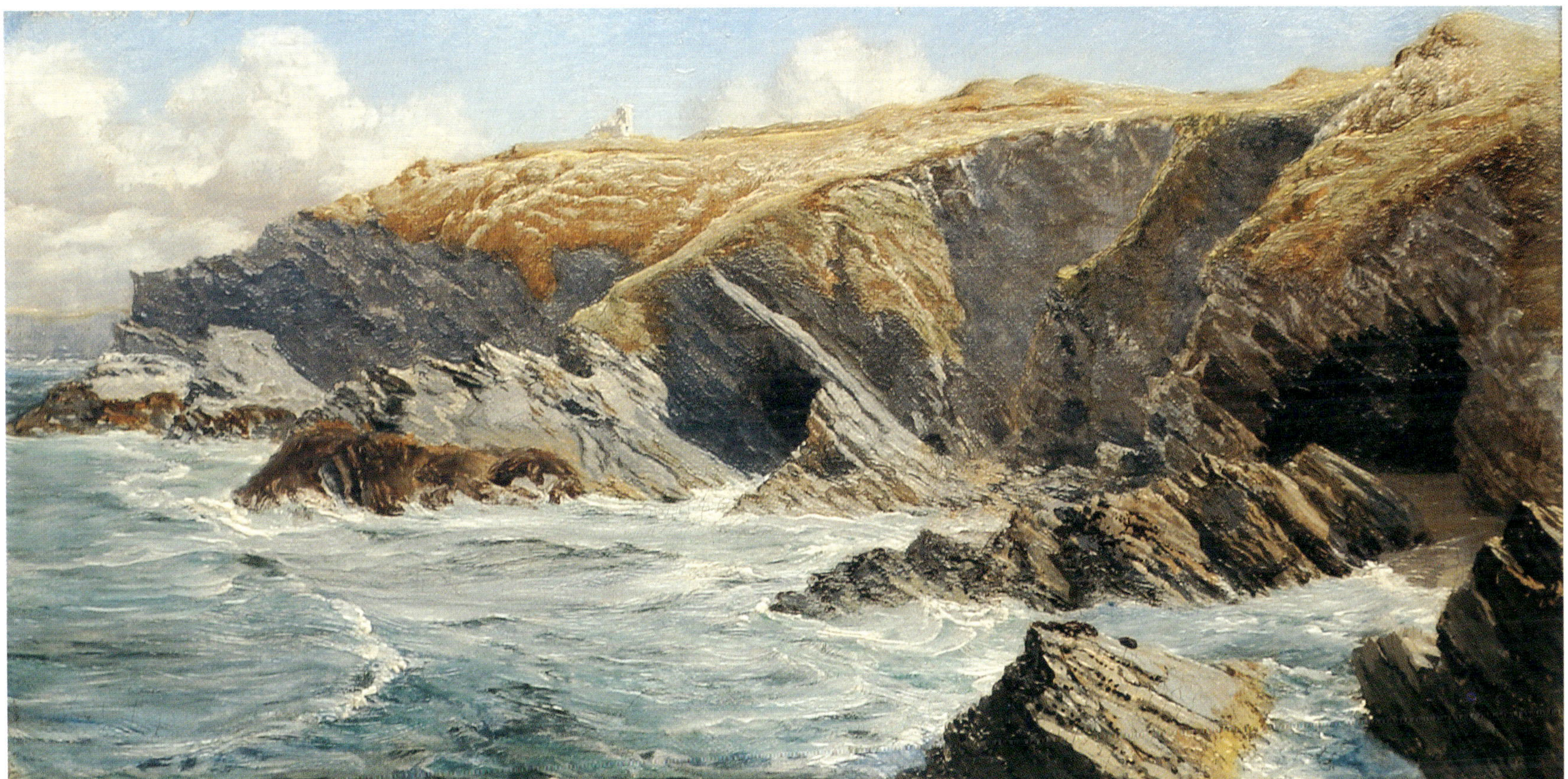

Off Falmouth
1883, Oil on canvas
17 x 35cm (6¾ x 13¾ins)
Inscribed *'Off Falmouth 16 July 83'*
Private Collection
Provenance: A.Tooth & Co; Bursman: Agnew's; through the sale rooms to the present owner

Brett acquired the schooner *Viking* in February 1883, and he and his family set off on their maiden voyage in her from Southampton on June 29 that year. Sailing via Swanage, Weymouth, Plymouth and Fowey, they arrived at Falmouth late in the evening of July 13, and remained there until July 24.

Falmouth, with its large and sheltered anchorage, had long been an important port. Formerly the base for the mail packets which served the Iberian peninsula, the Caribbean and the north Atlantic, it was also the first port of call for incoming cargo vessels from the Americas, which would receive instructions there as to their final destinations. The Fox family had been for several generations the principal shipping agents, and Howard Fox was an old friend of Brett's.

On July 16 he brought his young daughter Stella to lunch on board the Viking, and afterwards Brett had a tent erected on deck as a studio, where he 'tried to paint a sketch of the distant town.' It gives a delightful impression of the busy port, dominated on the right by Beacon Hill, with the waterfront buildings clearly delineated. But its main interest lies in the range of shipping Brett has depicted. Two gaff cutters, some distant luggers, a passenger steamer and a brig are painted with a precision typical of the artist, who had been observing boats closely for twenty years or more.

The sketch was bought from Brett by the Haymarket dealer Tooth for £22-10-0 in May 1884, and appeared in his spring exhibition the next year. It was sold in February 1886 to 'Bursman' for £25 (Tooth stock books, Getty Research Institute), and has subsequently passed through the sale rooms several times.

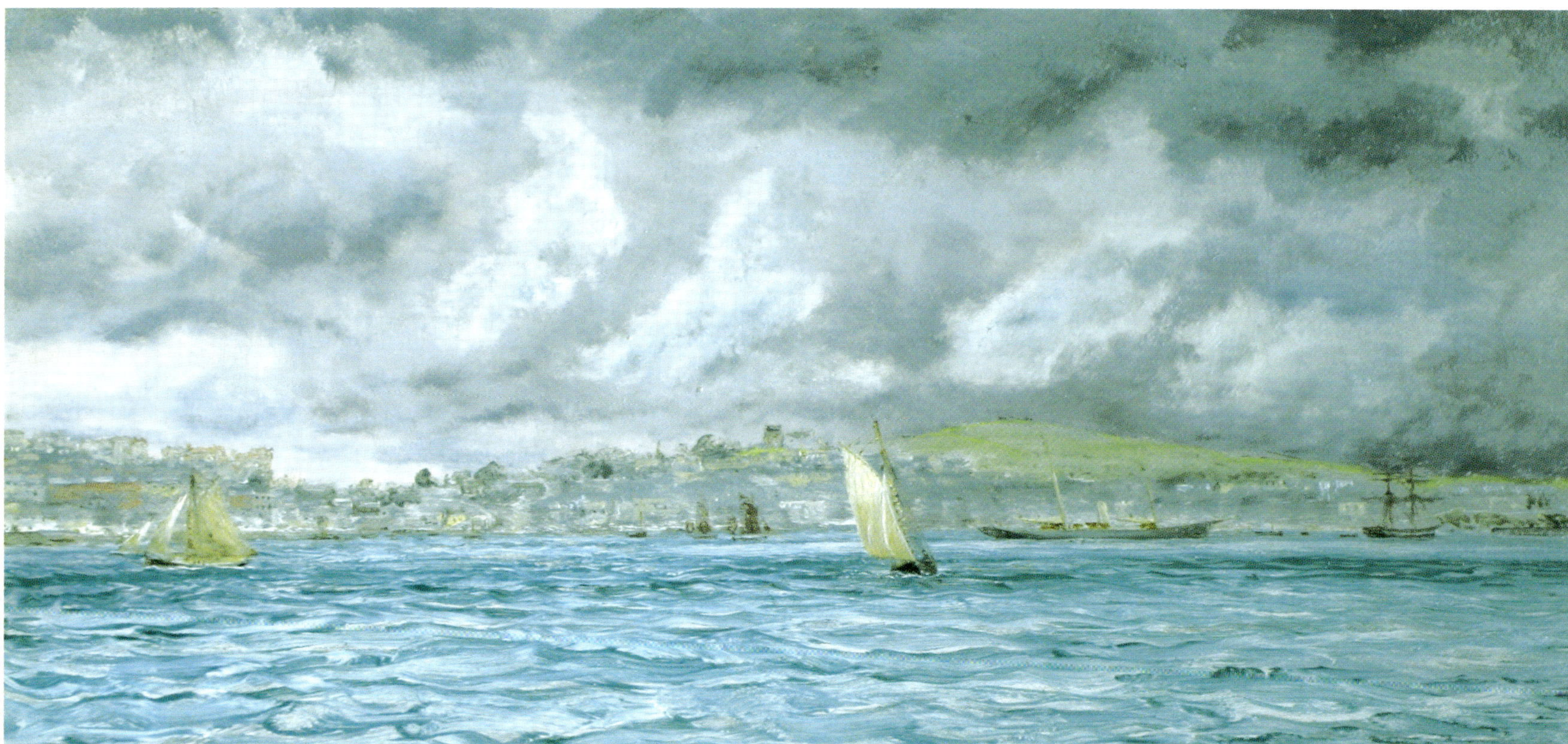

A south-westerly gale, Cornish coast
1884, Oil on canvas
61 x 122cm (24 x 48ins)
Signed and dated *'John Brett 1884'*
Private Collection
Provenance: Dr J. Watt Black; Sydney Public Gallery, NSW; returned 1889; Brett Studio sale 1902; Nasmyth; through the sale rooms to the present owner

This picture has a very interesting and rather chequered history. It began life as *A Strong sou'wester on an iron-bound coast*, and was commissioned in November 1883 by Brett's friend and patron Dr James Watt Black for £300. Brett's 'Book of Pictures' states that it was 'painted with copal & poppy & some lavender,' and was 'done from an old sketch of the Cowlow rock from Sennen belonging to (Alfred) Morrison.' As a young man, Black was consultant gynaecologist to Morrison's wife, and he must have seen and admired the sketch during visits to the Morrisons at 16 Carlton House Terrace. The work was finished in time for the Academy in 1884, where it appeared as *A south-westerly gale: Cornish coast*. The following year, however, Black decided it was too dark for his drawing-room, and exchanged it for another work.

Brett changed its title to *The Cowlow Rocks, Cornwall, in a SW gale*, and on the recommendation of T.L. Devitt, it was bought in February 1888 for the Public Gallery at Sydney, NSW for 200 guineas. But in Sydney the authorities took against it, and in March 1889 it was returned to England. As Brett wrote in his Studio Log, 'I found out that they knew that my best pictures at the RA fetched long prices (up to 1200) and as they wanted only a first rate specimen they despised a picture that only cost £210. And in fact sent it back (NB it is a thoroughly good picture)... Now the question is what shall I do with it? It is a picture rejected by a colonial corporation!!!! Everybody knows it and it has no selling value. Unlucky picture!!!'

In spite of attempts to sell it at exhibitions at the Guildhall (June 1890), Sevenoaks (1891), Oldham (Dec 1900) and York (Feb 1901), it remained unsold in Brett's lifetime. In the Studio sale after his death in 1902 it was sold as *Granite Boulders* to Nasmyth for 56 guineas. At its most recent appearance in the sale rooms it had acquired yet another identity, masquerading as *A friend in need* (a completely different work from 1896). But Brett was clearly justified in maintaining that it is a thoroughly good picture. The offshore Cowlow Rocks and the foreground boulders are painted with great precision, and the scene's stormy atmosphere is powerfully conveyed.

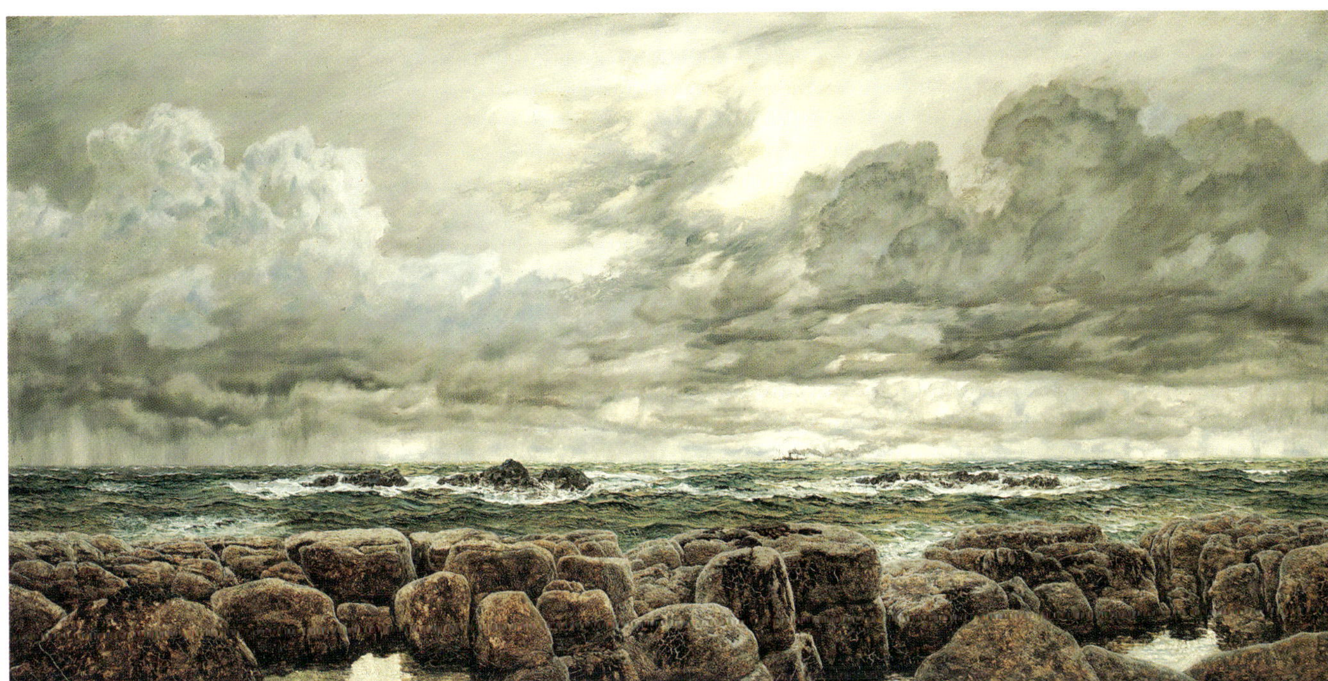

Entrance of Fowey Harbour
1884 Oil on canvas
38 x 76 cm (15 x 30 ins)
Signed and dated
'John Brett 1884'
Private Collection
Provenance: Arthur Tooth & Sons; Baker; by descent in the artist's family to the present owner

SUPPORTING IMAGE
Entrance of Fowey Harbour
J.M.W. Turner, engraved by W.B. Cooke 1820

This fine view of the entrance to Fowey harbour was based on a sketch done on 11 July 1883 during the *Viking's* maiden cruise (sold at Sotheby's 9 June 1994, lot 119). The viewpoint is the small beach on the western side of the harbour, close to one of the two blockhouses erected after the town had been burnt by the French in 1457. They were connected by a chain across the harbour. In the distance is St Catherine's Castle, added by Henry VIII to protect what was then one of England's busiest ports, and just visible on the top of the hill to its right is the Trinity House daymark on Gribbin Head, which lies beyond the Castle to the south-west. The view is easily recognisable today, although the blockhouse has virtually disappeared, and a terrace of houses has been built up on the right.

Interestingly, the same view was painted by both Turner (1816–17) and William Daniell (1823). Turner's view was engraved in *Picturesque views on the Southern Coast of England*, and it is possible that Brett knew this publication. His 1870 sketch of Lyme Regis from Charmouth (Private Collection) also reproduces Turner's viewpoint, and he seems to have been attracted to several of the other places illustrated in the book, including Lulworth Cove, Plymouth Sound, the Mewstone, Portsmouth and Deal.

The painting's provenance is a little puzzling. According to Brett's 'Book of Pictures', it was commissioned by the dealers Arthur Tooth and Sons in December 1883, and completed in February 1884. Tooth paid £135 for it, and it was shown in his spring exhibition that year. Almost immediately it was sold to 'Baker' (Tooth stock books, Getty Research Institute); but at some point it must have been bought back by a member of the Brett family, in which it has passed down by inheritance.

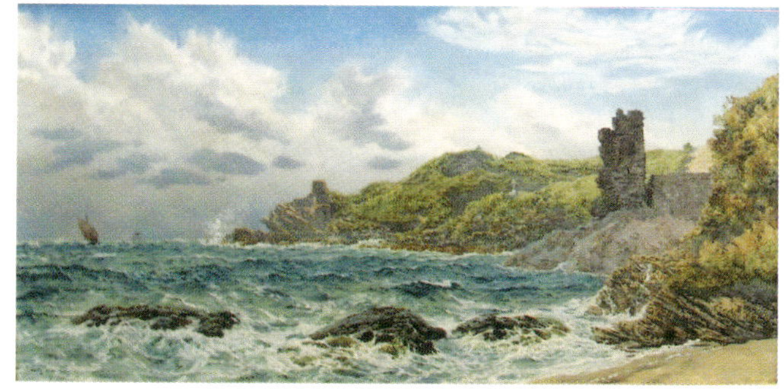

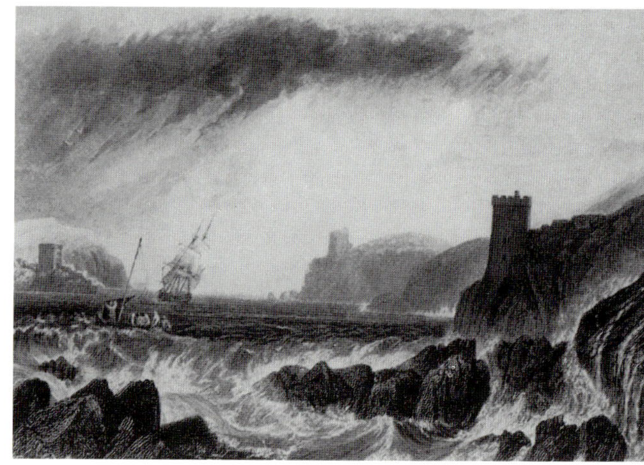

The Lion Rock
1888. Oil on canvas
25.4 x 48.2cm (10 x 19ins)
Inscribed *'The Lion 2 Oct 88'*;
on the reverse *'A.E. Cumberbatch Esq/12 Portland Place/from John Brett 38 Harley Street/13th April 89'*
Private Collection
Provenance: A.E. Cumberbatch; through the sale rooms to the present owner

This is one of the eight sketches Brett painted at Kynance Cove in 1888 as preparatory studies for *The Lion, the Lizard and the Stags* (p.122–3). He and Mary ('Pollie') arrived at Kynance on September 27, having travelled down by the night train. On September 30 he made a pencil sketch of the Lion Rock (Sketchbook 11), and two days later this delightfully fresh work was painted.

It is clearly one of the principal sources for the later work, as the Lion Rock, the serpentine cliffs to the left, and the cornfield visible between them are very similar in both works. However, in this sketch the tide is much further up, and the sky quite different. Of the other sketches done at this time two originally belonged to C.H. Stanton, Brett's landlord at Newquay in 1881, and have recently passed through the sale rooms. A third, *Serpentine Rock, Kynance*, is in the Metropolitan Museum, New York.

Brett's Studio Log records that he sold two works to A.E. Cumberbatch on March 27, 1889. One was this sketch, sold for £50. It was delivered to Cumberbatch's residence, 12 Portland Place, on April 13, presumably after he had paid for it. Not only did Cumberbatch live close to Brett's Harley Street studio, but his neighbour at 10 Portland Place was C.H.T. Hawkins, who had bought *The Grey of the Morning* in 1882.

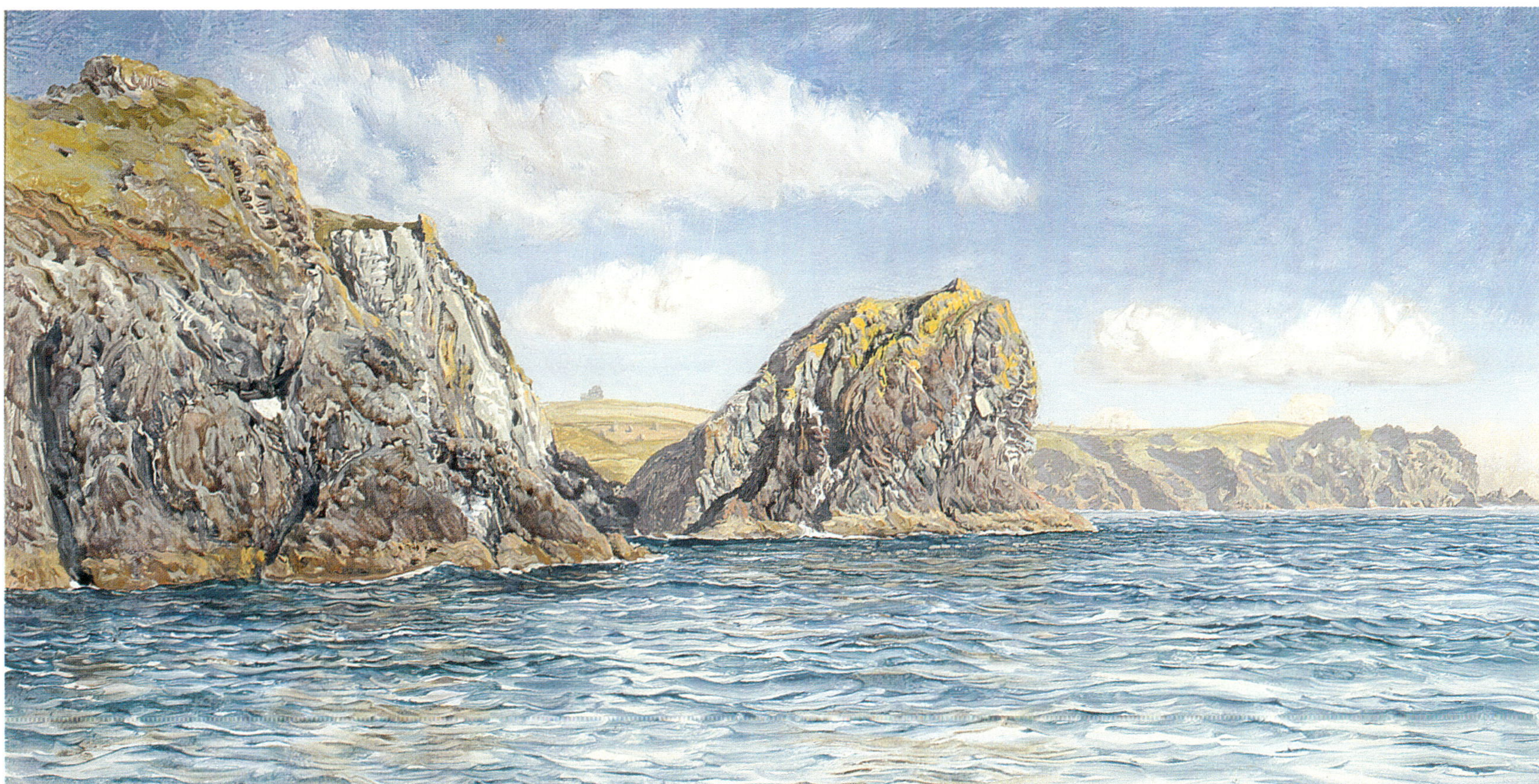

The Lion, the Lizard and the Stags
1889, Oil on canvas
107 x 214cm (42¼ x 84¼ins)
Signed and dated 1889
© Christie's Images Ltd
Provenance: Sydney Public Gallery, NSW 1890; de-accessioned 1956; through the sale rooms to the present owner

This magnificent work, described by Brett as 'the Lizard promontory from Asparagus Island, showing the principal view of the Cornish serpentine and some porphyry rocks with a rippling summer sea', has a complicated history (related in detail by Christopher Gridley in The British Art Journal Vol VI no 1, 2005).

After the rejection by the Sydney Gallery of *The Cowlow Rocks* (p.119), Brett was clearly anxious to persuade them to accept something else in its place. In August 1888 he therefore sent his friend T.L. Devitt, one of the committee delegated to select works for the Gallery, a study based on a drawing of the Lion Rock he had made in 1870 (Sketchbook 35) as a suggested subject. Encouraged by Devitt's reaction, he hurried off to Kynance Cove to make detailed sketches. Several of these relate to the final work. One is *The Lion Rock* (p.121), and another the *Study for my RA picture of the Lizard no 5*, later sold to Edward Atkinson. A further significant source was the pencil *Profile of the Staggs* (Sketchbook 11), which corresponds closely with Brett's painting of the group of offshore rocks. A photograph of the view, now lost, may also have been used. Finally, a 10 x 19ins sketch, dated 1889, probably served as a colour study (sold at the Omell Gallery, London, in 1978).

Brett's pocket diary for 1888 indicates that he must have begun the big picture soon after his return from Cornwall. By 12 November the sky was finished, and further references include 'painted distant Lizard' (16 Nov), 'begun Lion Rock in Lizard picture' (17 Nov), and 'painted on Lion Rock' (24 Nov). Work then had to stop as winter darkness set in. It was resumed the following February, at first slowly. But in March the light improved, and on the 27th the Studio Log states: 'My picture for the RA is now finished. I rather like it but it is less impressive than I expected for so fine a subject.' It was sent in at £1,000, F.G. Stephens describing it in *The Athenaeum* as 'a very brilliant Cornish coast picture of great beauty.' But it failed to sell there or at Manchester in the autumn. Eventually, in May 1890, Brett recorded its sale to the Sydney Gallery. 'They are to pay me 600 guineas together with the picture they rejected in March 1889' (i.e. a total of 800 guineas). 'I afterwards took out and repainted the nearer sea-gull and retouched the picture in many parts to its great improvement.'

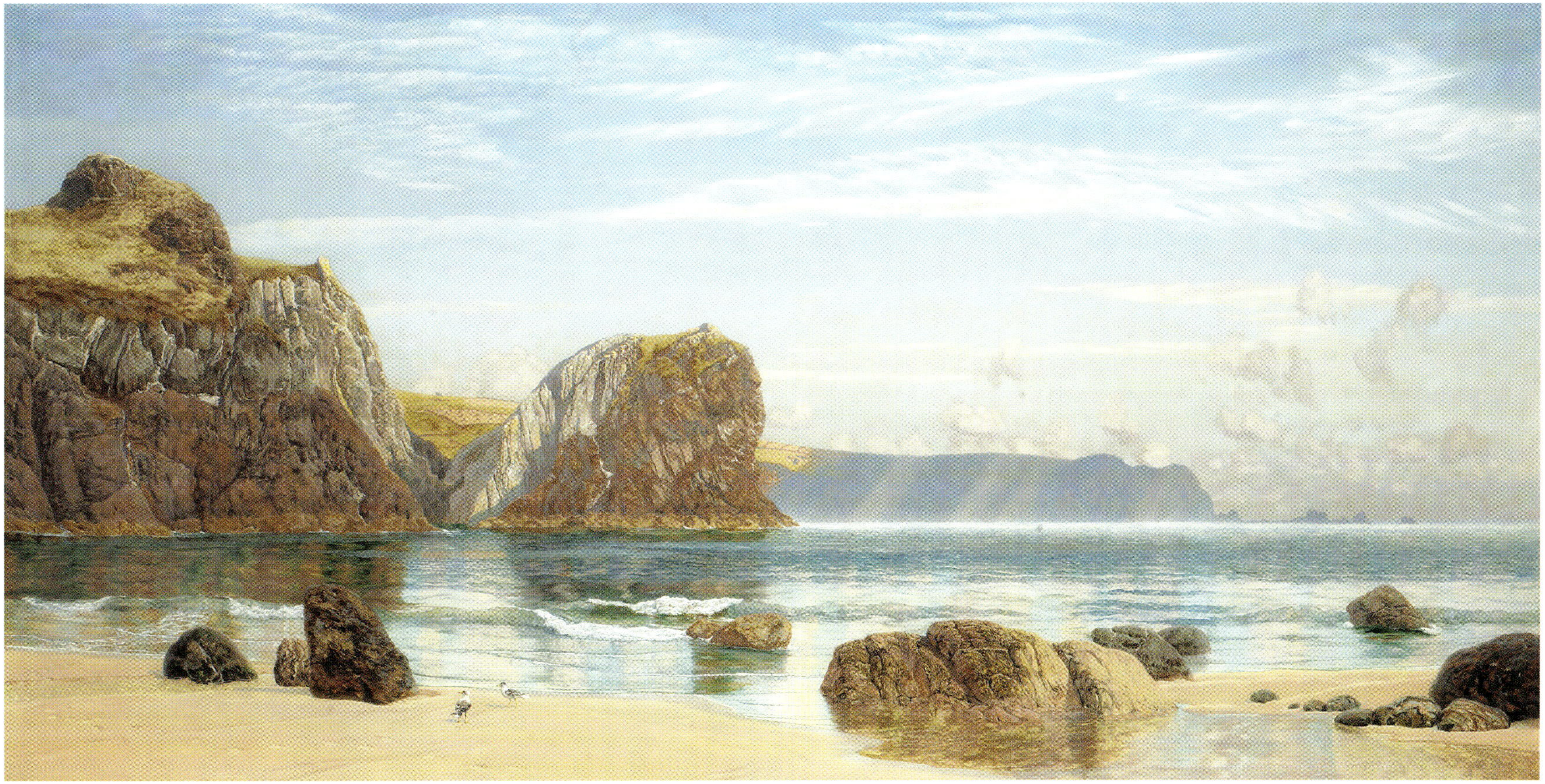

Newtrain Rocks
1889, Oil on canvas
16.5 x 35cm (6½ x 13¾ins)
Inscribed *'Cornish coast 2 Aug 89'*
Private Collection
Provenance: Dr Fitzpatrick; through the sale rooms to the present owner

Mary's entry in the 'Early Travels' for Sunday August 4 1889 records that on the previous Friday:

> we made a pic-nic; the two small children, Daddie and I driving in the trap, while the others with Miss Barrett (the governess) started off to walk! We arrived at Newtrain bay (about 2½ miles off) at eleven, and after waiting for the tide to go further down, we all bathed.

Newtrain Bay, also known as Cowrie Bay from the shells found there, is the more westerly of the two bays at Trevone, the other being sandy and ideal for bathing. Brett must have painted this sketch that afternoon on the incoming tide.

He was particularly fond of Trevone, and sketched there a good deal, both in 1889 and 1897. It offered a wide variety of subjects from studies of the slate rocks and pools, like this work, to more extended vistas showing Gulland Rock to the north, or Cataclews Point and Trevose Head to the west. He also noted that:

> a clever carpenter here… has built an embryo terrace at Trevone, on speculation, and is selling these little houses freehold at £300 each.

This was Atlanta (or later, Atlantic) Terrace, which is situated immediately above Newtrain Bay. Here several generations of Brett's descendants have spent happy summer holidays.

Although inscribed merely *Cornish coast*, this is likely to be the work entitled *Newtrain Rocks* in Brett's 1889 catalogue of sketches. It was sold on 13 April 1894 for £25 to Dr Thomas Fitzpatrick of 30 Sussex Gardens, Hyde Park.

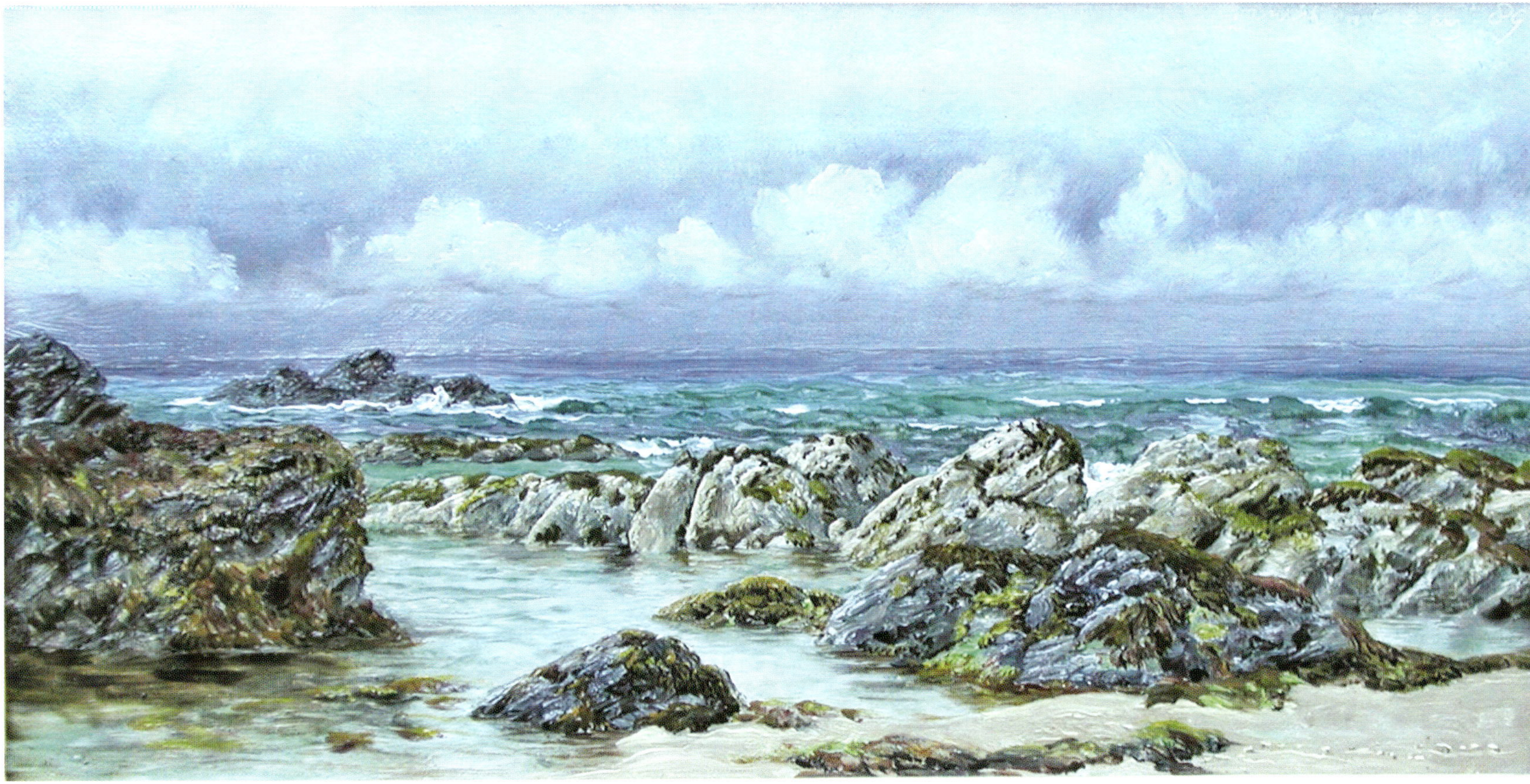

Mouth of the Camel River
1889, Oil on canvas
25.5 x 48cm (10 x 19ins)
Inscribed '*Mouth of the Camel River 15 Aug 89*'
Private Collection
Provenance: JB Studio sale 1902; George Aitchison RA; Sir T.L. Devitt Bt; by descent to the present owner

SUPPORTING IMAGE
The Camel Estuary from Dinas Hill, Padstow
Photograph: Cécile Brett

Brett's sketchbook 66 contains a pencil drawing dated July 10 89 which accords so closely with the view shown in this work as to suggest that the oil was painted from the pencil sketch rather than from nature. The sketch identifies the subject as 'Entrance to Padstow from Dinas Hill', and the vantage point is close to the obelisk which stands on the hill top above Dennis House, where the family stayed that summer. This obelisk, which commemorates Queen Victoria's 1887 Jubilee, was under construction in 1889, and may well have drawn Brett to the spot.

His view shows the Camel estuary looking north, with the tide well up. On the left is the entrance to Padstow harbour, and beyond it St Saviour's Point, from which the ferry crosses to Rock immediately opposite. Beyond Rock lies Daymer Bay, with Trebetherick Point to the north, and in the distance, at the entrance to the estuary, Pentire Point, in Brett's opinion 'a remarkably fine headland'. A boat is shown making its way up the centre of the channel, which is even narrower today owing to movement of the sandbanks, and the silting up of the estuary. The view has otherwise changed little since 1889, although the fields in the left foreground have been built over as the town has spread to the south.

Brett clearly enjoyed his high vantage point, which opened up a long vista, invariably a source of romance in his work. In its depiction of the river from such a great height, in delicate shades of blue and green, this sketch invites comparison with works like *Porth Curnow* (page 101). Although unsold in the artist's lifetime, it was acquired for 9 guineas at the 1902 Studio sale by his friend George Aitchison, best known as the architect of Leighton House. On his death in 1910 it entered the collection of Brett's most loyal patron, Sir Thomas Devitt.

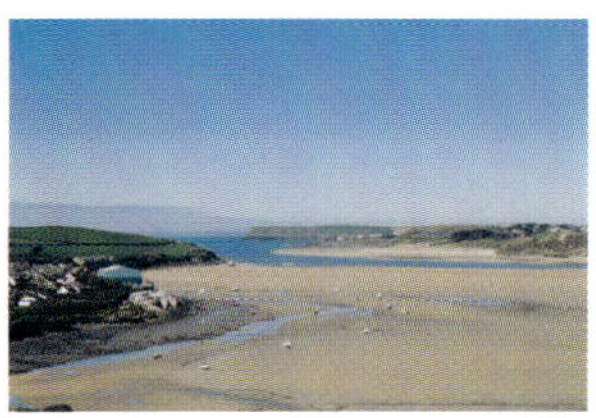

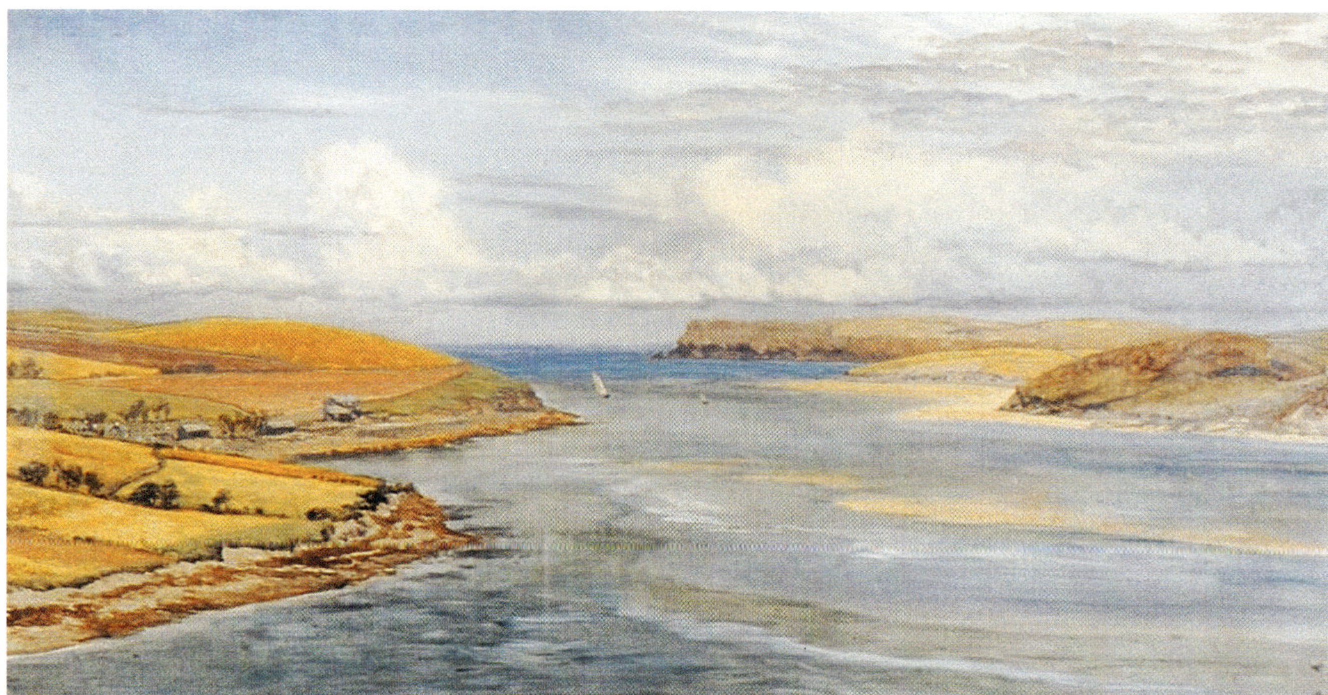

St George's Well
1889, Oil on canvas
18 x 35.5cm (7 x 14ins)
Inscribed '*St George's Well 27 Aug 89*'
Private Collection
Provenance: through the sale rooms to the present owner

St George's Well lies on the western side of the Camel estuary just to the north of St Saviour's Point and the Rock ferry, and according to legend never runs dry. Another legend attributes the shape of the cove through which it flows to its origin as the first hoof print of St George's horse on his arrival in England. St George is also associated with the traditional May Day ceremonies at nearby Padstow involving the hobby-horse parade, where songs are sung in his honour.

The well is depicted in the left foreground of this sketch, with Stepper Point beyond it. Pentire Point encloses the estuary on the right, and Newland Rock is visible some way out to sea. Across the centre stretches the notorious Doom Bar, which looks benign enough here, but can be treacherous in rough weather. Three hundred vessels are known to have been wrecked or stranded on it over the last century and a half.

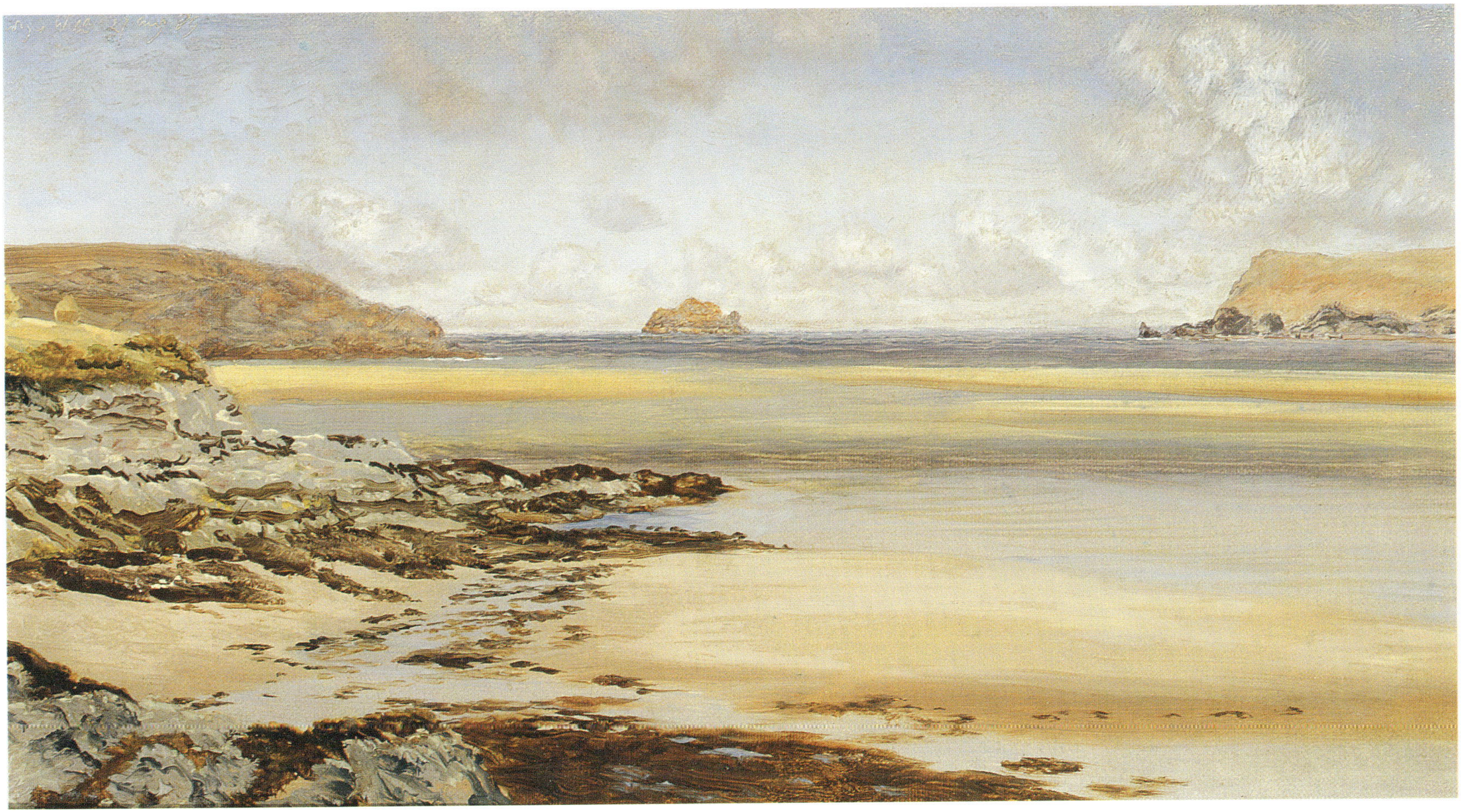

Treyarnon Bay
1889, Oil on canvas
25.5 x 48cm (10 x 19ins)
Inscribed *'Treyarnon 11 Sep 89'*, and on a label on the reverse *'I certify that this picture of Treyarnon/Bay was painted by me and was/sold to R.A. McAndrew Esq on the/29th July 1893. It measures 19 x 10/ inches on canvas/John Brett'*

Provenance: R.A. McAndrew; through the sale rooms to the present owner

This attractive sketch is one of at least four views of the beautiful little bay at Treyarnon Brett produced during the summer of 1889, and was certainly one of the principal sources for his Academy picture the next year, *Echoes of a far-off storm* (p.132–3).

Treyarnon is situated just to the south of Trevose Head, and Brett has chosen a diagonal view across the beach towards the group of offshore islands known as the Quies. It is a cloudy day, and the tide is out, leaving behind shallow pools in the sand amongst rocks covered with mussels and barnacles. Treyarnon Point is shown on the far side of the bay, striking an imposing note.

The sketch is a study in browns, set off by a beautiful range of soft pastel shades in the sky, which are reflected in the pools. As Brett remarked in the 'Early Travels', his choice of medium – 'Manders Copal 3 parts, chloroform 1 part, & Bells Oil of white linseed 4 parts' – caused the finished picture to dry very hard.

The Studio Log records that it was sold on July 29, 1893 to Mr and Mrs R.A. McAndrew, new clients 'introduced by Miss Hinson of W. Wickham', together with the 10 x 19ins *Rocket Cove, Aberporth* of 1891. Brett received £40 for each picture.

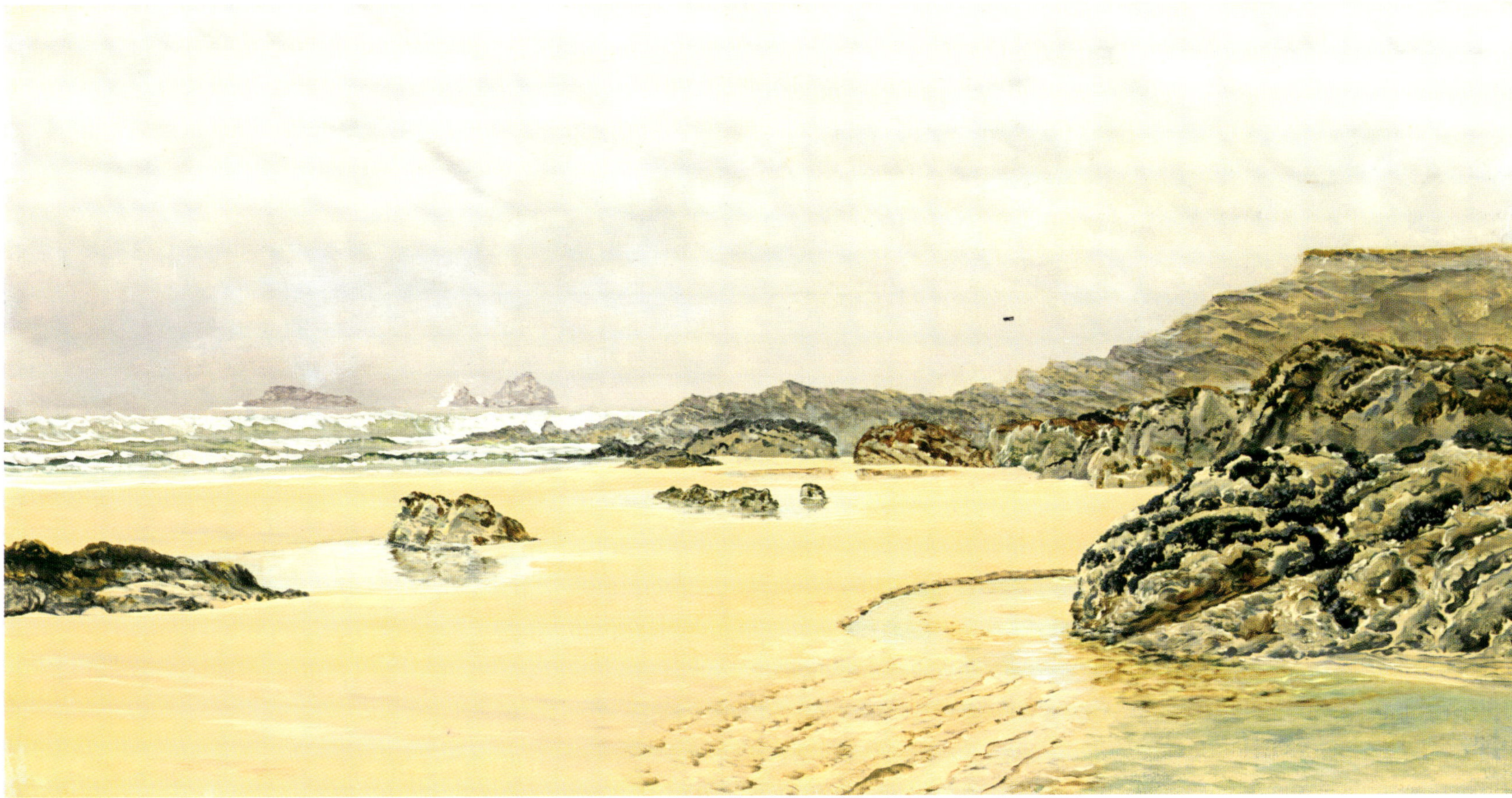

Gunver Head
1889, Oil on canvas
25.5 x 48cm (10 x 19ins)
Inscribed *'Gunver Point 16 Sep 89'*
and signed *'John Brett 1889'*
Private Collection
Provenance: through the sale rooms to the present owner

Although incorrectly inscribed *Gunver Point*, this lovely work is almost certainly *Gunver Head*, no 34 in Brett's 1889 catalogue of sketches, where it was priced at £60.

The view is from the north-western corner of Harlyn Bay, looking east. Now known as Onjohn Cove, in Brett's day it was called Perleze or Portledge Bay, and was the base for a pilchard seine. The fish cellars still exist, but the small pier built in 1794 to protect the fishery has long since disappeared. From this point the three headlands – Gunver Head, Stepper Point (crowned by its daymark) and Pentire Point – are all visible. Brett's masterly treatment of the scene, from the seaweed-covered foreground rocks to the long vista down the coast, suffused in a romantic glow, lends support to his conviction that his work was not declining in quality.

After returning to Putney in October, Brett painted a 24 x 48ins picture based on this sketch, which he called *A mist off the sea*, and sold to James Fairfax of Sydney, a friend of T.L. Devitt (Witt Library). The sketch itself is unusual in being signed as well as inscribed with place and date, perhaps an indication of its origin as a commissioned work.

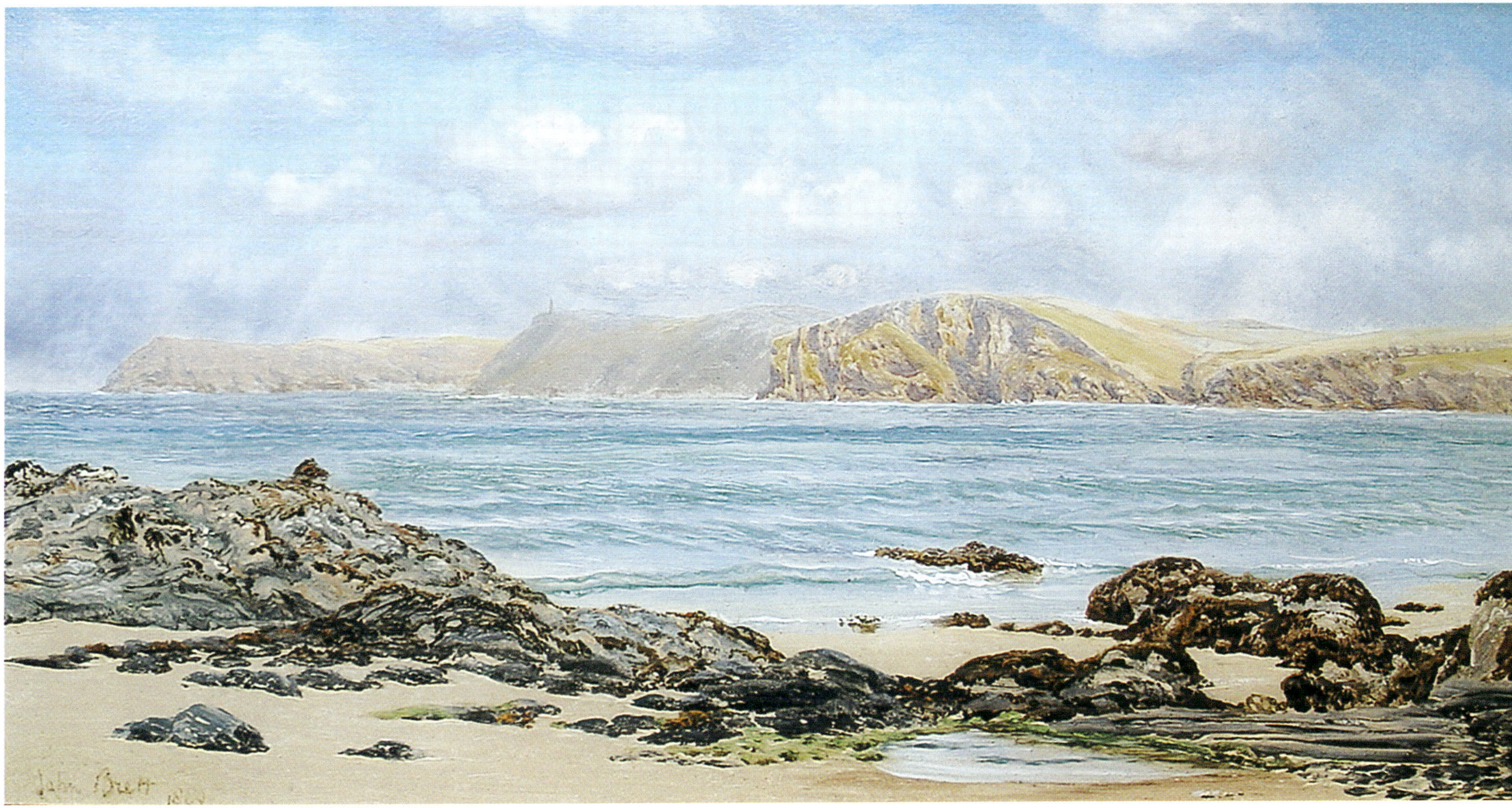

Echoes of a far-off storm
1890. Oil on canvas
106.68 x 213.36cm (42 x 84ins)
Signed and dated
'John Brett 1890'
© Guildhall Gallery,
Corporation of London/
Bridgeman Art Library
Provenance: JB Studio sale
1902; Sir T.L. Devitt Bt,
by whom it was presented
to the Gallery in 1918

This work, one of the finest of Brett's later seascapes, shows Treyarnon Bay in the aftermath of a fierce storm. A dark bank of cloud is moving towards the horizon, giving way to blue sky, with a few wisps of cirrus. The angry sea has receded, although breakers are still throwing up spray on the distant Quies rocks and Treyarnon Point beyond the headland. The tide has left behind great hollows scooped out of the sand, among which groups of plover timidly make their way.

This is a well documented work. Brett's Studio Log records on November 26 1889: 'Bright days lately. Have made a pastel study for a 7 foot picture of the North Cornwall cloud with an immense sand pool in the foreground from sketch 33 which I think will be both new and effective.' The sketch in question was entitled *Sand-pool at Treyarnon*. Other sketches undoubtedly related to the work were *The North Cornwall cloud*, and *Treyarnon Bay* (p.128–9), from which Brett seems to have derived his painting of the offshore Quies rocks, and some of the barnacle-encrusted rocks on the beach.

According to a note on one of the tacking edges, the work was begun on Christmas Day 1889, but progress the next year was interrupted when Brett succumbed to 'flu, and on March 12 he wrote: 'I have been so ill of late that there is a prospect of my big RA picture falling through.' But he did manage to finish it in time to send in on April 7. Surprisingly, in view of its dramatic power, he was not satisfied with it, complaining that it 'would have been much better if I had been well, but I could hardly hold a brush. The sandpool is not nearly equal to the sketch, and the headland is positively bad.'

His reservations were borne out by its failure to sell, and it became a much-travelled work in his vain attempts to find a buyer. The Studio Log records that it was sent to Liverpool (summer 1891), Hobart (July 1894 at £800), St Petersburg and Moscow (Nov 1897 at £500), the Walker Gallery, Liverpool (Aug 1899), and the Glasgow International Exhibition (Jan 1901 at £800). It remained unsold at Brett's death, and fetched only 42 guineas in the Studio sale in February 1902. It was later acquired by his old friend Sir Thomas Devitt, the shipowner and great City figure, who in 1918 presented it to the Guildhall Art Gallery.

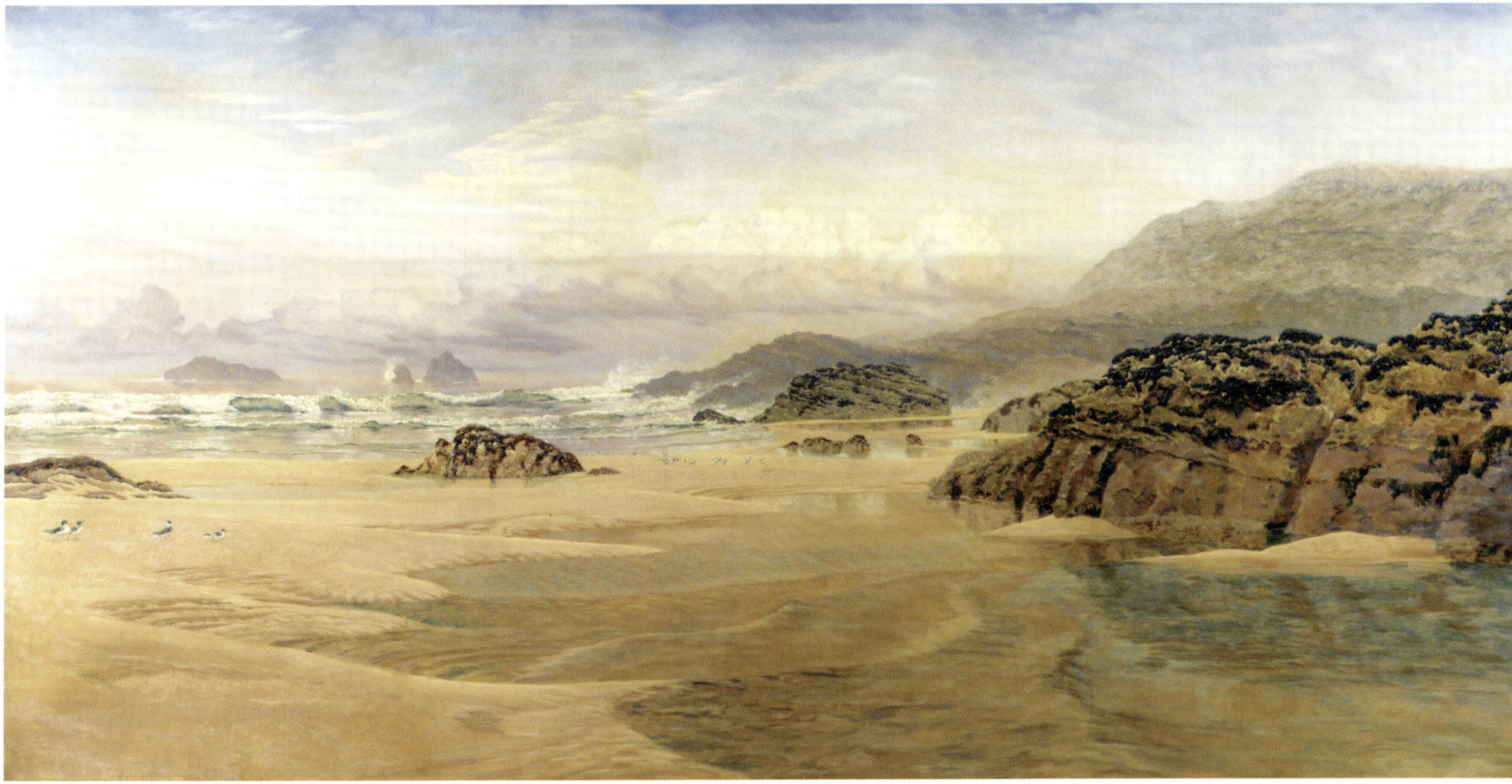

Harlyn Sands
1890, Oil on canvas
38 x 76cm (15 x 30ins)
Signed and dated
'John Brett 1890'

Provenance: G. Nelson Haden; through the sale rooms to the present owner

This picture, like *Gunver Head* (p.130–1), was painted at Harlyn Bay, but from a point near its eastern end. From this viewpoint Gunver Head occupies a central position, but both Stepper Point and Pentire Point are hidden behind it, and the Newland Rock is also invisible in the haze that envelops the far distance. Instead, St Cadoc's Point, which marks the eastern boundary of the bay, is on the immediate right, with the much higher Roundhole Point beyond it. Between the two, out of sight, lies Trevone. The picture has an interesting history.

Work began on Brett's new house, Daisyfield, in March 1888 (the first brick was laid by his eldest daughter, Daisy, on March 3). Although the contract stipulated September 30 as the finishing date, things dragged on, and the builders finally left on June 8 1889. Even then there was still plenty to do, including the installation of central heating, quite a luxurious item for those days. Meanwhile, the cost had escalated beyond the original estimate of £5,800. Brett, who was finding it increasingly hard to sell his work, was obliged to pay the heating engineers, Hadens of Trowbridge, in pictures, handing over three works worth £130 on June 5 as a first instalment.

The Studio Log entry for 29 Jan the next year reads:

> I have undertaken a commission from George Nelson Haden Esqr of Homefield House, Trowbridge to paint a picture measuring 30 x 15 inches in the course of next spring. The subject to be sketch no 16 of the 1889 series, but in clearer weather. The price to be £100, to set against his bill for the heating of Daisyfield.

Harlyn Sands is this work. The final account for the house was not settled until 4 June 1895, when Brett sent Barnsley the builder *Sea Mists, Cardigan Bay*, valued at £250, 'to balance his bill for Daisyfield', adding, with an audible sigh of relief, 'there is now nothing owing on D.'

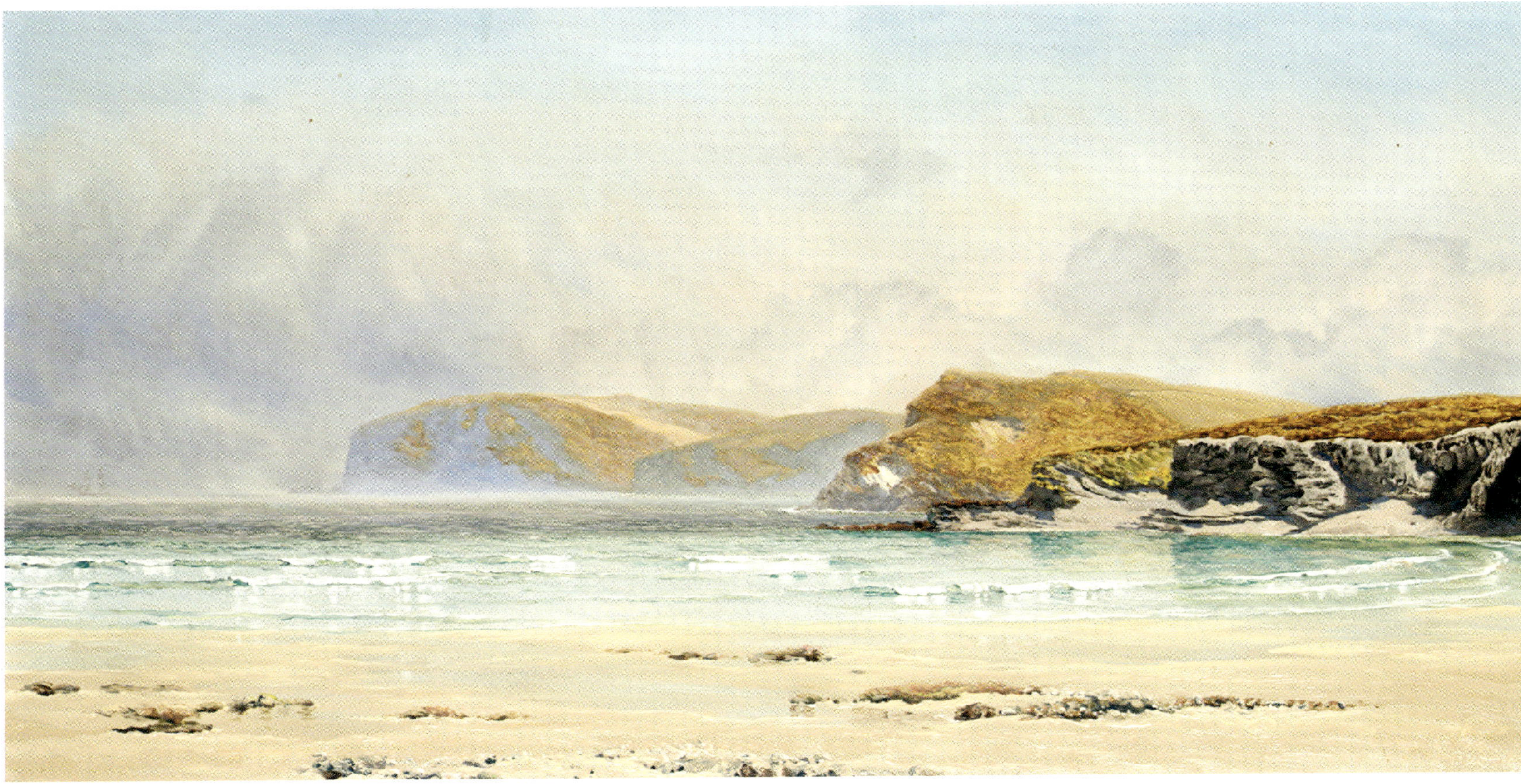

Trevose Head
1897, Oil on canvas
107 x 214cm (42 x 84ins)
Signed and dated
'John Brett 1897'
National Museums Liverpool
(The Walker)
Acquired for the Gallery by
Liverpool Corporation from
the artist in 1900

This view of Trevose Head from Newtrain Bay, Trevone, was Brett's last major Cornish work. As usual with his large pictures, he drew on several sources, including two 1897 Trevone sketches – the 7 x 14ins Trevose Head, sold in 1899 to the Gallery at Grahamstown, South Africa, and *Cataclew Point*, unlocated since its exhibition at the RA in 1901. Then there are two significant pencil drawings, dated 2 and 4 Aug 97, and a further drawing of the Trevone Reef of 24 Aug which seems to relate to the foreground (Sketchbook 72). These are accompanied by detailed colour notes, showing that Brett's powers of observation, and description, were unimpaired:

> Surface of sea granulated like morocco leather and of intensest greens & purples mingled in distance, but in the near sea the purple makes a more or less distinct pattern laid on a ground of melting green near lemon yellow in the lightest parts. Out of this lovely carpet project at intervals rocks of orange colour telling light decorated with Burnt umber patches of seaweed. The nearer bits grey below with a few strays and patches of quartz of strong orange. Weed intense brown, where it is sparse the appearance is dappled like a pied animal, the rock being buff.

The picture was begun on October 7 1897 (Studio Log). It was sent in to the RA the next year at 500 guineas, but at the private view Brett was dismayed to find that 'my big picture is hung next Herkomer's scarlet picture in the big room and utterly smashed.' To hang such a restrained, almost valedictory work beside a jingoistic scene of Guards veterans in scarlet uniforms cheering the Queen at the Jubilee does seem to have been insensitive. But the Art Journal reacted favourably. 'Mr Brett's incisive colouring is manifest in all his exhibits, of which Trevose Head is the most effective.'

Unsold at the Academy, it went on to Manchester, then to Oldham, reaching its final destination, the Walker Art Gallery, Liverpool, in August 1900. As Mary wrote to their daughter Daisy in a letter of 18 November (Private Collection), 'the Liverpool people have made an offer for Trevose Head. Dad gave the price £300 they offer £200, so Dad has written to say he will accept £250 on consideration of being represented in their permanent gallery. I only hope they will agree & send the cash quickly!' But they refused to raise their offer, and Brett reluctantly had to accept £200. The badly needed cheque eventually arrived on 15 December.

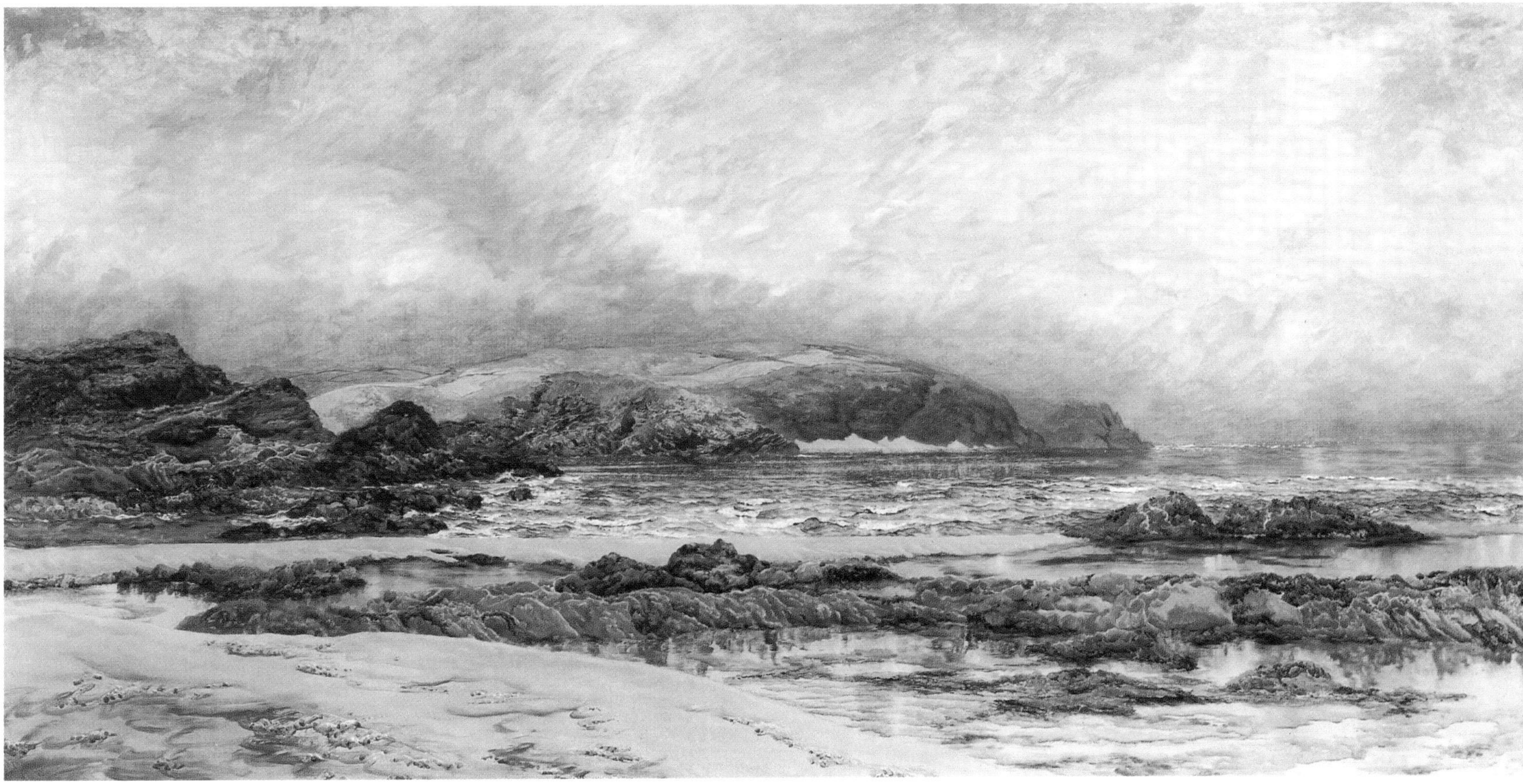

LIST OF ILLUSTRATIONS

OIL UNLESS OTHERWISE STATED

JOHN BRETT A.R.A. (1831–1902)

ROSA BRETT (1829–82)

JOHN RUSKIN (1819–1900)

J.M.W. TURNER R.A. (1775–1851)

PHOTO CREDITS

SUPPORTING IMAGES ARE IN BRACKETS

Nicholas Balaam p.91
Chris Beetles Gallery p.121
Birmingham City Art Gallery fig. 35
Blackburn's Academy Notes (p.114)
Elizabeth Blake pp.83,118
Cécile Brett figs 7,15,34,37; pp.60,61,63,65,66,68,(69),70,(71),72,76,78,(80),88,(88),89,(98),(110),116,(126)
Charles Brett figs. 42,47,49, pp.2,(120)
Martin Brett figs. 2,4,52
Bridgeman Art Library figs.3,22
British Museum fig.29
Brian Brooke-Smith figs.16,44,45,(p.108)
Christie's pp.(67),123
Jeremy Clarke p.62
A.C. Cooper figs.38, p.81
Detroit Art Institute p.8, fig.6
Fitzwilliam Museum fig.30, p.69
Christopher Gridley fig.23
Guildhall Art Gallery p.133
Richard Guise fig.36, pp.67,120
Michael Hickox fig.28
Johannesburg Art Gallery (p.88)
Jack Knecht pp.73,84,105,131
David Loundes fig.40
Maas Gallery fig.1, pp.77,97,127
Manchester City Art Gallery p.111
Peter Meagher p.125
National Maritime Museum figs.10,11,13,14,21,24,25,26,27,39, 41,pp.(76)
Nottingham Castle Museum fig.43, p.109
Elizabeth Padmore fig.53, (p.106)
Robert Hawkes Preston (p.72)
Peter Rand pp.101,126
Royal Exchange Gallery pp.93,100
Royal Holloway College p.99, front cover
Russell-Cotes Art Gallery & Museum pp.103,107
Sotheby's figs.5,8,17,32,33, pp.28,44,75,79,(86),87,95,113, 115,119,129,135
Tate London figs.12,18,31
Walker Gallery, Liverpool fig.20, pp.6,71,137
Robert Wallers figs.46,48,50,51
Jack Watson figs.9,19
Leo Wilkinson p.117
Christopher Wright p.35

BIBLIOGRAPHY

PRIMARY SOURCES

'John Brett, Diary 1851–61', typescript, ed. Charles Brett (Private Collection)

'Charles Curtis Brett, Diary 1863–5', typescript, ed. Charles Brett (Private Collection)

'Georgina Weldon, Diary 1864–71', typescript, ed. Charles Brett, taken from the Treherne family MSS by kind permission of Dr Joanna Martin

John Brett's address book dating from 1874 to c.1897 (Private Collection)

Sketchbooks: 72 of John Brett's sketchbooks, covering the period 1856–99 (National Maritime Museum, Greenwich)

Memoranda of the Early Travels of our children 1879–97, by John and Mary Brett (Private Collection)

Viking: a History, by John Brett 1883 (Private Collection)

Viking Log: Logbook of the schooner *Viking*, kept by John Brett from 11 June 1883–12 October 1883 (Private Collection)

John Brett's Pocket Diary for 1888 (Private Collection)

'Book of Pictures: being a record of the size, subject, price and destination of my principal productions from this year 1879.' This covers 1879–86 (Private Collection)

Studio Log kept by John Brett ARA at 38 Harley Street, London (1887–94) (Private Collection)

Studio Log, Daisyfield, Putney 1894. Containing Records of Pictorial Transactions, by John Brett ARA (1894–1901) (Private Collection)

Miscellaneous letters from John and Mary Brett (Private Collections)

MS Catalogue of Pictures belonging to Thos L. Devitt, c. 1890 (Private Collection)

Stockbooks of Arthur Tooth & Co (Getty Research Institute, USA).

Wandsworth Rate Books 1874–8

OTHERS

Anon, 'A Pre-Raphaelite Exhibition'. *Saturday Review,* July 4 1857, pp.11–12

Anon, 'Fine Art Gossip', *The Athenaeum*, July 11 1857, p.886

Anon, 'Artists' Houses', *The Art Journal*, 1882, pp.57–8

Bartram, Michael, *The Pre-Raphaelite Camera,* Weidenfeld and Nicolson 1985

Bates, Robin and Scolding, Bill, *Beneath the Skin of the Lizard,* Cornwall County Council 2000

Bendiner, Kenneth, *An Introduction to Victorian Painting*, New Haven and London, 1985

Bennett, Alan, *The Great Western Railway in West Cornwall,* Runpast Publishing 1995

Bennett, Alan, *Images of Cornwall,* Runpast Publishing 1992

Blackburn, Henry, *Academy Notes 1875–99,* Chatto and Windus

Bonney, T.G., 'A Geologist's Notes on the Royal Academy', *Nature 24* (May–October 1881)

Brett, Charles, 'John Brett and *Aurora Leigh*', *The Review of the Pre-Raphaelite Society*, Vol XI, Summer 2003, pp.14–20

Brett, Charles, 'John Brett and his Patrons', *The Review of the Pre-Raphaelite Society*, Vol XII, Summer 2004, pp.1–22

Brett, Charles, 'John Brett and Ruskin's *The Elements of Drawing*', *Burlington Magazine*, CXLVII, September 2005, pp.613–6

Brett, John, 'Realism in Painting', *The Contemporary Review*, No.402, June 1899, p.830

Chapel, Jeannie, *Victorian Taste,* Royal Holloway College 1993

Christie, Manson and Wood, Ltd, Sales catalogues

Clark, Kenneth, *Ruskin Today,* Penguin, 1967

Cook, E.T., and Wedderburn, A, eds., *The Works of John Ruskin*, Library Edition, 39 vols., 1903–12

Crook, J. Mordaunt, *The Rise of the Nouveaux Riches,* John Murray 2000

du Maurier, Daphne, *Vanishing Cornwall,* Penguin 1972

Dunning, Martin, *Francis Frith's Around Newquay,* Frith Book Company Ltd 2001

Fowles, John, *Shipwreck,* Sphere Books Ltd 1981

Girouard, Mark, 'An Open Plan in the 1880s', *Country Life*, March 29, 1962, pp.720–2

Gridley, Christopher, 'Two round trips to Sydney', *The British Art Journal* Vol VI, no 1, 2005

Hannigan, Des, *Francis Frith's Around St Ives,* The Francis Frith Collection 2005

Hewison, Robert, ed., *Ruskin's Artists: Studies in the Victorian Visual Economy*, Ashgate, 2000

Hickox, Michael, 'John Brett and the Rossettis', *The Journal of Pre-Raphaelite Studies*, Vol V, No.2, May 1985, pp.105–110

Hickox, Michael, 'John Brett and Ruskin', *The Burlington Magazine*, Vol CXXXVIII, 1996

Hickox, Michael, 'Religion and

Science in the Pre-Raphaelite work of John Brett', *The Victorian W[illegible]*

Hickox, Michael, 'The Royal Academy's rejection of Brett's *Florence*', *Review of the Pre-Raphaelite Society*, Vol III, No. 1, 1995, pp.10–16

Hickox, Michael, 'John Brett's *The Stonebreaker*', *Review of the Pre-Raphaelite Society*, Vol. IV, No.1, 1996, pp.3–7

Hickox, Michael, 'The unpublished correspondence of Ruskin and Brett', *The Ruskin Gazette*, Vol 1, No.8, 1995

Hickox, M., and Payne, C, 'Sermons in Stones: John Brett's *the Stonebreaker* reconsidered', in Ellen Harding, ed., *Re-framing the Pre-Raphaelites: Historical and Theoretical Essays*, Scolar Press, 1995, pp.99–114

Hudson, Derek, *Munby – Man of Two Worlds*, John Murray 1972

Hunter, W.V., *Cornwall's Coastal Footpath*, Tor Mark Press, Truro

Isles of Scilly Standard Guidebook, Bowley Publications Ltd 1975

John Brett: A Pre-Raphaelite on the Shores of Wales, National Museum and Gallery, Cardiff, 2001

Kelly's Directory for Cornwall, 1873, 1883, 1889, 1897

Ironside, Robin and Gere, John, *Pre-Raphaelite Painters*, Phaidon, 1948

Kittridge, Alan, *Cornwall's Maritime Heritage*, Twelveheads Press, Truro 2003

Lewis, David, 'Pondered Vision: the Art and Life of John Brett, A.R.A., 1830–1902', unpublished PhD thesis, Indiana University, 1995

Linder, Leslie, (ed.), *The Journal of Beatrix Potter 1881–97*, Frederick Warne & Co 1966

Lynch, T.T., *Memorials of Theophilus Trinal, Student*, Longman, Brown, Green and Longmans, 1850

Maber, Richard, and Tregoning, Angela, (eds.), *Kilvert's Cornish Diary*, Alison Hodge 1989

Macadam, John, *South West Coast Path, Padstow to Falmouth*, Aurum Press 2002

McEvansoneya, P., 'The Cosmopolitan Club Exhibition of 1863: the British *salon des refuses*', in Ellen Harding, ed., *Re-framing the Pre-Raphaelites: Historical and Theoretical Essays*, Scolar Press, 1995, pp.27–42

McEvansoneya, P., 'More light on the Royal Academy's rejection of Brett's *Florence*', *Review of the Pre-Raphaelite Society*, Vol IV No.1, 1996, pp.19–23

Mais, S.P.B., *The Cornish Riviera*, Great Western Railway Company 1928

Marriott, Sir J.A.R., *England since Waterloo*, Methuen & Co Ltd 1959

Marsh, Jan, *Chrstina Rossetti: a Literary Biography*, Jonathan Cape 1994

Massé, H.J.L.J.,*The Art Workers Guild 1884–1934*, Shakespeare Head Press 1935

Matthews, G. Forrester, *The Isles of Scilly*, George Ronald 1960

Panoramas of Cornwall, J. Salmon Ltd 2002

Nunn, Pamela Gerrish, 'Rosa Brett, Pre-Raphaelite', *Burlington Magazine*, CXXVI, October 1984, pp.630–2

Pevsner, Nikolaus, *The Buildings of England: Cornwall*, Penguin 1951

Plomer, William, (ed.), *Kilvert's Diary*, Penguin 1978

Polsue, Joseph, *Lake's Parochial History of the County of Cornwall*, 4 vols 1867–72

Shanes, Eric, *Turner's Rivers, Harbours and Coasts*, Chatto and Windus 1981

Sotheby's, Sales catalogues

Staley, Allen and Newall, Christopher, *Pre-Raphaelite Vision*, Tate Publishing, 2004

Staley, Allen, *The Pre-Raphaelite Landscape*, New Haven, 2001

Stanier, Peter, *Francis Frith's Cornwall a Century Ago*, Frith Book Company Ltd 2004

Stillman, W.J., *The Autobiography of a Journalist*, Vol. 1, Grant Richards, 1931

Surtees, Virginia (ed), *Sublime and instructive: letters from John Ruskin to Louisa, Marchioness of Wateford, Anna Blunden and Ellen Heaton*, Michael Joseph, 1972

Tooth, Arthur & Co, Exhibition catalogues (National Art Library)

Underhill, Harold A., *Sailing Ship Rigs and Rigging*, Brown, Son & Ferguson Ltd 1955

Ward, Lock & Co, *A Pictorial and Descriptive Guide to Falmouth*, 1928

Ward, Lock and Co, *A Pictorial and Descriptive Guide to Newquay*, 1930

Ward, Lock & Co, *A Pictorial and Descriptive Guide to Penzance*, 1934

Annual Register, The, 1870

Art Journal, The, 1877, 1881, 1897

Art Workers Guild, Annual Report, 1891

Athenaeum, The, 1889

British Census Returns, 1861, 1871, 1881, 1891

Burke's Landed Gentry

Dictionary of Business Biography

Navy List, 1877

Sculpture Journal, The, Vol 1, 1997

Post Office Suburban Directory 1876

Who's Who, 1849–

Who Was Who, 1897–1916

ABOUT THE AUTHORS

CHARLES BRETT

Charles Brett, a great-grandson of the artist, is a professional musician, who has had a distinguished career as a solo counter-tenor, conductor and teacher. He has been researching Brett's work for some years, with the aim of producing a definitive list of his known pictures. He has edited Brett's diaries, and contributed a number of articles on various aspects of his output to periodicals, including *The Burlington Magazine*. He also acts as a consultant to Sotheby's on the artist.

MICHAEL HICKOX

Michael Hickox taught Politics at South Bank University from which he recently retired. He became interested in John Brett through conversations with his step-aunt Winifred Watson, Brett's granddaughter, and he has published a number of pieces on the artist in the *Review of the Pre-Raphaelite Society* and elsewhere.

CHRISTIANA PAYNE

Christiana Payne is a Senior Lecturer in the Department of History of Art at Oxford Brookes University. She first became seriously interested in John Brett while researching her exhibition catalogue, *Toil and Plenty: Images of the Agricultural Landscape in England 1780–1885* (Yale University Press, 1993), and she is now working on a full-length study of his life and art. Her forthcoming book, *Where the Sea Meets the Land: Artists on the British Coast in the Nineteenth Century,* will be published by Sansom & Company in 2007.